THE POWER OF PROBLEM-BASED LEARNING

A Practical "How To" for Teaching Undergraduate Courses in Any Discipline

Edited by Barbara J. Duch,
Susan E. Groh,
and Deborah E. Allen

STERLING, VIRGINIA

Published in 2001 by
Stylus Publishing, LLC
22883 Quicksilver Drive
Sterling, Virginia 20166

Library of Congress Cataloging-in-Publication Data

The power of problem-based learning: a practical "how to" for teaching undergraduate courses in any discipline / edited by Barbara J. Duch, Susan E. Groh, and Deborah E. Allen.—1st ed.
    p. cm.
    Includes bibliographical references and index.
    ISBN 1-57922-036-3 (alk. paper)—
    ISBN 1-57922-037-1 (pbk- : alk. paper)
      1. Problem-based learning. 2. Problem-solving—Study
    and teaching (Higher) I. Duch, Barbara J., 1944—II.
    Groh, Susan E., 1952—III. Allen, Deborah E., 1952–

LB 1027.42 .P69 2001
378.1'7—dc21   00-066130

First edition, 2001
ISBN: hardcover 1-57922-036-3
ISBN: paperback 1-57922-037-1

Printed in the United States of America

All first editions printed on acid free paper

10 9 8 7 6 5 4 3

CONTENTS

About ten years ago, a handful of faculty at the University of Delaware, searching for a better way to teach, adapted problem-based learning (PBL) to their introductory science courses. Subsequently, committed to helping their colleagues discover the same satisfaction and renewed excitement about teaching they experienced upon adapting PBL, they founded an Institute for Transforming Undergraduate Education (ITUE). ITUE Fellows attend workshops and programs (led by seasoned PBL faculty) that provide them with hands-on experience with PBL and other active learning strategies. Since 1992, when the first PBL courses were designed and implemented, over one-third of the University of Delaware's faculty across almost every discipline have participated in ITUE or related PBL workshops.

This volume is an outgrowth of the faculty-driven reform of undergraduate education on the University of Delaware campus. It is meant to serve as a practical "how to" guide for the instructor contemplating a change to PBL. Unlike Boud and Feletti's *The Challenge of Problem-Based Learning*, we present here little in the way of theoretical discussion or justification for PBL. Rather, our emphasis has been to try to address the issues and practical questions we have often been asked by interested colleagues: "Where do I start?" "How do you find problems?" "What about using groups?" "How do you grade in a PBL course?"

The book is organized into three parts. Part One deals with institutional issues: we outline how the PBL program at the University of Delaware developed, the model for faculty mentoring we have developed, and the role that administrations need to play to promote reform on campus. In Part Two, we address some of the practical questions involved with course transformations and planning for effective problem-based instruction. Finally, in Part Three, we present a series of case studies from a variety of disciplines and colleagues who have incorporated PBL into their courses. We hope that this compilation of our experiences will assist others in their journeys into problem-based instruction.

We would like to acknowledge the support of the many students whose positive responses to our efforts to vitalize our teaching fueled (and continues to fuel) our enthusiasm. We would also like to acknowledge the many faculty who contributed to our collective experience above and beyond the chapters in this volume. In addition, support of the University of Delaware administration (from the President and Provost to individual department chairs) was a key factor in the transformation of our fledgling, grassroots effort into a thriving, campuswide reform. Finally, we gratefully acknowledge the following agencies and foundations, whose support helped us to extend our vision beyond our own courses and campus: the National Science Foundation's Division of Undergraduate Education (for development of the first PBL courses in the introductory sciences and creation of the ITUE), the U.S. Department of Education's Fund for the Improvement of Postsecondary Education (for development of the peer group facilitator program), the Howard Hughes Medical Institute (for development of PBL courses in the biomedical sciences and support of peer group facilitators), and the Pew Charitable Trusts (for expansion of PBL laterally across the disciplines).

B. J. D., S. E. G., and D. E. A.

PART ONE

INSTITUTIONAL ISSUES

Part One deals with some institutional issues associated with the adoption of problem-based learning. Here we describe the problem-based learning effort at the University of Delaware, discuss the role played by the faculty-led Institute for Transforming Undergraduate Education in furthering the use of PBL on campus, and present some ideas concerning the nature of effective administrative support for educational reform.

I

WHY PROBLEM-BASED LEARNING?

A CASE STUDY OF INSTITUTIONAL CHANGE IN UNDERGRADUATE EDUCATION

Barbara J. Duch, Susan E. Groh, and Deborah E. Allen

Chapter Summary

The past decade has seen major changes in how we communicate, do business, access information, and use technology. How we teach must also change in order to prepare our students to cope with these new situations: students need more than ever to be able to pose questions, seek and find appropriate resources for answering these questions, and communicate their solutions effectively to others. Problem-based learning is one educational strategy that helps students build the reasoning and communication skills necessary for success today. This chapter describes the basic tenets of problem-based learning and outlines the development of a university-wide program of problem-based learning at one institution, the University of Delaware.

Introduction

The last several decades have seen monumental change in all aspects of our lives—how we communicate, conduct business, access information, and use technology. Today, our students must be prepared to function in a very different working world than existed even ten years ago. The problems that these future professionals will be expected to solve will cross disciplinary boundaries, and will demand innovative approaches and complex problem-solving skills. Those of us who teach undergraduates in higher educational institutions are obligated to rethink how we teach and what our students need to learn in order to prepare them for this challenging time.

With few exceptions, college and university faculty embark upon the business of teaching with very little instruction or training in pedagogy: we simply teach as we were taught. For most of us, that experience revolved around lectures. In a traditional undergraduate classroom, lectures are usually content-driven, emphasizing abstract concepts over concrete examples and applications. Assessment techniques focus on recall of information and facts, and rarely challenge students to perform at higher cognitive levels of understanding. This didactic instruction reinforces in students a naïve view of learning in which the teacher is responsible for delivering content and the students are the passive receivers of knowledge.

Why Change the Way We Teach?

What worked in the classroom a decade (or two or three) ago, however, will no longer suffice, for the simple reason that past approaches fail to develop the full battery of skills and abilities desired in a contemporary college graduate. In June of 1994, a Wingspread Conference brought together state and federal policymakers, and leaders from the corporate, philanthropic, higher education, and accreditation communities to discuss quality in undergraduate education. This conference was sponsored by the Education Commission of the States (ECS), the Johnson Foundation, the National Governors' Association, and the National Conference of State Legislatures. The discussion that took place was based on the assertion that substantial improvement in American undergraduate education is needed to prepare students to function successfully in current business and industrial environments. The Conference developed the following list of important characteristics of quality performance of college and university graduates (Wingspread, 1994):

- High-level skills in communication, computation, technological literacy, and information retrieval to enable individuals to gain and apply new knowledge and skills as needed

- The ability to arrive at informed judgments—that is, to effectively define problems, gather and evaluate information related to those problems, and develop solutions

- The ability to function in a global community through the possession of a range of attitudes and dispositions including flexibility and adaptability, ease with diversity, motivation and persistence (for example, being a self-starter), ethical and civil behavior, creativity and resourcefulness, and the ability to work with others, especially in team settings

- Technical competence in a given field

- Demonstrated ability to deploy all of the previous characteristics to address specific problems in complex, real-world settings, in which the development of workable solutions is required

Survey results (Czujko, 1994) of all physics baccalaureates who were employed in either the private sector or government/national labs confirmed the Wingspread Conference conclusions. With approximately 80 percent response to the question, "What skills have you found to be most useful in your work?", problem-solving, interpersonal skills, technical writing, and management skills were cited (greater than 60 percent) over physics knowledge. More recently, the Carnegie Foundation's report, *Reinventing Undergraduate Education: A Blueprint for America's Research Universities* (1998) stated that "traditional lectures and note-taking were created for a time when books were scarce and costly and lecturing to large numbers of students was an efficient means of transferring knowledge." Lecturing is *still* efficient and has persisted as the traditional teaching method largely because it is familiar, easy, and how *we* learned. It does little, however, to foster the development of process skills to complement content knowledge.

There are teaching practices, however, that do foster such skill development without forsaking content. Quoting John Dewey's observation that "true learning is based on discovery guided by mentoring rather than the transmission of knowledge," (Boyer, 1998, p. 15) the Boyer report urged universities to

> . . . facilitate inquiry in such contexts as the library, the laboratory, the computer, and the studio, with the expectation that senior learners, that is, professors, will be students' companions and guides. . . . The research university's ability to create such an integrated education will produce a particular kind of individual, one equipped with a spirit of inquiry and a zest for problem solving; one

possessed of the skill in communication that is the hallmark of clear thinking as well as mastery of language; one informed by a rich and diverse experience. It is that kind of individual that will provide the scientific, technological, academic, political, and creative leadership for the next century. (Boyer, 1998)

Student-centered, inquiry-based instruction, particularly problem-based learning, falls right into line with this philosophy; indeed, the Boyer Commission pointed to the PBL efforts at the University of Delaware as one example of how to help students reach the important goals highlighted in the report.

What Is Problem-based Learning?

We believe that problem-based learning (PBL) provides a forum in which these essential skills will be developed. The basic principle supporting the concept of PBL is older than formal education itself; namely, learning is initiated by a posed problem, query, or puzzle that the learner wants to solve (Boud & Feletti, 1991). In the problem-based approach, complex, real-world problems are used to motivate students to identify and research the concepts and principles they need to know to work through those problems. Students work in small learning teams, bringing together collective skill at acquiring, communicating, and integrating information. Problem-based instruction addresses directly many of the recommended and desirable outcomes of an undergraduate education: specifically, the ability to do the following:

- Think critically and be able to analyze and solve complex, real-world problems

- Find, evaluate, and use appropriate learning resources

- Work cooperatively in teams and small groups

- Demonstrate versatile and effective communication skills, both verbal and written

- Use content knowledge and intellectual skills acquired at the university to become continual learners

The PBL Cycle

PBL in the sciences traces its roots to the medical school setting where small groups of intellectually mature, highly motivated medical students work in small groups with a dedicated faculty tutor to learn basic science concepts in the context of actual clinical cases. The process of problem-based instruction (Boud & Feletti, 1997) follows:

- Students are presented with a problem (case, research paper, videotape, for example). Students working in permanent groups organize their ideas and previous knowledge related to the problem and attempt to define the broad nature of the problem.

- Throughout discussion, students pose questions called "learning issues" that delineate aspects of the problem that they do not understand. These learning issues are recorded by the group and help generate and focus discussion. Students are continually encouraged to define what they know and—more importantly—what they don't know.

- Students rank, in order of importance, the learning issues generated in the session. They decide which questions will be followed up by the whole group and which issues can be assigned to individuals, who later teach the rest of the group. Students and instructor also discuss what resources will be needed to research the learning issues and where they could be found.

- When students reconvene, they explore the previous learning issues, integrating their new knowledge into the context of the problem. Students are also encouraged to summarize their knowledge and connect new concepts to old ones. They continue to define new learning issues as they progress through the problem. Students soon see that learning is an ongoing process and that there will always be (even for the teacher) learning issues to be explored.

PBL fosters the ability to identify the information needed for a particular application, where and how to seek that information, how to organize that information in a meaningful conceptual framework, and how to communicate that information to others. Use of cooperative working groups fosters the development of learning communities in all classrooms, enhancing student achievement (Johnson, Johnson, & Smith, 1991). Students who learn concepts in the context in which they will be used are more likely to retain that knowledge and apply it appropriately (Albanese & Mitchell, 1993). They will also recognize that knowledge transcends artificial boundaries since problem-based instruction highlights interconnections between disciplines and the integration of concepts.

The Origins of PBL at the University of Delaware

The systemic incorporation of problem-based learning into curricula at the University of Delaware (UD) began in 1992 with the proposed revision of several courses connected with the Medical Scholars Program. (In this collaborative program with Thomas Jefferson Medical College in Philadelphia, selected Delaware undergraduates gain early admission to Jefferson and complete some of their medical school requirements through courses taken at UD.) While problem-based learning had been on the medical school scene for some time, this technique was much less well known among undergraduate faculty. Given Jefferson's desire to include more problem-based learning in their curriculum, Delaware faculty associated with the Medical Scholars Program were invited to attend a workshop at Jefferson on PBL, presented by faculty from the University of New Mexico, one of the proponents of this technique. The interest generated by this workshop led Barbara Duch, then affiliated with UD's Center for Teaching Effectiveness (CTE), to invite the New Mexico faculty to present a second workshop on PBL at the UD campus, open to all interested faculty. As a result of these workshops, two PBL courses were introduced at UD in the fall of 1992 in physiology and physics. Another PBL workshop offered in January was attended by over thirty faculty and resulted in the introduction of two more PBL courses that spring. In addition, three faculty members received seed money from CTE to support the incorporation of PBL into their general biology, chemistry, and physics courses.

With several other instructors excited about the possibilities of PBL for improving undergraduate science education on campus, this small core of faculty submitted a proposal to National Science Foundation (NSF) in June of 1993 to further the transformation of introductory courses in biology, biochemistry, chemistry, and physics. That summer, the science faculty presented a workshop on problem-based learning but with an emphasis on moving away from the "medical school model" of mature, motivated students working with individual faculty tutors, to adaptations that would be more successful in a typical undergraduate setting. (Indeed, in 1996–97 several faculty received funding from both the Fund for the Improvement of Postsecondary Education (FIPSE) and NSF to develop a training program for peer tutors in PBL classes, as discussed by Allen and White in Chapter 8.) By the spring of 1994, additional PBL courses became available in biology, chemistry, geology, and political science. NSF funding of the introductory science proposal made it possible to continue to offer workshops each summer and winter to satisfy the growing interest in problem-based learning. By 1996, more than 175 faculty had participated in PBL workshops, representing all ranks and nearly every discipline, and over thirty courses had been transformed to incorporate problem-based learning. Off-campus participants included K–12 educators and faculty from institutions throughout the United States and as far away as Australia, Europe, and South Africa.

Despite the advantage of improving the undergraduate experience that problem-based learning offers, it became clear that, for many instructors, the adoption of PBL as a mode of instruction was a change not undertaken lightly. Giving up the safety and authority of the podium can be unsettling for faculty accustomed only to a traditional, teacher-centered lecture format. Attempts to promote PBL further, therefore, would have to be accompanied by broader efforts to change the campus culture to one more accepting of active, student-centered, and inquiry-based learning.

Realizing that many instructors were unfamiliar with (and intimidated by) active student-centered learning in general, a core of PBL-active faculty created, with the support of NSF's Institution-Wide Reform program, an Institute for Transforming Undergraduate Education (ITUE). The goals and methods of this Institute will be discussed in more detail later by Watson and Groh (Chapter 2); in short, faculty selected as ITUE Fellows attend workshops and programs providing them with hands-on experiences with PBL and other active learning strategies, as well as the effective use of technology in their courses. The organizing faculty and Fellows from previous years serve as mentors to help their colleagues negotiate this somewhat unnerving paradigm shift in teaching.

In 1997 and 1998, the first two years of the Institute, over 100 faculty Fellows participated—twice the number originally anticipated. Although the PBL effort was based originally in the College of Arts and Sciences, ITUE helped to spread its influence rapidly throughout the campus: teams from the political science, biology, mechanical and electrical engineering departments, for example, attended ITUE in preparation for transforming their undergraduate curricula. The success of the Institute led the university administration to make ITUE an integral part of faculty development. By the summer of 2000, more than 230 Fellows had received training through the Institute with problem-based learning being incorporated into more than 150 courses and experienced by over 4000 students.

Assisted by the creation of this Institute, visibility of the PBL effort increased dramatically both on and off campus. By sharing their experiences with their colleagues, Visiting Fellows from other institutions, both in the United States and abroad, generated further interest both in problem-based learning and in UD's approach on their own campuses. In 1997, UD was one of only ten institutions nationwide to receive an NSF Recognition Award for the Integration of Research and Education (RAIRE) for its leadership and vision in research-based education, and was also singled out in the recent Boyer report (Boyer, 1998) for its emphasis on research-based learning. The promotion of PBL as a means of allowing students to experience the excitement of discovery in the classroom, as well as in the lab, was highly praised in both of these awards. A report commissioned by NSF in 1997 cited the University of Delaware in recommending problem-based learning as ideally suited for instruction in the analytical sciences (NSF, 1997). In 1998, the University received a grant from the Pew Charitable Trusts to support (1) the introduction of problem-based learning into large general education courses in the social sciences and humanities, and (2) the establishment of a national electronic clearinghouse for problem-based learning. Now in the beta testing stage, this repository of problems, teaching notes, articles, and other materials will serve as an invaluable resource for other educators seeking to use problem-based learning in their classrooms. In 1999, the University of Delaware was awarded the Theodore M. Hesburgh Certificate of Excellence in recognition of its enhancement of undergraduate teaching through the ITUE faculty development program.

In looking for elements that have been critical to the development of the PBL program at Delaware, one finds a critical mass of individuals committed to the improvement of instruction; success in garnering external funding to leverage support and provide outside validation for the effort; a mechanism for training and mentoring other faculty in the new pedagogy; and administrative support. At Delaware, a handful of science faculty, concerned about how well their students were learning, were drawn to PBL by its potential for providing a richer learning experience for their students. Successful proposals to respected national organizations not only provided financial support for the project but even more importantly, demonstrated that this undertaking was considered both credible and valuable in the eyes of outside experts. The ITUE made it possible to encourage and support other faculty in making their transition to a more active, student-centered mode of instruction, helping to change the culture of teaching and learning at the university. Finally, while this has been a grassroots-level call for change in teaching rather than a management-driven program, the support of the administration (which Cavanaugh discusses in Chapter 3) has been crucial in helping to sustain the effort.

Authors' Biographies

Barbara J. Duch is Associate Director of the Mathematics & Science Education Resource Center at the University of Delaware.

Susan E. Groh, Ph.D., is Assistant Professor in Chemistry and Biochemistry and an affiliated faculty member of the University Honors Program at the University of Delaware.

Deborah E. Allen, Ph.D., is Associate Professor and Undergraduate Programs Director in the Department of Biological Sciences and an affiliated faculty member of the University Honors Program at the University of Delaware.

References

Albanese, M. A., & Mitchell, S. (1993). Problem-based learning: A review of literature on its outcomes and implementation issues. *Academic Medicine, 68,* 52–81.

Boud, D., & Feletti, G. (1997). *The challenge of problem-based learning* (2nd ed.). London: Kogan Page.

Boyer Commission on Educating Undergraduates in the Research University for the Carnegie Foundation for the Advancement of Teaching. (1998). *Reinventing Undergraduate Education: A Blueprint for America's Research Universities.* URL: http://notes.cc.sunysb.edu/Pres/boyer.nsf.

Czujko, R. (1994). Physics job market: A Statistical Overview. *Announcer, 24* (4), p. 62.

Johnson, D. W., Johnson, R. T., & Smith, K. A. (1991). Cooperative learning: Increasing college faculty instructional productivity. (ASHE-ERIC Higher Education Report No. 4). Washington, DC: George Washington University.

National Science Foundation. (1997). *Curricular Developments in the Analytical Sciences.* Arlington, VA: Author.

Wingspread Conference. (1994). Quality Assurance in Undergraduate Education: What the Public Expects. Denver, CO: Education Commission of the States.

2

FACULTY MENTORING FACULTY

THE INSTITUTE FOR TRANSFORMING UNDERGRADUATE EDUCATION

George H. Watson and Susan E. Groh

Chapter Summary

An essential feature of educational reform on campus is commitment from the faculty. At the University of Delaware, instructors with an interest in making the transition to more student-centered, active forms of learning receive support from the Institute for Transforming Undergraduate Education (ITUE), a faculty-driven program that combines instruction in pedagogy with personal mentoring by faculty who have already transformed their own teaching. This chapter describes the goals of ITUE, how it operates, and its role in promoting the adoption of problem-based learning on this and other campuses.

Origins of the Institute

In April 1997, the National Science Foundation (NSF) granted an award to the University of Delaware (UD) as part of a new national program for science education reform—the Institution-Wide Reform of Undergraduate Education in Science, Mathematics, Engineering, and Technology. The motivation behind this program is reflected in the following description from the NSF program announcement:

> To stimulate comprehensive reform of science, mathematics, engineering, and technology education and to provide national models of excellence, the [NSF] will make awards to colleges and universities that have demonstrated success in revitalizing undergraduate education and now wish to further infuse the institution with these gains. It is intended that by recognizing visionary, comprehensive plans based on successful and significant accomplishments, the awards will catalyze modifications in the institutional culture and infrastructure that are prerequisite to systemic reform.

Our proposal, titled "Catalysts for Change: Foundation Courses and Instructional Innovation," presented the University of Delaware as an institution poised on the brink of systemic educational reform as the result of a number of significant accomplishments at UD in the past few years. Particularly noteworthy were two recently funded NSF projects: Problem-Based Learning in Introductory Science Across Disciplines and Delaware's Innovative Science/Mathematics Collaborative for Undergraduate Success (DISCUS). Several principal investigators from these projects were represented on the proposal team.

The main component of the proposal was the creation of an Institute for Transforming Undergraduate Education (ITUE) to promote reform of undergraduate education through faculty development and course design. Institute leaders would share ideas for transforming courses by incorporating effective techniques for the promotion of active learning and use of technology in the classroom. Institute Fellows would be selected to receive hands-on experience in employing active learning strategies and technology in their courses to "infuse the institution" with transformed courses and faculty. Thus, the systemic reform envisioned by NSF might be realized at the University of Delaware by transforming our curriculum from the bottom up via this faculty-led initiative; broad dissemination of our model might then lead to its subsequent adoption by other institutions.

As described at the ITUE website http://www.udel.edu/itue, the underlying philosophies of the Institute are that undergraduate courses should help students to (1) think critically and enhance their ability to analyze and solve real-world problems; (2) develop skill in gathering and evaluating information needed for solving problems; (3) gain experience working cooperatively in teams and small groups; and (4) acquire versatile and effective communication skills. Toward this end, undergraduate courses should be student-centered, encourage students to "learn to learn," apply technology effectively where it will enhance learning, and provide opportunities for a variety of learning experiences. The goal of the Institute, then, has been to provide faculty with the training, resources, and support needed to transform their courses along these lines.

First Cycle of the Institute

The recruitment of faculty members interested in becoming Institute Fellows began immediately following the announcement of the award from NSF in early 1997. Although we had convinced the panel reviewers and program directors at NSF of the merit of our plan, we remained uncertain of the extent of faculty interest in this endeavor. By offering a modest incentive (a financial award for technology acquisitions or curricular materials), we hoped to attract at least twenty prospective Fellows.

During the spring semester, an informational meeting announced by campus media and direct mailing was held for faculty interested in the pending program, followed by a call for proposals due within one month. The qualities that we sought in aspiring Fellows were availability for participation in ITUE sessions, motivation for improving their courses with a reasonable goal in mind, and a course portfolio that overlapped somewhat with the interests of ITUE in science education reform. The response from the faculty was gratifying. The 1997 class of Institute Fellows was comprised of 55 members from 29 different academic departments, with each of UD's six colleges and the Parallel Program represented by at least one member.

At the general orientation meeting on the last day of the 1997 spring semester, the new Fellows met to consider aspects of education reform regarding active learning and use of technology in the classroom. Fellows discussed their experiences with active, hands-on, or group learning and with technology, as well as the barriers they perceived to further reform in their classrooms. Learning objectives were identified and interests prioritized for further exploration at the in-depth ITUE session coming in June.

The main ITUE session spanned three days in June. During that time, the ITUE leaders attempted to present a variety of active learning and technology approaches that reflected both the expertise of the leaders and the interests of the new Fellows. Included, for example, were sessions on writing cases and problems for a PBL course, experiencing PBL yourself, using active learning in large classes, and using the Web as a resource for student learning. (A complete listing of the sessions presented may be found in the appendix.) Active learning approaches were put into practice as part of the presentation of each topic. Each afternoon, the Fellows adjourned to several computer labs to explore on-line resources for their courses.

As a follow-up to the summer session, numerous special workshops were offered for Fellows throughout the year, amplifying elements that had not been addressed during the main session because of limited time. These included an extended discussion of syllabus design, hands-on sessions in moving course materials online, active learning strategies for large classes, and strategies for making groups work and managing conflict when they do not.

Evolution of the Institute

Analysis of the first cycle of the Institute and a review of program evaluations led to several immediate observations about ITUE's initial success. First, there was enormous faculty demand locally for this integrated program of teaching/learning workshops on active learning and instructional technology. Second, scheduling and coordinating activities and meetings across the calendar year would be difficult for the diverse group of faculty members interested in ITUE. Third, the rapid development of instructional technology, both hardware and software, and the diversity in faculty expertise would make supporting and mentoring faculty a major task. It was clear that some adaptations in how ITUE operated would be needed to meet each of these challenges.

Following the first summer ITUE session, faculty interest in participating in ITUE continued to grow through word-of-mouth and campus publicity. In addition, off-campus interest emerged because of the website that had been launched to promote and coordinate ITUE activities. A concentrated two-day introductory session was offered in January 1998, open for the first time to off-campus participants. Although we had originally envisioned solely an annual cycle of workshops, we felt strongly that we wanted to maintain a small-class environment in our training session and that going much beyond fifty participants would diminish their experiences and the program's effectiveness.

Follow-up programs and scattered special sessions became difficult to schedule for both the ITUE Fellows and leaders. Input and feedback from faculty who completed the first cycle allowed us to refine and consolidate the ITUE program into a full-week session offered twice annually. An outline of the most recent session of ITUE, held in June 2000, is provided in the appendix; in addition to the original workshop topics, the program now also addresses such issues as different models of PBL geared to particular learning situations and the use of peer tutors in PBL courses.

Fortunately for the development of the Institute's instructional technology component, a faculty technology center was created concurrently (but through separate channels). Practical Resources for Educators Seeking Effective New Technologies (PRESENT), was designed with several goals in mind: to coach faculty as creative technology users, to bridge the gap between learning technology and applying it to teaching, to provide hands-on experience in a simulated classroom environment, to create templates for faculty to benefit from innovative uses, and to provide follow through to ensure a successful connection of technology to teaching. The staff of PRESENT and ITUE quickly found a resonance in their objectives and joined forces. PRESENT staff now work closely with the ITUE Fellows, side-by-side with ITUE leaders, during the afternoon technology training sessions. Follow-up support in the facilities of PRESENT follows naturally as a consequence of this early interaction. ITUE helps to generate an informed clientele for PRESENT, a clientele interested in using technology for the pedagogical value added. Most of the individualized, one-on-one training of faculty is accomplished in the PRESENT facilities by professional staff and trained student assistants and has permitted ITUE to continue operating efficiently as a faculty-led effort without full-time staff. The synergy in the partnership between ITUE and PRESENT has been responsible in large part for the rapid expansion in the use of the Web among the faculty at UD.

Impact and Sustainability of the Institute

ITUE has successfully brought together a diverse group of faculty members for examination of best practices in the classroom and discussion of a broad range of active learning strategies and uses of on-line resources for instruction. The Fellows represented areas well outside the core of disciplines typically supported by the National Science Foundation. A conscious attempt to increase the rate of "infusion" throughout the university was made. We sought to expand the use of active learning and technology in science, mathematics, and engineering courses, while advocating best practices throughout the entire university community. Of the nearly 200 ITUE Fellows participating from the University of Delaware, 65 have been from SMET disciplines (Science, Mathematics, Engineering and Technology); clearly the reach of ITUE across the university has been broad.

In general, it appeared that two types of faculty were being attracted to participate in ITUE: those interested in PBL, and those interested in using the Web and other technologies in their teaching. Their transformation during the weeklong session was often striking. Those coming primarily for the technology portion (and for the supplemental funding to facilitate their acquisition of more technology) had their eyes opened to the possibility of PBL and other active learning strategies. Those coming primarily for PBL saw how the Web can be used to facilitate student learning in their courses and were empowered both to design problems with rich on-line resources and to publish them on the Web for their students. ITUE has continued with this two-pronged approach to faculty development that has, in our opinion, been an essential element in its success.

Perhaps one of the most important aspects of ITUE has been its identification as an initiative that arose from the faculty and remains faculty-led. The ITUE leaders are all active teaching faculty with experience in making the transition from lectures to more student-centered active learning instructional models. As much as one can be convinced intellectually that moving to an approach such as problem-based learning is pedagogically sound and desirable, taking that first step away from the lectern and surrendering even some of the responsibility for learning to the students can be unnerving. Being able to turn for advice and mentoring to other faculty who have already made that transition helps to ease some of those concerns. Besides having the opportunity for one-on-one consultations with the ITUE leaders, Institute Fellows are invited to visit classroom sessions of ongoing PBL courses to get a better sense of how these ideas play out with students. In addition, the fact that the ITUE program came out of faculty ranks rather than as a mandate from the administration has, we feel, been a positive factor in faculty buy-in. An instructor may make the decision to pursue the approaches espoused by ITUE freely, rather than as a result of pressure from the top.

The administration's strong support for the educational strategies promoted by ITUE has been made clear in a number of tangible ways: ITUE Fellows, for example, have been awarded matching support funds from their departments or colleges. The recently constructed Gore Hall is devoted solely to classroom use; it contains no large lecture halls; indeed, no room holds more than 80 people, and several classes were furnished explicitly for case study or PBL use. Campus recruiting programs are billed as "Delaware Discovery Days," with a strong emphasis on the theme of discovery-based education. An administrative orientation session for new faculty has been conducted in part using a problem-based format.

Expanding the leadership of ITUE to include faculty members from disciplines outside of natural sciences has been key to sustaining interest across the spectrum of disciplines represented at the University. Two ITUE leaders have been added from Health Science and Sociology & Criminal Justice, both demonstrating best practice in the use of PBL, as well as instructional technology. Expansion of the leadership team has permitted ITUE to expand and refine its programs without burning out the founding leaders.

Another successful model that ITUE has supported focuses effort on departments seeking to transform their curricula broadly and coherently. In the first cycle of ITUE, nine members of Biological Sciences, six members of Mechanical Engineering, and five members of Civil and Environmental Engineering participated in ITUE activities, as well as a three-member team from Linguistics. Not surprisingly, collaborative efforts are more likely to lead to systemic reform in departmental curricula. Departments with at least ten ITUE Fellows over the past four years include Political Science & International Relations (17), Biological Sciences (14), Education (13), Sociology & Criminal Justice (10), and Consumer Studies (10). Development of vertical integration of PBL through the major's curriculum is well underway as a result in most of these units.

Since 1988, ITUE has welcomed off-campus participants; to date we have hosted 66 Visiting Faculty Fellows from 29 institutions, including 36 SMET faculty members. The international reach of ITUE has been a delightful surprise and a tribute to the representation of PBL at UD by its practitioners at professional conferences and via its Web presence. At this point, international visitors have participated from Slovakia, Belgium, Mexico, Australia, and Korea. Curriculum reform teams have been highly visible in their ITUE participation; groups have participated from a diverse set of institutions: Colorado College (4), Defense Systems Management College (3), Samford University (6), Florida A&M University (4), Middlesex Community College (5), North Dakota State University (6), and Universite Catholique de Louvain (8). We have recently expanded our program to include visiting K–12 Fellows, integrating local middle and high school teachers into our week long programs, coordinated with UD's Math/Science Education Resource Center.

Creation of an active visitors program has affected ITUE in several beneficial ways. First, several representatives of the UD PBL effort are regularly solicited for on-site workshops, both nationally and internationally, for the benefit of specific audiences. Typically, more requests are received than can be honored because of time and travel constraints. The regular availability of UD ITUE sessions allows participants from those institutions to travel instead to Delaware, interact with educators from diverse institutions and disciplines, and return to their institutions with the background and resources needed to begin introducing PBL at their home institutions. Optional afternoon workshops to train prospective trainers are now offered as needed in the ITUE program.

The second benefit is for the UD faculty. ITUE attracts leading proponents of curriculum reform and incorporation of active learning and instructional technology at their respective institutions. UD faculty members have the opportunity to interact with interested participants beyond their own department and campus, interested enough to make the trip to Newark, Delaware, during their academic year break. The Visiting Fellows bring great vitality to the ITUE sessions and raise the importance of ITUE in the eyes of the UD faculty as they recognize the opportunities available to them through the local resources of ITUE, its leaders, and established base of Faculty Fellows.

The strategy in promoting active and problem-based learning at UD has been to target introductory-level courses, in order to develop critical habits of mind in students as soon as possible. We also hope that early exposure to these exciting teaching methods will stimulate student demand for more courses like them, helping to spread the reform effort throughout the curriculum. Thus far, over 100 lower-level courses either have been or are slated for transformation to utilize active and problem-based learning. The recent awarding of a Pew Charitable Trusts grant to UD to incorporate problem-based learning into large, general education courses in the social sciences and humanities will enhance this effort even more.

Toward this end, ITUE has supported small teams of faculty members for development of multidisciplinary courses, especially those that would serve nonscience majors and first-year students in meeting curricular requirements. As originally envisioned in our project proposal to NSF, these Foundation Courses would approach topic areas in science from a multidisciplinary point of view, challenging students to learn by solving real-world problems or working through cases in groups or teams. A similar approach was adopted by the University of Delaware in Spring 2000 as a key feature of the university's new General Education Program. First-year interdisciplinary "Pathways to Discovery" courses are thematic, integrative courses for first-year students designed to introduce students to the academic resources of the university and to teach basic intellectual skills required for a successful undergraduate experience. Many of the faculty members designing and offering courses for this initiative have participated fully in ITUE. The widespread adoption of PBL that resulted from the creation of ITUE framed the discussion of general education reform and is apparent in its stated aims to ensure that every student will be able to do the following:

1. Attain effective skills in oral and written communication, quantitative reasoning, and the use of information technology

2. Learn to think critically to solve problems

3. Be able to work and learn both independently and collaboratively

4. Engage questions of ethics and recognize responsibilities to self, community, and society at large

5. Understand the diverse ways of thinking that underlie the search for knowledge in the arts, humanities, sciences, and social sciences

6. Develop the intellectual curiosity, confidence, and engagement that will lead to lifelong learning

7. Develop the ability to integrate academic knowledge with experiences that extend the boundaries of the classroom

8. Expand understanding and appreciation of human creativity and diverse forms of aesthetic and intellectual expression

9. Understand the foundations of U.S. society, including the significance of its cultural diversity

10. Develop an international perspective in order to live and work effectively in global society

Summary

In 1993, the term "problem-based learning" was virtually unknown on the campus of the University of Delaware. Seven years later, it has become a byword, and the university has established an international reputation as the leader in the development of problem-based learning in undergraduate education. At the heart of this change in campus culture has been the Institute for Transforming Undergraduate Education. To date, over 25 percent of the UD faculty have participated either in PBL workshops or ITUE programs, and more than 150 courses have been or are targeted for transformation. ITUE's efforts toward the improvement of undergraduate education through faculty development were recognized in 1999 through the Theodore M. Hesburgh Certificate of Excellence.

What began as a search on the part of a few faculty members for a better way to teach is changing the face of undergraduate education at UD and providing a viable model for other institutions to emulate. The initial proposal to use PBL in a handful of courses has led to the following:

- A full-scale development program to train faculty in using PBL and other active learning strategies and technologies in their courses

- A number of initiatives aimed at transforming individual courses and whole curricula into more active, student-centered and inquiry-driven formats

- National recognition as a resource of information and insight for others interested in change

Perhaps the most important change, though, has been in attitude—in the renewed interest expressed throughout the university in the importance of undergraduate teaching aimed at meeting the real needs of our students, in ways that are invigorating and effective for both students and faculty.

We invite you to participate in an upcoming ITUE session!

Authors' Biographies

George H. Watson is Professor of Physics and Astronomy at the University of Delaware.

Susan E. Groh is Assistant Professor of Chemistry and Biochemistry and an affiliated faculty member of the University Honors Program at the University of Delaware.

APPENDIX TO CHAPTER 2

Table 2.1. Sessions Presented during the 1997 Summer ITUE Program

Wed.	Experience It Yourself	Example of class structured around a problem.
	Getting Started—The Syllabus	Building the framework of your course; elements of a good syllabus.
	The Internet as a Learning Resource	Finding information on the Web and using the Web as a resource for student learning.
Thurs.	Incorporating Active Learning in the Classroom	Active learning and larger classes.
	Getting Started with Groups	Why use groups? What works?
	Problems and Cases: Writing Material for Your Course	Characteristics of good problems or cases; Bloom taxonomy and higher-order thinking skills.
	Internet Resources for Your Course	
Fri.	Panel Discussion on Student Assessment	Reexamining how we assess students.
	Assessment Strategies	Nontraditional assessment strategies to try.
	Evaluation of Transformation Projects	

Table 2.2. Sessions Offered at the June 2000 ITUE Program

Mon.	**An Introduction to Active Learning and Problem-based Learning**	Why use student-centered inquiry methods? What instructional models can be used in typical undergraduate courses?
	Experience It Yourself A model for active/problem-based learning for all classes	Participants work through a PBL problem, exploring a variety of strategies to use in problem-based instruction.
	Fellows '99	Each day following lunch, past Fellows present transformation projects from prior years.
	Scouring the Web Finding the resources you need	Search strategies and techniques are modeled by reviewing several web searches.
	Searching the Web Bringing the real world into your classroom	Participants exercise several search engines and refine their Internet search techniques to find information relevant to the problem of the day.
Tues.	**Getting Started I**	PBL instruction is different from traditional teaching in many ways. This session helps participants plan for course and syllabus revisions.
	Writing Effective Problem-based Materials	Participants learn to write materials suitable for a PBL course. By the end of this day, participants have a draft of a problem for their course.
	Building the Web Publishing course resources	The rudiments of publishing course materials on the Web will be presented.
	Publishing on the Web Preparing your own problem for the Web	Participants finish developing their PBL problem, learn how to publish it in web-ready form, and select and list Internet resources.
Wed.	**Getting Started II**	This session helps participants to plan for course revisions, including how to introduce students to PBL instructional methods and group work.

Wed. *cont.*	**Group Dynamics** How groups work effectively	Participants learn effective strategies for forming groups, initiating group activities, and helping students work cooperatively in their groups.
	PBL Syllabi on the Web	Examples are shown of syllabi for PBL courses.
	Expanding the Web Starting your course web page	Participants activate their homepages, create a course web page, and learn how to post course materials.
Thurs.	**Assessment of Learning in Student-Centered Courses**	Participants learn a variety of methods for assessing higher-order thinking skills and group activities related to their own course goals.
	Working the Web Why have a website for your course?	How can a course website improve student learning and the undergraduate experience?
	Moving to the Web Converting existing materials for on-line use	Participants learn how to convert existing documents and move them online.
Fri.	**Models for Problem-Based Learning in Small, Medium, and Large Classes**	Participants learn about a variety of models of problem-based instruction.
	Peer Tutors A Multilayered Learning System	Participants learn about the strengths and benefits of using peer tutors in their courses.
	Picking Our Brains	Participants or teams of participants work with ITUE leaders as they write problems, syllabi, or assessment items.
	Taking Care of Loose Ends	Open computer lab to help with specific questions or hands-on training.

3

MAKE IT SO

ADMINISTRATIVE SUPPORT FOR PROBLEM-BASED LEARNING

John C. Cavanaugh

Chapter Summary

Experience and research evidence demonstrate that problem-based learning (PBL) greatly improves the teaching and learning environment. However, without appropriate support from key administrators, PBL cannot emerge as a viable instructional option. This chapter discusses ways administrators can help facilitate the successful introduction of problem-based learning on campus.

Introduction

Arguably the most difficult challenge facing an academic administrator is designing successful, sustainable curricular or pedagogical reform (Ewell, 1997). In part, this is due to faculty reluctance to change well-established habits without extensive evidence that the proposed approach is better, and in part to administrative reluctance to push the need for currency in view of empirical research on the efficacy of alternative approaches. The unfortunate consequence is that too often the opportunities for true innovation and improvement of student learning are lost because of faculty and administrative proclivity to become bogged down in seemingly endless discussion and turf protection.

This book offers an alternative, grounded in pedagogical and cognitive developmental theories and empirical evidence. As such, it provides a blueprint for successful and meaningful change that simultaneously addresses the need for greater achievement in student learning through alternative curricular and pedagogical approaches. Taken together, the chapters in this book provide the basis needed by academic administrators and the faculty to effect the kinds of changes that leaders in both groups typically envision at the outset of a reform effort, but rarely achieve. Most important, these changes help faculty and academic administrators take learning seriously (Shulman, 1999).

The present chapter provides a brief overview of the steps academic administrators can and should take to help maximize the success of a reform effort based on PBL (for a related perspective, see Ewell, 1997). The focus will be on five major topics: (1) the role of senior administration in promoting PBL; (2) cost-benefit implications of PBL; (3) faculty roles and rewards; (4) long-term sustainability of PBL reform efforts; and (5) documenting outcomes. Each of these topics will be discussed in turn. The chapter will conclude with recommendations for putting the ideas into practice.

Role of Senior Administration

In order for curricular or pedagogical change to be successful, it will need the support of senior administrators, especially the chief academic officer and campus chief executive. Such support can often be the element that makes or breaks the reform effort. Perhaps because of the critical nature of senior administrative support, it is also one of the most delicate matters involved in reform. That is, silence or lukewarm support from individuals "at the top" for reform efforts generally lowers the likelihood of success; however, these same individuals can be overly zealous and similarly doom reform by mandating it. Thus, the first issue to consider is how senior administrators can be most effective in helping to promote curricular or pedagogical reform.

In general, there are two strategies senior administrators adopt in promoting reform: top-down and bottom-up. The top-down approach entails individuals, such as the chief executive officer, who announce a major initiative concerning curricular or pedagogical reform as a way to enhance student learning. Trustees and other key academic administrators, e.g., chief academic officer, deans, may also promote the effort. Top-down strategies ensure that the campus is made aware of the priorities of the administration and can set a particular agenda for change.

Used appropriately, top-down strategies can be effective in motivating and energizing faculty to change. Top-down approaches often take the form of goals for the campus as outlined by the chief executive officer or the chief academic officer in annual reports to the faculty. Ideally, well-stated goals can then be turned over to the appropriate faculty governance group(s) for further refinement and implementation. However, top-down strategies also run the risk of being perceived as mandates that are simply pronouncements made without room for discussion. For example, a chief executive officer may simply declare that the faculty *will* change the curriculum or change the way they teach. In these cases, a top-down strategy may not be effective and may delay reform efforts, and in the worst case it may completely stifle any chance of support by the faculty.

In contrast, bottom-up strategies begin with faculty coming together in support of an initiative that is subsequently supported by senior administrators. In this case, a faculty-led initiative, such as the initial PBL initiative at the University of Delaware described elsewhere in this book (Chapter 1), garners support from key administrators only after it is clear that a core group of faculty are strongly committed to the change initiative, and there is a reasonable probability of success. At this point, senior administrators may step forward and champion the project.

The advantages of a bottom-up strategy are that there is no question of faculty support, there usually are successful demonstrations of the new curriculum or pedagogical approach, and potential faculty leadership on the initiative is likely to have emerged. There may also have been successes at procuring extramural funds to support the early stages of the project. Senior administrative support at this point makes it appear that faculty are clearly in control of the curriculum and that success is being rewarded and encouraged. The disadvantage is that if the support from senior administrators is too slow in coming or is mistimed, the initial excitement and motivation of the faculty change agents may be lost. For example, if there is an overt attempt by senior administrators to wrest control of the project from its faculty base, either rhetorically or in fact, then the initial success is unlikely to be sustained, and faculty may abandon the effort.

Clearly, the best situation involves the right balance between top-down and bottom-up strategies. For example, a faculty-led initiative to improve student learning through PBL that enjoys early success in improving student performance and results in significant reinvigoration among faculty for their teaching is supported publicly by senior academic administrators. Three key ingredients that maximize the likelihood of a successful blend of top-down and bottom-up strategies can be identified: (1) getting the rhetoric right, (2) removing the barriers to innovation, and (3) making adequate resources available.

One often-overlooked aspect of helping to ensure the success of any initiative is getting the rhetoric about the initiative right. In the case of PBL, that means using consistent definitions of PBL, discussing and agreeing on the same critical outcomes, and agreeing on the scope of the effort. Of these, the one most often given insufficient attention is the consistent use of the same terms. As discussed elsewhere, PBL refers to a specific type of teaching and learning. Substitution of other labels, such as collaborative learning, can confuse the issue and divert attention from the main goals. Senior administrators must work closely with the key faculty involved in the initiative to ensure that consistent terminology is used.

One of the most important (and usually cost-free) roles that senior administrators can play in ensuring the success of a curricular or pedagogical change effort is removing barriers to innovation. Barriers may exist at the individual level (e.g., tenured faculty strongly discouraging untenured faculty from engaging in innovation in teaching), unit level (e.g., a department refuses to give faculty "credit" toward merit pay increases for working on curricular or pedagogical efforts), or structural level (e.g., institutional research only attributing student credit hours to a single department, even when courses are team taught by faculty in different departments). Senior academic administrators have the power to make sure that such barriers are removed; for example, a chief academic officer can take curricular or pedagogical efforts into consideration during review for tenure or promotion and, if necessary, reverse inappropriate decisions made at lower levels. Administrators can also obtain extramural funds to support an institutionwide reform effort.

Using the power of administration wisely to help ensure the success of a reform effort such as PBL is critical. Not only does it directly address (and presumably solve) potential reform-killing problems, it also sends a strong message of support to the campus. Although these types of interventions are no substitute for the provision of the necessary resources for the reform effort, they often make the difference between success and failure. For even if resources are provided, if barriers to change are allowed to remain, then the long-term success of the effort will always remain in doubt.

Finally, senior academic administrators are the only people who can provide the resources needed for a curricular or pedagogical reform that will ensure long-term success. Making a reform effort such as PBL a sufficiently high budget priority clearly signals that it has become a high institutional priority and is another way of demonstrating support for the initiative. The form of resource support can vary as will be described later. Irrespective of whether it is in the form of cash, administered workloads, or some other approach, providing resources is an essential role for senior academic administrators.

The role of senior administrators, then, is deceptively simple: Know which faculty-led initiative on curricular or pedagogical reform to support publicly, state that support publicly, and take the appropriate steps to ensure success. The deceptive parts involve knowing which initiatives to support and the timing of the support. Supporting the "wrong" initiatives (or, worse yet, every initiative) may result in a climate of indiscriminate efforts that are misguided and ineffective. Poor timing of support may result in the perception of a top-down mandate, if the support is stated too early, or in a too-little-too-late perception if the support is rendered too far into the effort. The trick is for academic administrators to work very closely with key faculty engaged in reform efforts, as well as staying in close touch with key faculty leaders who can provide advice on the timing of statements of support. Such partnerships are the best way to ensure success.

Faculty Roles and Rewards

Irrespective of how well intentioned any curricular or pedagogical reform may be, unless faculty have sufficient incentives to change, it is unlikely that there will be the motivation to do so. These incentives can include a wide variety of options, including salary, merit increases, release time, professional development opportunities, and other support (e.g., laptop computers). In addition, it is important to recognize that any curricular or pedagogical change entails significant risk and expenditure of time, which affects both workload issues, as well as evaluation and compensation (Seldin, 1998).

Deciding which incentives to use to motivate (and ultimately sustain) change is much more complex than it may appear at first glance. There is a tendency for academic administrators to focus almost exclusively on financial incentives (e.g., salary), probably because they are the easiest to implement through the usual annual evaluation process for merit increases. In many cases, such financial incentives work well and provide a workable approach to implementing change.

Although many faculty respond positively to money, it is the case that the most precious commodity for many faculty is *time*. A major barrier to adopting new teaching techniques (among other things) is that faculty are increasingly being asked to do more, resulting in an additive model of faculty workload. When a curricular or pedagogical reform is proposed, the effort expended is typically considered to be *in addition to* the ongoing workload, creating a situation forcing faculty to choose whether they can afford (in terms of risk and time) to adopt the proposed changes. In such cases, no amount of financial incentive is likely to work if faculty perceive (accurately or not) that they simply do not have the time to work on change. In such cases, an effective alternative would be to provide faculty release time from other obligations (e.g., course, committee work) to prepare a PBL course. In short, the best approach for designing incentives for faculty is to have a range of options that can be tailored to the needs of individuals.

Unfortunately, no matter how flexible and individually tailored the incentive system is, it may not address the most difficult issue facing early career faculty—the danger of taking risks concerning their teaching. The issue is straightforward. Early career faculty are (in too many cases correctly) concerned that adopting a new instructional approach could result in less positive teaching evaluations than their tried-and-true (but possibly less effective) approach. Many senior faculty exacerbate the situation by strongly dissuading early-career faculty from attempting any innovations in their teaching for fear that it will affect their reappointment and tenure and promotion decisions negatively. Thus, many early-career faculty are risk averse when it comes to trying a new approach in their teaching.

It is critical that academic administrators, especially chairs and deans, make it very clear what the stakes are for early-career faculty. If a climate favorable to innovation is to be established, then mechanisms must be in place to protect early-career faculty who decide to be innovative. For example, means by which early-career faculty receive meaningful credit for engaging in curricular or pedagogical reform efforts could be implemented. In any case, it is often the responsibility of academic administrators to ensure that early-career faculty who choose to try alternative instructional approaches are not affected negatively.

Cost/Benefit Implications of PBL

As documented in several other chapters in this volume (Part Three), PBL results in comparable or better student learning compared with traditional lecture formats. Moreover, students over the long run strongly endorse PBL as a teaching-learning method. Given these significant and consistent findings, a key question is why these results have not led to wholesale adoption of PBL across all disciplines in all courses.

As with any innovation, the answer lies in a careful analysis of the costs versus benefits of PBL. Because the benefits of PBL in terms of improved learning are detailed in several other chapters, we will focus here on the costs and other benefits. In general, only if it can be shown that the benefits of PBL outweigh the costs is it likely that PBL will be widely adopted.

The costs of PBL include both obvious ones (e.g., faculty incentive pay, professional development and training, consultants) and less obvious ones (e.g., increased course preparation time for faculty). These costs can be examined at four levels of analysis: (1) individual, (2) department, (3) college/school, and (4) institutional.

At the individual level, costs can be measured in terms of time spent preparing for and teaching a course, as well as in terms of financial resources, such as merit increases or increased professional development funds as a direct result of using a particular teaching-learning approach. For example, a faculty member may find that preparing for a PBL course takes longer than for a traditional lecture course and may risk receiving somewhat lower merit funds as a result of changing from traditional lecture format to PBL. In addition to benefits in terms of improved (over the long run) teaching evaluations, which in turn may lead to higher merit increases, benefits of PBL may also accrue in terms of having access to additional professional development or extramural funds. For example, faculty who use PBL may be eligible to receive funds to attend workshops, such as those described by Watson and Groh (Chapter 2). Although costs and benefits to individual faculty are both real and highly salient, they are difficult to compare across individuals. Thus, most cost-benefit analyses for comparison purposes are conducted at the development, college/school, and institutional levels.

Most cost analyses at the department, college/school, and institutional levels focus exclusively on the actual dollars expended per full-time equivalent (FTE) student or some similar index. Such benchmark data permit direct comparisons across departments and institutions and rely on common definitions of terms. Using such indices can provide a consistent measure of costs of instruction based on different teaching-learning methods. However, comparisons between traditional lecture, for example, and PBL approaches must include all relevant aspects (e.g., faculty development, laptop computers, teaching assistants) in order to be meaningful.

As the level of aggregation increases, the types of benefits that become important also change. For example, at the department (and in some cases college/school level), benefits may include overall passage rates on certification examinations following PBL courses, summative evaluation of majors and courses of study, number of papers and presentations made by faculty concerning PBL, and the like. At the institutional level, a benefit of widespread PBL use may be the ability to use PBL as a student (and faculty) recruitment tool in order to uniquely position the institution in relation to its peers.

The cost-benefit analysis computed at various levels of analysis is extremely important. In general, PBL is likely to be more costly (at least in terms of expenditures per FTE student and faculty time) during the initial development and implementation phases. Thus, it is essential to define specific benefits by which PBL will be evaluated in advance. Furthermore, these benefits should include both those that involve student learning (e.g., content learning, critical thinking, problem-solving skills) and those focused on faculty (e.g., improved teaching ratings, increased motivation for teaching, scholarly publications on teaching). The decision point at which PBL will be supported even in the face of greater costs should also be specified in advance; otherwise, it will be difficult to evaluate the point at which PBL is too costly even when the benefits are clearly demonstrated. Equally important to these analyses is the continued monitoring of the cost-benefit data over time. Ideally, costs should stabilize or decline as faculty become more proficient at PBL and larger sections of PBL courses are implemented.

In sum, the analysis of cost-benefit data is a key aspect of determining the long-term viability of PBL. If the models described elsewhere in this book are implemented, especially those describing large section PBL courses, use of undergraduate peer tutors, and faculty-to-faculty peer mentoring, over the long run, costs of PBL instruction should not be significantly greater than traditional lecture formats.

Achieving Sustainability

Getting a curricular or pedagogical reform underway and gaining the necessary support from senior academic administrators represent only a beginning of true change. In order to effect true change, it is essential that the change effort be sustained over the long run. The secrets to sustainability are relatively simple: (a) Establish an ongoing faculty development program. (b) Maintain the right mix of incentives. (c) Create a demand for the new curriculum or pedagogy. (d) Generate publicity and recognition.

Of the various models of faculty development, one that has worked extremely well at the University of Delaware is the faculty-to-faculty model described by Watson and Groh in Chapter 2. By focusing on developing a critical mass of faculty who use PBL and having those faculty serve as peer tutors, a self-sustaining faculty development and support program was developed. This program creates PBL experts in every department, ultimately making department faculty (rather than a director of a teaching center) the locus of assistance. This is a very important shift; by focusing on departments, barriers based on discipline-based differences in instruction are greatly reduced.

A second key to sustainability involves maintaining the right mix of incentives for faculty to continue using an innovation such as PBL. Earlier in this chapter, the issues pertaining to incentives were discussed (e.g., salary, administered workloads, etc.). Too often, these incentives are created in order to get the initiative started and are subsequently withdrawn and moved to the next new project. A secret to sustaining a curricular or pedagogical innovation is leaving the incentives in place and keeping them current. This latter point involves assessing incentives periodically to make sure they reflect the set of faculty needs at the time. For example, one popular incentive early in an initiative is support to create a course using an innovation such as PBL. At some point, though, course development needs may significantly diminish. However, a need for advanced training in PBL techniques may emerge. Unless the incentive system keeps pace with changing faculty needs, there is likely to be a mismatch between incentives and need. Successful innovations manage to maintain a match between the two by periodic review of incentives by faculty and academic administrators.

A third critical element of sustainability involves creating a demand for the innovation. In the case of PBL, this would entail getting and keeping students excited about taking PBL courses. In large part, this depends on the faculty delivering dynamic courses that provide excellent learning opportunities, but academic advisors encouraging students to take PBL courses is also important. When students are excited about learning through PBL, they put pressure on departments to provide additional PBL opportunities, which helps sustain PBL.

Finally, publicity about a curricular or pedagogical innovation like PBL is critical to keep faculty (and academic administrators) motivated. Faculty-staff publications, department newsletters, local newspapers, and alumni magazines all offer ways of getting the word out about an innovation. Teaching and research awards should include opportunities for faculty who use the innovation. Like anyone, faculty need to be recognized and rewarded for being willing to explore new ways of doing their jobs, which in turn helps maintain the innovation.

Documenting Outcomes

The great increase in the need to document the outcomes of curricular or pedagogical innovations for accreditation and other purposes means that the appropriate data need to be collected to show the effectiveness of the innovation. Such documentation includes measurement of student learning, students' critical thinking, pass rates on licensure examinations, course evaluations, and faculty self-evaluation of teaching. Many examples of outcome measures are discussed throughout this book (Part Three) (see also Mierson & Parikh, 2000).

Summary and Conclusions

In summary, academic administrators have an important role to play in creating and sustaining curricular or pedagogical innovations such as PBL. Most important, they need to work with the faculty in developing the right balance between top-down and bottom-up approaches to innovation, to create appropriate incentive systems that recognize different needs among the faculty, to monitor the cost-benefit trade-off of an innovation and to define both costs and benefits in appropriate ways, to ensure that the necessary elements are in place to sustain the innovation, and to collect the appropriate data that provides measures of the innovation's effectiveness.

The ideal situation is one in which senior academic administrators act as facilitators for the faculty during a curricular or pedagogical innovation. Administrative support is essential, but ideally it should be done in such a way that the focus remains on the faculty. In this way, a true partnership can be created that fosters and sustains each group. If that happens, then the stage is set for successful innovations that can transform the teaching-learning experience.

Author Biography

John C. Cavanaugh is the Provost and Vice Chancellor for Academic Affairs at the University of North Carolina at Wilmington. He previously held the office of Vice Provost for Academic Programs and Planning at the University of Delaware.

References

Ewell, P. T. (1997). Organizing for learning. *AAHE Bulletin, 50* (1), 3–6.

Mierson, S., & Parikh, A. A. (2000). Stories from the field: Problem-based learning from a teacher's and a student's perspective. *Change, 32* (1), 21–27.

Seldin, P. (1998). How colleges evaluate teaching: 1988 vs. 1998. *AAHE Bulletin, 50* (7), 3–7.

Shulman, L. S. (1999). Taking learning seriously. *Change, 31* (4), 10–17.

PART TWO

PLANNING FOR EFFECTIVE PROBLEM-BASED INSTRUCTION

Part Two deals with broad topics of general interest to faculty who are contemplating a change to problem-based instruction. These include discussions of different models for PBL classes, the process of writing problems, ways to use groups effectively, issues to consider in getting started in PBL, the utility of peer tutors, assessment strategies, and ways to incorporate technology in a PBL course.

4

MODELS FOR PROBLEM-BASED INSTRUCTION IN UNDERGRADUATE COURSES

Barbara J. Duch

Chapter Summary

Problem-based learning is a teaching technique used in many medical schools to facilitate learning basic science concepts in the context of clinical cases. This model is not generally applicable to many typical undergraduate courses for a variety of reasons, including class size. This chapter discusses several instructional models used in medium to large classes.

Introduction

In the early 1990s when I first became aware of problem-based learning (PBL) in the medical school setting, I was immediately interested in it because I believed that the process of learning in PBL most closely mimics how we question and learn in our professional lives. I was also aware, however, that what worked in a medical school setting might not transfer well into a typical undergraduate setting for a variety of reasons, including intellectual maturity and motivation level of the students. I found that in order to incorporate PBL in undergraduate courses, it was necessary to develop models of instruction that allow one faculty member to teach large numbers of typical undergraduate students. There are a variety of instructional decisions that need to be made based on several factors, including size of class, intellectual maturity of students, course objectives, preference of instructor, and availability of undergraduate peer tutors or graduate teaching assistants.

Instructional Models

When the "early PBL reformers" at the University of Delaware started to develop their first problem-based courses, each instructor made his or her own decisions on the best way to use problem-based instruction for their students. At the same time, those faculty members were talking to one another, sharing what was working in their course, what wasn't working, and brainstorming ideas for overcoming some of the problems they encountered in adopting problem-based techniques in their typical undergraduate classes. Out of those discussions and early adoptions, several models of problem-based instruction were identified and have been used by increasing numbers of faculty who teach undergraduates in a variety of undergraduate institutions.

Medical School Model

Problem-based learning is a teaching technique used in many medical schools to facilitate learning basic science concepts in the context of clinical cases (Boud & Feletti, 1997). In many cases, students are assigned to groups of eight to ten, and each group is assigned a faculty member who plays the role of tutor or discussion leader as the students work through a case or problem. This model is very student-centered, with little or no formal class time. Instead, groups schedule time that they will meet to discuss the materials. Since typical undergraduate classes are larger, most instructors would be unable to use the classic medical school model, except in smaller, senior-level seminar-type classes.

Some faculty have used graduate students, recruited outside professional experts, or invited other faculty into their course to serve as additional tutors in their course in order to mimic the medical school model as closely as possible. Others have recruited undergraduate students to serve as peer tutors (see Chapter 8 for more detail).

Floating Facilitator Model

A variety of instructional strategies can be used to facilitate the learning of multiple groups of students in larger size classes. When it is not possible to have a dedicated faculty tutor lead discussion, answer questions, and ensure equal participation from all students, it is best to limit the size of each group to four, at most five students. Johnson, Johnson, and Smith (1991) recommend that students be assigned to groups of four in order to improve student accountability and assure that each student gets his or her own "talk time." It is also easier to plan group activities that require the effort of four students rather than a larger group.

In this model, only a portion of class time will be devoted to individual group discussion, while the instructor as the "floating facilitator" moves from group to group asking questions and probing for student understanding. Other periods of time will be spent having each group report to the whole class on the results of individual discussions. Minilectures and whole class discussions will also play a role in this model, as well as other activities, such as debates and presentation of project results or problem solutions. Using a variety of learning activities has the advantage of appealing to the diverse learning styles of the students in the course.

The following is an example of activities in a typical class the day after the first stage of a problem has been introduced and the students have had an opportunity to do research on their initial learning issues:

- Introduce the schedule for the day.

- Students within their groups discuss the findings of their research on learning issues that were previously identified for the first 15–20 minutes. Groups then rank, in order of importance, the learning issues from the previous class and add new learning issues that have emerged from group discussions. Students use this time to teach each other what they have learned so far about the concepts targeted in the problem. During this time, the instructor moves from group to group asking questions, directing discussion, and checking for understanding. It is important not to get stopped by one group for too long. All groups want to feel that they have access to the teacher during the individual group time. One common student complaint will be, "We were stuck and wasted class time waiting 15 minutes to get help." If all groups seem to be "stuck" on the same issue, it is best to suspend group discussion while the instructor clarifies the topics through a minilecture or whole-class discussion.

- Each group reports to the whole class on what their top-ranked learning issues are and what they have learned so far through their research. This "reporting out" procedure is helpful to the instructor, as well as to each of the groups. When listening to other groups' learning issues and findings, each group will be getting feedback on their own choices and research. If most groups' top-ranked learning issue was at the bottom of another group's list, those students will have an opportunity to rethink how they have approached the problem before going further. If the groups are split, the instructor has an excellent opportunity to initiate a discussion on the rationale used by various groups and perhaps redirect some students who were missing the "big ideas" and important concepts in the problem. This is also a good time for the faculty member to recommend helpful learning resources for students if they don't appear to have found them.

- Once a list of the groups' learning issues has been generated, and there has been a discussion about the research done on those questions, the instructor may want to conduct a class discussion or plan a minilecture to focus on the questions that are outstanding with most groups. One may choose to reflect on the major learning objectives addressed by the problem, particularly if the students seem confused or lack direction. At the same time, PBL practitioners will highlight important learning issues students have not identified and direct students to other materials and resources they have missed in their research.

- After some whole-class activities, the instructor can cycle back to individual group work, asking students to reevaluate their list of learning issues after hearing the responses from other groups and instructions from the teacher. They also may identify new questions that may have been generated by the class discussion or minilecture. While students are discussing issues in their group, one can circulate among them listening to group discussion and questions.

Before introducing the second stage, the faculty member may want to summarize the first stage of the problem, soliciting remarks from each student group in terms of answers to questions and resolution of important learning issues. The cycles between group discussion and whole-class activities will help the instructor keep informed of what and how the groups are doing and will also be a mechanism for timing the progress of all of the groups, ensuring that a few groups don't get too far ahead or behind.

Peer Tutor Model

Undergraduate peer or near-peer tutors can be utilized to extend the ability to check the functioning of individual groups and assure that the group discussions probe for deeper levels of understanding. Peer tutors can help incorporate an instructional model that is closer to problem-based instruction in medical schools. Peer tutors are especially effective in the following ways:

- They help smooth the group and problem-solving process, accentuating the positive aspects of group learning and minimizing the negative ones.

- They serve as a role model in the PBL process for inexperienced students, facilitating student response and participation from everyone in the group. Peer tutors who were previous students in the course can reassure and support students, particularly freshmen, when they feel challenged.

- Peer tutors check the content of the discussion, looking for conceptual understanding.

- They also make decisions about when to answer student questions and when to throw questions back to the students.

- Tutors serve as the instructor's window into their groups, informing him or her of what is working well and what is not. Feedback from peer tutors is very informative to the instructor.

Just as in the medical school model, peer tutors can serve the role of group facilitator to a larger group (six to eight students) since they will be in a position of monitoring the group function on a regular basis. In large classes where there are not enough tutors for each group, they can serve in a rotating or "floating facilitator" role with two or three groups of four students. This role is more difficult for peer tutors (as it is for faculty). If this model is used, it may be desirable to script appropriate probing questions and dialogue for the peer tutors to use as they move from group to group. This strategy, although somewhat structured, ensures that each group is effectively guided toward achieving the course instructional goals. More details about peer tutors and how to prepare undergraduates to be successful group facilitators are found in Chapter 8 of this book.

Large Class Models

Problem-based instruction can be implemented in large courses, although the structure of the class will need to be more teacher-centered than in the previous models. Undergraduate peer tutors or graduate assistants can be used in this model as floating facilitators to provide support that will assist in group discussions and classroom management. When implementing PBL in large courses, teachers need to design additional structure into group activities during class time. The instructor's role will be similar to that of the discussion leader's—asking students to do the following:

- Discuss instructor-generated questions.
- Rank learning issues.
- Report results.
- Share resources.
- Ask probing questions.

A PBL instructor will want to plan to use many teaching strategies that will challenge students to develop critical thinking skills and communication skills and still support them in a way that allows them to accept the challenges of learning from themselves and their peers. When planning a PBL class, recognize that it will be important to cycle through many instructional activities that will include minilectures, whole-class discussion, and small group discussion. The daily routine may be somewhat like the one mentioned under the "floating facilitator" model, but the faculty member will need to limit the time that groups spend in individual group discussion. Rather than plan for a twenty-minute period of group discussion, it will be more successful to break the group discussion time into two ten-minute periods with whole class discussion or a minilecture in between. More details about teaching large classes using PBL can be found in Chapter 14.

Conclusion

Incorporating PBL into typical undergraduate courses, particularly at research universities, is a challenge that is worth meeting in order to help undergraduate students develop the lifelong learning skills that will help them succeed in college and beyond. Many models for successfully using PBL in medium- to large-size classes have been discussed in this chapter, and more details of these models are discussed in Part Three of this book. Each faculty member intent on using problem-based instruction will make many decisions based on the size of their class, the intellectual maturity of their students, the type of course (survey course, introductory, majors' upper level), and the availability of graduate or undergraduate peer tutors.

Author Biography

Barbara J. Duch is Associate Director of the Mathematics & Science Education Resource Center at the University of Delaware.

References

Boud, D. & Feletti, G. (Eds.). (1997). *The challenge of problem-based learning* (2nd ed.). London: Kogan Page.

Johnson, D. W., Johnson, R. T., & Smith, K. A. (1991). Cooperative learning: Increasing college faculty instructional productivity. *ASHE-ERIC Higher Education Report No. 4.* Washington, DC: George Washington University.

5

WRITING PROBLEMS FOR DEEPER UNDERSTANDING

Barbara J. Duch

Chapter Summary

One of the keys to success in implementing problem-based learning in undergraduate courses is the type of problem you use. This chapter will discuss ways to find or write PBL problems if there are no sources of them in print.

Introduction

A common complaint heard from college faculty is that their students seem to lack the ability or motivation to go beyond factual material to a deeper understanding of course material. The reasons for superficial rather than deep understanding on the part of students are many, including how we test, what expectations we set, and what learning materials we use when we teach. This chapter will focus on using new materials and problems in a problem-based environment to help students achieve in-depth knowledge of the concepts central to their understanding course material.

Standard college textbook problems in science and other disciplines tend to reinforce the students' naive view of learning because they can successfully answer homework end-of-chapter problems through memorization of facts and equations and using novice "pattern-match" problem-solving techniques. Typical problems do not foster the development of effective problem-solving and analytical skills (Heller & Hollabaugh, 1992) nor do they challenge students to develop critical thinking skills and logical reasoning (Mazur, 1996). In a successful PBL course, the selection of appropriate problems and material is crucial for students to go beyond a superficial understanding of the important concepts and principles being taught.

Characteristic of Good PBL Problems

There may be more characteristics of good PBL problems than those in the following list, and those characteristics may vary somewhat according to the discipline. However, many practitioners of problem-based instruction will probably identify the following as important characteristics of a good PBL problem:

1. An effective problem must first engage students' interest and motivate them to probe for deeper understanding of the concepts being introduced. It should relate the subject matter to the real world as much as possible. If the problem is placed in a context in which the students are familiar, they will feel that they have a stake in solving the problem.

2. Problems that work well sometimes require students to make decisions or judgments based on facts, information, logic and/or rationalization. In this kind of problem, students will be asked to justify their decisions and reasoning based on the principles being learned. Problems may require students to decide what assumptions are needed (and why), what information is relevant, and/or what steps or procedures are required in order to solve the problem. Not all the information given in the problem needs to be relevant to a solution, as is the case in "messy" real-world situations, and not all the information needed for a solution will be given to the student right away. For this reason, many PBL problems are designed with multiple stages, to be given to student groups one at a time, as they work through the problem. The second stage of the problem may give additional information to students related to issues raised in the first stage of the problem.

3. The problem should be complex enough that cooperation from all members of the student group will be necessary in order for them to effectively work toward a solution. The length and complexity of the problem or case must be such that students soon realize that a "divide and conquer" effort will not be an effective problem-solving

strategy. It may be necessary and, in fact desirable for groups to assign different learning issues to individuals to research. The power of problem-based learning, however, lies in the ability of the group to synthesize what they have learned and connect that new knowledge to the framework of understanding that they are building, based on the concepts in the course. This requires cooperative learning and group discussion as opposed to individual compartmentalized learning. For example, a problem that consists of a series of straightforward "end of chapter" questions will be divided by the group and assigned to individuals and then reassembled for the assignment submission. In this case, students end up learning *less* not *more*.

4. The initial questions in the first stage of a problem should be open-ended, based on previously learned knowledge, and/or be controversial so that all students in the groups are initially drawn into a discussion of the topic. This strategy keeps the students functioning as a group, rather than encouraging them to work individually at the outset of the problem. Again, the initial discussions will help students remember what they already know and help them build connections to previously learned concepts and material.

5. The content objectives of the course should be incorporated into the problems, connecting previous knowledge to new concepts, and connecting new knowledge to concepts in other courses and/or disciplines. Many faculty share the content objectives of the problem with students after they finish the problem to ensure that all groups researched each objective, and if not, they still have an opportunity to do so. Instructors usually prefer to wait until students are through so that they will not limit the scope of their investigations, but they do want to give students the benefit of seeing the instructor's objectives as a check on their learning. PBL practitioners may also choose to share the broader objectives of the problem at the beginning of the problem to focus students before they identify learning issues. The problem's questions should challenge students to develop higher-order thinking skills, moving them beyond Bloom's (1956) lower cognitive levels of knowledge and comprehension to the higher Bloom levels, where they analyze, synthesize, and evaluate (Table 5.1). These are the skills that are so important for our students to develop in order to succeed in any profession.

Table 5.1 Bloom's Cognitive Levels

Cognitive Level	Student Activity
Knowledge	Remembering facts, terms, concepts, and definitions
Comprehension	Explaining and interpreting the meaning of material
Application	Using a concept or principle to solve a *new* problem
Analysis	Breaking material down into its parts to see interrelationships
Synthesis	Producing something new from component parts
Evaluation	Making a judgment based on criteria

Suggestions for Writing PBL Problems

Finding good PBL problems is a challenge in most disciplines. They generally are not found in traditional texts, so the search for material for a problem-based course takes a certain amount of creativity. Some faculty use video clips, stories, novels, articles from the popular press, and research papers as the basis of a problem. Frequently, veteran PBL faculty may use a typical textbook problem and rewrite it as an open-ended, real-world problem. The process of developing a multistage PBL problem may differ from one discipline to another, but generally, the following steps can help instructors write problems for any course:

Step 1.   Choose a central idea, concept, or principle that is always taught in a given course, and then think of a typical end-of-chapter problem, assignment, or homework that is usually assigned to students to help them learn that concept. List the learning objectives that students should meet when they work through the problem.

> *For example: In an introductory physics course, I teach conservation of momentum. In a typical textbook for this course, students would be expected to solve simple collision problems (two objects colliding, such as pool balls, a bullet and a stationary block of wood, two cars) in which most or all of the necessary information is given. As stated by Mazur (1996), with these typical problems students tend to pattern-match and then "plug and chug" to find a solution.*
>
> *My content objectives in a traditional course would include the following:*
>
> 1. *Understand and be able to solve conservation of momentum problems involving elastic and inelastic collisions.*
> 2. *Understand and be able to explain the role of force, motion, and energy in elastic and inelastic collisions.*

Step 2. Think of a real-world context for the concept under consideration. Develop a storytelling aspect to an end-of-chapter problem, or research an actual case that can be adapted, adding some motivation for students to solve the problem. A complex, ill-structured problem will challenge students to go beyond simple plug-and-chug to solve it. Look at magazines, newspapers, and articles for ideas on the story line. Some PBL practitioners talk to professionals in the field, searching for ideas of realistic applications of the concept being taught.

> *For example: I decided to use an automobile accident scenario as the context for my problem. My new objectives would be expanded to include the following. Students should be able to do the following:*
>
> 1. *Use understanding of the principles of forces, motion, momentum, and energy to design a plan to reconstruct a car accident.*
> 2. *Explain how frictional forces related to varying surfaces affect the motion of an object.*
> 3. *Calculate the velocities of two vehicles before and after impact using physics principles, such as forces, motion, mechanical energy, and conservation of momentum.*
> 4. *Evaluate real-world data related to a car accident in order to make a judgment about the drivers' fault.*
> 5. *Find and use appropriate learning resources to aid in reconstructing the accident.*
> 6. *Explain how safety devices, such as seat belts, airbags, and crumple zones work in terms of force, motion, momentum, and energy.*

Generally, the learning objectives for students in a problem-based course include objectives beyond the content objectives found in a traditional course. Problem-based learning objectives may be more complex and involve process skills objectives, such as number 5 in the previous list. Chapter 9 of this book describes the importance of learning objectives in more detail.

Step 3. The problem needs to be introduced and staged so that students will be able to identify learning issues that will lead them to research the targeted concepts. Some questions that may help guide this process follow:

- What will the first page (or stage) look like? What open-ended questions can be asked? What learning issues should be identified?
- How will the problem be structured?
- How long will the problem be? How many class periods will it take to complete?

- Will students be given information in subsequent pages (or stages) as they work through the problem?

- What resources will students need?

- What end product will students produce at the completion of the problem?

Many times, PBL problems are designed as multistage or multipage and may take student groups a week or more to complete. Not all the information needed to solve the problem is given in the problem, or chapter, or perhaps even in the textbook. Students will need to do some research, discover new material, and arrive at judgments and decisions based on the information learned. The problem may have more than one acceptable answer, based on the assumptions students make.

> *For example: The problem I wrote about a car crash ("A Day in the Life of John Henry" is at the end of this chapter) begins by asking students to decide what questions a police officer needs to be able to answer in order to decide who is at fault in an accident. What measurements and data need to be gathered? What physics principles will be needed to analyze the crash scene? These questions are designed to encourage students to talk about what they already know about car crashes and what they have already learned about the physics involved.*
>
> *The four-page problem takes students a week to work through, as they research and learn about momentum, accident reconstruction, safety devices, and then they apply that knowledge to make assumptions and judgments about the cause of the accident.*

Step 4.   Write a teacher guide detailing the instructional plans on using the problem in the course. If the course is a medium- to large-size class, a combination of minilectures, whole-class discussion, and small group work with groups regularly reporting may be necessary (see Chapter 4). The teacher guide can indicate plans or options of cycling through the pages of the problem interspersing the various modes of learning.

> *As students worked on the "John Henry" problem, they spent time in their individual groups discussing answers to questions posed in the problem, sharing information they learned in individual research, and arriving at conclusions based on their assumptions and calculations. The student group time was interspersed with whole-class discussion, allowing time for individual groups to share with other groups their*

findings, conclusions, and questions. I also intervened with minilectures to clarify issues or demonstrate specific models for analyzing certain aspects of the problem. They also had the opportunity to develop hands-on experience in a laboratory setting. The end product that groups produced was a group written report of their solution to the problem, justifying their position by citing physics principles involved.

Step 5.   The final step is to identify resources for students. Students need to learn to identify and utilize learning resources on their own, but it can be helpful if the instructor indicates a few good sources to get them started. Many students today will want to limit their research to the Internet, so it will be important to guide them toward the library as well.

Conclusion

Writing problem-based learning problems may be time consuming, challenging, and sometimes frustrating. However, the process of thinking through the learning priorities of a course and finding, adapting, or writing complex, realistic materials to meet those learning priorities will change how an instructor views his or her course in the future. Any magazine or newspaper article, documentary, news report, book or movie that is seen will become possible material for new problems for a course. Faculty will gain a new appreciation for the concepts and principles that they teach, and the connections that should be made to concepts in other courses and disciplines. It is always revealing to grapple with such questions as "How is the knowledge of this concept used in the world outside the classroom?" or "Why do my students need to know this?" or "How will my students use this knowledge in future courses?" I believe that writing PBL problems can help faculty develop into more reflective teachers.

Author Biography

Barbara J. Duch is Associate Director of the Mathematics & Science Education Resource Center at the University of Delaware.

References

Bloom, B. S. (Ed.). (1956). *Taxonomy of educational objectives: The classification of educational goals.* New York: Longman.

Heller, P., & Hollabaugh, M. (1992). Teaching problem-solving through cooperative grouping. *Am. J. Phys., 60,* pp. 637–644.

Mazur, E. (1996). The problem with problems. *Optics and photonics news, 7,* 59.

APPENDIX TO CHAPTER 5

SAMPLE PBL PROBLEM: A DAY IN THE
LIFE OF JOHN HENRY, A TRAFFIC COP

Barbara Duch, 1993; Revised 1995.

Part 1

At 13:20 on the last Friday in September 1989, a frantic call was received at
the local police station. There had been a serious automobile accident at the
intersection of Main Street and State Street, with injuries involved. Lt. John
Henry arrived at the scene ten minutes after the phone call and found that
two cars had collided at the intersection. In one car, the driver was unconscious, and in the other car, both driver and one passenger were injured.
After the emergency vehicles transported the injured to the hospital,
Lt. Henry's responsibility is to investigate the accident in order to determine
whether one of the drivers (or both) are responsible. With the severity of
injury in this accident, the investigation is critical because there may be a
fatality involved.

- What questions does John Henry have to answer in this investigation?

- What measurements does he need to take?

- What data should he collect?

- What other information does he need to record in order to aid the
  investigation?

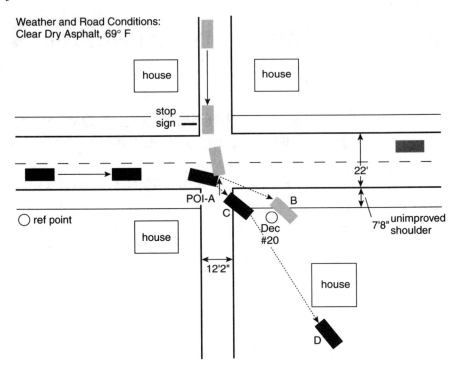

FIGURE 5.1. Police sketch of accident scene

- What physics principles will John Henry need to use in order to help analyze the data and answer his questions?
- If two cars moving at right angles to each other collide, in what direction do you expect the cars to be moving after the collision?
- What factors will influence the direction and distance traveled after impact?

Part 2

The sketch of the accident scene is shown in Figure 5.1. Main Street, a thoroughfare, has a 45 miles per hour speed limit. State Street also has a 45 miles per hour limit but has a stop sign on either side of the road. Vehicle 2, which weighs 5800 lbs, skidded for 24 feet before coming to a stop next to the utility pole, marked Dec #20. Vehicle 1, which weighs 2060 lbs, showed no skid marks after the impact and came to a rest next to the house on the corner. Looking at the impact areas of the cars, it was clear to Lt. Henry that the cars collided at right angles, hitting the front right bumper of vehicle 2 and the front left bumper of vehicle 1. After impact, they initially were traveling in the same direction. Lt. Henry noted that the weather was clear and sunny, the temperature was 69°F and the roadway was dry.

Before John Henry got any further in his analysis, he was informed that the driver who was unconscious at the scene of the accident died at the hospital.

- Can you make an educated guess about which driver died based on the evidence so far? Justify your answer.

- Why would John Henry note the weather and the condition of the road?

- Why did vehicle 1 travel further than vehicle 2?

John Henry has to determine whether the driver of vehicle 2 ran the stop sign and/or if the driver of vehicle 1 was speeding. Outline a procedure that Lt. Henry can use to answer these important questions. Be sure that your reasoning is sound, since he will have to testify in court on the evidence.

- Does John Henry have all the information he needs to determine the velocities?

Lt. Henry used a drag sled to determine that the coefficient of friction between the tires and road was 0.60. He cannot use the drag sled to determine the coefficient of friction between the tires of vehicle 1 as they roll over the roadway and grass.

- Does he need this information?

- What procedure can he use to find out this information?

Part 3

Using your outlined procedures, find the velocities of the two vehicles just prior to impact, and estimate the coefficient of friction between the rolling tires of vehicle 1 and the roadway and grass. Be sure to state any assumptions that you make and justify them.

- During the collision, which vehicle delivered the greater force of impact. Justify your reasoning using physics principles.

- How can Lt. Henry determine the speeds of both vehicles just before they applied their brakes? What further information will he need?

Part 4

Lt. Henry measured the skid marks made by both vehicles prior to impact. The skid marks for vehicle 1 were 20 feet in length and for vehicle 2 were 7 feet in length.

- How fast were both cars going just prior to hitting their brakes?

- Which driver do you recommend John Henry cite in the accident? Justify your answer, since Lt. Henry will need to make an airtight case in court.

Resources for Students

Brake, Mary L., (1981). Physics in accident investigations. *The Physics Teacher, 19,* 26–29.

Calkin, M. G., (1990). The motion of an accelerating automobile. *American Journal of Physics, 58,* 573–589.

Fountain, C. R., (1942). The physics of automobile driving," *American Journal of Physics, 10,* 322–327.

Smith, Richard C., General physics and the automobile tire. *American Journal of Physics, 46,* 858–859 (1978).

Whitmire, Daniel P. & Alleman Timothy J., (1979). Effect of weight transfer on a vehicle's stopping distance. *American Journal of Physics 47,* 89–92.

http://www.pbs.org/wgbh/nova/escape/resourcescar.html
http://www.nhtsa.dot.gov/
http://www.hwysafety.org/
http://c-design.com/c-design/accrec.html

6

STRATEGIES FOR USING GROUPS

Deborah E. Allen, Barbara J. Duch,
and Susan E. Groh

Chapter Summary

In problem-based learning, students are asked to work together to analyze and resolve problems, and to communicate, evaluate, and integrate information from diverse sources. Effective performance of these group learning tasks requires the development of new skills on the part of both the student and instructor. This chapter discusses strategies an instructor can use to maintain functional groups in the classroom—groups in which all members work effectively to enhance their own and each other's learning.

Introduction

A team of students had four members called Everybody, Somebody, Anybody and Nobody. There was an important job to be done. Everybody was sure that Somebody would do it. Anybody could have done it, but Nobody did it. Somebody got angry about that because it was Everybody's job. Everybody thought Anybody could do it but Nobody realised that Everybody wouldn't do it. It ended up that Everybody blamed Somebody when Nobody did what Anybody could have done. (Gibbs, 1995)

Collaborative learning is an essential feature of problem-based learning (PBL). Working in PBL groups toward common goals can benefit students by lessening their sense of isolation (Seymour & Hewitt, 1997) and thereby fostering the development of learning communities (MacGregor, 1987). Courses that incorporate small-group learning can have a positive effect on students' academic achievement, persistence through courses and programs, and attitudes toward learning when compared to their more traditionally taught counterparts (Bonwell & Eison 1991; Johnson, Johnson, & Smith, 1991, 1998; Springer, Stanne, & Donovan, 1999). Frequent exposure of students to collaborative and cooperative learning reinforces the collaborative nature of scholarship and inquiry (American Association for the Advancement of Science, 1989). It introduces a new social structure to the classroom—one of negotiated relationships between students, and between student groups and the instructor, helping students to become articulate, autonomous, and socially mature (Michaelson & Black, 1994).

Conversely, classroom experiences with collaborative and cooperative grouping can leave students feeling (to varying degrees) cheated by group members who have not pulled their weight, held back by slower students, discounted by more assertive group members, or shortchanged by the course instructor because they have had to teach themselves. As Felder and Brent point out (1996), although student-centered instruction can yield tangible benefits, "they are neither immediate nor automatic." There are many ways that groups can fail (Feichtner & Davis, 1985).

For that reason, activities that promote a good atmosphere for collaborative learning are never a waste of classroom time. They can lead to more productive learning and reduce the time that both students and instructor might otherwise spend diagnosing and mediating the sources of group conflict. This chapter will focus on practical strategies (accessible to any instructor) for promoting the development of student groups that act cohesively, yet display a high degree of individual accountability for the work required.

Getting Started with Groups

Most instructors using a student-centered method, such as problem-based learning, recommend that group work be started early in the course—preferably the first day of class. If the enrollment of the course is not stable at this point, these earliest groups need not be the permanent ones in which students will work later on. On the first day of class, a common strategy is for the instructor to explain why he or she thinks using groups is a good strategy, then ask students to report on past experiences they have had working in teams. Student accounts of negative experiences can prompt opportunities to reassure the class with a point-by-point description of the mechanisms in place to help prevent negative experiences in the present course.

The first day of class is also a good occasion to conduct what will be the first of many activities that promote positive group interactions. Examples of these first-day activities include the following:

1. Writing a group biography (including such items as hometowns, career goals, and favorite courses)

2. Taking a short pretest on course content given first to individuals, then to groups. Students will no doubt find that the group score is better than any individual score within the group. (This can also serve double-duty as a preassessment mechanism for uncovering students' misconceptions about the upcoming course material.)

3. Completing a learning style survey such as the Kolb Learning Style Inventory (1985). The results can be used for group discussion of the effect that the individual preferred learning styles might have on group function.

4. Engaging in mental games that require the skillful use of teamwork to complete or that make a point about the distinction between student- and instructor-centered learning environments, such as "Stand and Deliver," described in Chapter 7.

Forming Groups

Creation of heterogeneous groups can expose students to new ideas and distribute assets and liabilities evenly (Michaelson & Black, 1994). Heterogeneous groups can either be selected intentionally or randomly (by counting off on the course roster or by having students count off in class, for example). Information for intentional selection of attributes to be balanced across groups can be based on student records (major, year in school), or on information provided by students (existence of special skills, desired grade in the course, course and work schedules on- or off-campus residence, etc.). Collaborative learning can be a particular success story for minority students (Fullilove & Treisman, 1990; George, 1994). Felder et al. (1995), however, recommend that minority students (ethnic minorities or women in traditionally male disciplines) not be isolated in groups, in order to reduce the possibility of the discounting or devaluing of their ideas.

Monitoring Groups

Instructor's Role

In the early model of PBL, each faculty "tutor" guided a single student group. Although the role of the well-functioning classic PBL tutor is far from easy, the one-on-one nature of his or her interaction with a group allows for spontaneous and informal interventions that continually fine-tune the reasoning process, assure evenness of participation, keep the group moving forward in the problem, promote good interpersonal relationships, and help the group learn how to direct its own learning. In all but the smallest of undergraduate classes, the instructor must resort to other strategies, often more structured and formal, to help optimize the functioning of the multiple-classroom groups. These strategies include (1) having well-defined group activities, (2) using PBL problems that allow for instructor interventions at key points (in a large class, for example, at roughly 10–15 minute intervals) to bring the class together for discussion and/or clarification, and (3) walking around the classroom as groups work to look for and help remedy obvious signs of group dysfunction. These signs include conversations that are off task; students who don't take part in the discussion or conversely, dominate it; and physical behaviors, such as reading while others are talking, or sitting back and slightly apart from other group members.

Peer Group Facilitators

An excellent way for a PBL instructor to extend his or her observational and group guidance range is to invite undergraduates who have taken the course to return and serve as peer group facilitators. Strategies for recruiting, preparing, and supporting the efforts of these peer group facilitators are discussed in Chapter 8.

Ground Rules

Another way to encourage students to take ownership of their effective performance as a group is to ask them to establish and enforce group ground rules in the first week or two of class, before negative behaviors have a chance to take root. This set of standards and expectations, written after groups have discussed the behaviors that they will not tolerate, helps to establish norms for group behavior. Many instructors, particularly in courses taken by students who are new to collaborative learning, provide examples of "rules of the road" that are minimally essential for good group function: (1) come to class on time, (2) come to class prepared, (3) notify members of the group ahead of time if class must be missed for any reason, and (4) respect the views, values, and ideas of other members of the group. Some instructors mandate that these essential behaviors be included in the ground rules, allowing student groups to draft additional codes of behavior they feel are necessary.

As in the world outside the classroom, rules tend to be broken or ignored if they have no teeth. For this reason, in many PBL courses, ground rules are not considered complete unless there are stated consequences for violators. Some examples of consequences that student groups have drafted are to have the instructor lower the violator's grade (to zero if appropriate) for assignments to which he or she didn't contribute, or to give extra assignments or share of responsibilities to make up for missed work. Students seldom suggest permanent or even temporary shunning of a group member, despite being informed by the instructor that this is conceivable and would be upheld. Some instructors perceive that their students seldom resort to imposing their own penalties for ground rule violation, and instead distribute a description of recommended steps to take when disturbed by another group members' behavior (see "Conflict Resolution"). In most courses, groups are asked to sign two copies of their ground rules and consequences, give one copy to the instructor, and keep one in a group notebook.

Group Roles

When each student feels individually accountable for his or her own performance, "free riders" are discouraged and contributors to the group effort are rewarded. One way to promote individual accountability and lower barriers to participation is to ask students to take on roles of responsibility in their groups. Common strategies include formulating a role for each student in the group and asking students to rotate the roles among group members every week or after every problem or assignment. This discourages students from sticking to roles that come to them easily and gives them additional experience in those that they find more challenging.

Commonly assigned roles of responsibility include the following:

- Discussion Leader. Keeps the group on track; maintains full participation.

- Recorder. Records assignments, strategies, unresolved issues, data; convenes group outside of class.

- Reporter. Reports during whole-class discussion; writes final draft of assignments.

- Accuracy Coach. Checks group understanding; finds resources.

Some practitioners of collaborative teaching and learning strategies depend on assignments, practices, and their grading systems to foster the development of group cohesion (Michaelson, 1997–1998), rather than rotating roles.

Evaluation

Allowing classroom opportunities for students to provide constructive verbal and written feedback to individuals and their groups is another strategy for reinforcing positive group behaviors and maximizing individual accountability. Verbal group feedback sessions work best if scheduled at the end of each problem (at least two to three times a semester) or whenever a group is not functioning well. Feedback sessions typically begin with each individual in the group stating what the group did well since the last session and how he or she thinks the group needs to change or improve to function better. Sessions should ideally end with each group setting goals that will help remedy any perceived problems. For example, if a group tends to drift into talk about personal issues, it may decide to monitor the accuracy coach and discussion leader roles more closely in the future to help keep the discussions on task.

After the overall functioning of the group has been discussed, many instructors ask students to rate their individual contributions to the group effort using written evaluation forms (see Allen & Duch, 1998 and Chapter 11 for examples of these forms). Typically, the instructor predetermines the ratings criteria on these forms. Each student fills out the form in a confidential manner, rating the effort of the other members of the group as well as him- or herself on a scale of one to five and writing a few sentences of specific comments for each individual student. Instructors then compile the average ratings and summarize all comments to be given to each student, ensuring that students can be candid in their comments. The results of the ratings should be factored into each student's grade.

This feedback is not only an important reality check for students, but is invaluable in helping the instructor detect the signs of a malfunctioning group. When evidence that group members are not contributing well presents itself in these forms, early intervention is possible. Before the first feedback session of the course, it helps to review for the class the basic guidelines for giving good feedback (Gibbs, 1995). That is, good feedback is specific, focuses on behaviors and actions rather than personality or similar personal attributes, describes rather than criticizes or demeans, is presented as perceptions or feelings rather than as absolutes, and focuses on behavior that can be controlled or changed.

Finally, larger group projects, assignments, and products may also require feedback about the extent and nature of each group member's participation to ensure individual accountability and discourage free riders.

Group Activities
Jigsaw Grouping

In a PBL course, students gradually become accustomed to discussing learning issues within their group, doing research, and teaching each other in order to work through a problem. For some problems, use of a jigsaw group scheme can be an effective way to encourage students to research one point of view or learning issue in depth with others before sharing that information with his or her permanent (base, or home) group (Slavin, 1995). In a jigsaw group scheme operating in a PBL context, students begin a problem in their permanent group and are then assigned a new group (the jigsaw or expert group) in which to work with others who are also gathering evidence to support a particular viewpoint or researching the same learning issues. Each individual in the permanent, home group chooses a distinct point of view for which he or she will become an advocate. All students now form the new (jigsaw) groups that are specific to their point of view. In a jigsaw group, discussion focuses on issues that will influence that group's position on the problem. Each member of the jigsaw group is assigned learning issues to research, then shares information and constructs evidence to support the group's viewpoint. Students then return to their base to advocate for their jigsaw groups' position. Typically, the base groups must then reach consensus on a position with regard to a dilemma or proposal linked to the original problem and list the reasons for the group decision. Whole-class discussion or debate can then follow, with all groups (ideally) fully prepared to provide substantive evidence for their consensus opinion.

Assignments

In a problem-based learning course, the instructor may plan to have groups work through a series of problems, design and implement a project related to a problem or specific concepts in the course, develop a concept map (Allen & Duch, 1998), research and develop a problem of their own, complete a homework assignment, or a variety of additional activities. A number of decisions need to be made in planning such activities, including how to structure an assignment so that all group members will be involved, whether individual students or the entire group will be responsible for a written or presentation product, and whether the product will be graded or not. Assignments requiring an out-of-class component, such as library or web research, can be designed to allow division into parts; joining these parts into a coherent whole, however, should require the resources of the entire group working together. This presents a challenge for the instructor: Students will quickly use a "divide and conquer strategy" if they perceive that the individual parts can just be assembled for the final product with no group interaction. One strategy to increase group cohesiveness is to require members to make a concrete decision based on the analysis of a complex issue. Students quickly realize that the group effort is invaluable in this type of assignment, since individual members' input is such a valuable resource.

At the same time, it is essential to make provisions to ensure individual accountability in group assignments. One suggestion used by many PBL practitioners is to have students individually or collectively distribute the total points for the assignment among themselves in proportion to the effort each one put into it. Another is to call randomly on individual team members to present sections of project reports or critical solutions to problems, with everyone in the group getting a grade based on the selected student's response (Felder & Brent, 1995). Similarly, one might assign each student the responsibility of writing his or her own solution to a problem after the group discussions; this, however, can become burdensome to the instructor if the class is large.

Resolving Conflicts

Group ground rules, roles of responsibilities, documenting the activities of the group and individuals within the group, and peer pressure within the group all provide ways to help group members avoid conflict. The instructor should communicate clearly to the class that each student is responsible for monitoring the functioning within his or her group, as well as the academic standards of the discussions, assignments, and research reported. If students are in a group with another person who resists working as hard as the rest of the members, then the group-monitoring methods stated previously will provide safe, objective mechanisms through which the group can give the errant individual truthful and direct feedback concerning his or her performance and the group's expectations. The instructor should also make it clear to students that she or he will assist them in dealing with group conflict, including direct intervention if necessary. This intervention may take the form of a request that a group rewrite their ground rules and consequences, or the suggestion that the group conduct an extra feedback session, or a requirement for the group to meet regularly with the instructor until the conflict is resolved. It is important to remember that conflict is not entirely negative and that it is good training for students to learn to resolve conflict and facilitate troubled groups.

Conclusions

For the many faculty members who did not experience group learning as students, undertaking an instructional shift from traditional lecture (with its emphasis on individual learning) to group-centered problem-based learning may be rather intimidating; the same will certainly be true for many students. It is important, therefore, to reassure both students and faculty that the benefits of cooperative learning are well documented (see Johnson, Johnson, & Smith, 1991 & 1998). By structuring a course with group ground rules, roles of responsibility, and individual accountability, the PBL practitioner can greatly curtail, if not eliminate entirely, the ability of "slackers" to benefit from the hard work of others in the group. Knowing that their individual efforts will be recognized and protected gives students the freedom to take full advantage of the power of groups in developing knowledge with and for one another.

Authors' Biographies

Deborah E. Allen is an Associate Professor in the Department of Biological Sciences at the University of Delaware and an affiliated faculty member in the University Honors Program.

Barbara J. Duch is Associate Director of the University of Delaware's Mathematics & Science Education Resource Center.

Susan E. Groh is an Assistant Professor in the Department of Chemistry and Biochemistry and an affiliated faculty member of the University Honors Program at the University of Delaware.

References

Allen, D. E., & Duch, B. J. (1998). *Thinking toward solutions: Problem-based learning activities for general biology.* Philadelphia, PA: Harcourt Brace.

American Association for the Advancement of Science. (1989). *Science for all Americans: Project 2061.* New York: Oxford University Press, p. 148.

Bonwell, C. C., & Eison, J. A. (1991). Active learning: Creating excitement in the classroom. *ASHE-ERIC Higher Education Report No. 1.* Washington, DC: George Washington University.

Feichtner, S. B., & Davis, E. A. (1985). Why some groups fail: A survey of students' experiences with learning groups. *The Organizational Behavior Teaching Review, 9,* 58–73.

Felder, R. M., & Brent, R. (1996). Navigating the bumpy road to student-centered instruction. *College Teaching, 44,* 43–47.

Felder, R. M., Felder, G. N., Mauney, M., Hamrin, Jr., C. E., & Dietz, E. J. (1995). A longitudinal study of engineering student performance and retention. III. Gender differences in student performance and attitudes. *J. Engr. Education, 84,* 151–174.

Fullilove, R. E., & Treisman, P. U. (1990). Mathematics achievement among African American undergraduates at the University of California, Berkeley: An evaluation of the mathematics workshop program. *J. Negro Education, 593,* 463–478.

George, P. G. (1994). The effectiveness of cooperative learning strategies in multicultural university classrooms. *Journal of Excellence in College Teaching, 51,* 21–30.

Gibbs, G. (1995). *Learning in teams: A tutor guide.* Oxford: Oxonian Rewley Press.

Johnson, D. W., Johnson, R. T., & Smith, K. A. (1991). Cooperative learning: Increasing college faculty instructional productivity. *ASHE-ERIC Higher Education Report No. 4.* Washington, DC: George Washington University.

Johnson, D. W., Johnson, R. T., & Smith, K. A. (1998). Maximizing instruction through cooperative learning. *ASEE PRISM,* February, 24–29.

Kolb, D. (1985). *LSI: Self-scoring inventory and interpretation booklet.* Boston: McBer & Co.

MacGregor, J. (1987). Intellectual development of students in learning community programs, 1986–1987. *Washington Center Occasional Paper No. 1.* Olympia, WA: Evergreen State College.

Michaelson, L. K. (1997–1998). Three keys to using learning groups effectively. *Teaching Excellence: Toward the Best in the Academy, 9* (5).

Michaelson, L. K., & Black, R. H. (1994). Building learning teams: The key to harnessing the power of small groups in higher education. In S. Kadel & J. Keener (Eds.) *Collaborative learning: A sourcebook for higher education Vol. 2.* State College, PA: National Center for Teaching and Learning Assessment, pp. 65–81.

Seymour, E. & Hewitt, N. (1997). *Talking about leaving: Factors contributing to high attrition rates among science, mathematics, and engineering undergraduate majors.* Boulder, CO: Westview.

Slavin, R. E. (1995). *Cooperative learning.* Boston, MA. Allyn & Bacon.

Springer, L., Stanne, M. E., & Donovan, S. (1999). Effects of cooperative learning on undergraduates in science, mathematics, engineering, and technology: A meta-analysis. *Review of Educational Research, 69,* 21–52.

GETTING STARTED IN PROBLEM-BASED LEARNING

Harold B. White, III

Chapter Summary

The transition from traditional instruction to a problem-based approach to learning requires many changes and, without proper preparation, can frustrate the best intentions. Among the issues one needs to address are preparing a syllabus that reflects revised learning objectives, finding appropriate problems to address content, introducing students to group process and learning skills, and dealing with the uncertainty of a different classroom strategy.

Introduction

It takes a certain amount of independence and determination to change the way one teaches. It also takes time and involves risks. Where do instructors acquire the commitment to get started with problem-based learning (PBL)? Frequently, commitment grows out of the recurring frustration most instructors experience when they realize how little their students understand or remember from a semester of charismatic lectures. If not ignored, that frustration leads to reflection on what it means "to teach" and "to learn." Problem-based learning addresses these issues and offers an attractive alternative to traditional education by shifting the focus of education from *what faculty teach* to *what students learn*. Content remains important, but emphasis shifts more to the process. For those used to lecturing, the trade-offs can intimidate, but the promise of greater student understanding sustains the effort. Fundamentally, adopting PBL requires a transformation of the classroom role of the instructor from a "sage on the stage to a guide on the side" (King, 1993). With that change in perspective comes the commitment to accept the risks and take the time. However, commitment alone is insufficient. Advanced planning is necessary to anticipate pitfalls encountered by blind enthusiasm (McKeachie, 1986; White, 1996a).

Getting Started Ahead of Time
Mentoring
Getting started begins well before the semester begins. Sometimes the idea of transforming a course to one with a PBL format incubates for several years. The change in perspective requires getting used to. Finding others who have experience helps this transition, because few instructors have themselves been taught in a PBL classroom, and it is sometimes difficult to envision how a PBL class operates or to anticipate all the situations one might encounter. Instructors who use PBL have traveled the same path and appreciate the problem. In most cases, they welcome visitors to their classes. Those getting started should take advantage of such opportunities and find a mentor. An occasional coffee break or lunch with others using PBL can help deal with new situations. Most concerns relate to process; thus, colleagues from diverse disciplines can contribute constructively to each other's effective teaching. The University of Delaware PBL website (see electronic resources for PBL at the end of the list of references for this chapter), and related PBL listserver also provide information and a forum for discussion.

Decisions
While circumstances may limit choices, some ways of getting started are easier than others. Occasionally, one might start by creating an entirely new course with a PBL format, but more often, instructors will transform one of their existing lecture-based courses into one that uses PBL. Because existing courses are already built into the curriculum, they have an established content and clientele, and they constitute part of the regular workload. These factors legitimatize the effort. Most faculty choose to make the transition gradually by introducing a problem-based exercise every week or two at first. They also tend to start with smaller classes and courses within a major. Once comfortable with PBL, instructors often transform other courses they teach.

Course Goals and Learning Objectives

Once the decision to transform a course has been made, formulating a list of instructional goals focused on student learning helps subsequent decisions. Examples of such goals can be found elsewhere in this volume. Because PBL addresses behavioral issues in addition to content issues, the course goals probably will change the way a course is structured and conducted. For example, oral and written communication skills or the ability to find and use new resources often become explicit goals that may have been subordinated to content goals without a PBL format. The new priorities lead to new assignments and restructured schedules.

Finding Problems

With the exception of a few disciplines, notably medicine and business, good PBL problems usually do not appear in textbooks. As a consequence, an instructor needs to find problems, modify textbook problems, or write new problems that address the course content goals and learning objectives. The "learning issue matrix" (White, 1996b; White, Chapter 12 of this book) provides a strategy for selecting a set of problems that covers the course content. While having to write problems may be necessary and seem to be a significant barrier, most instructors find writing problems an enjoyable scholarly activity (White, 1995; Duch, Chapter 5 of this book). Furthermore, because of the need, there are outlets for publishing good problems. The *PBL Clearinghouse* and *Case Studies in Science* are two web-based opportunities, while educational journals, such as *Biochemistry and Molecular Biology Education* (see electronic resources for PBL at the end of the list of references for the URLs to these three sites) or the *Journal of College Science Teaching* will accept manuscripts describing PBL problems.

Using the Syllabus to Get Started

Because the syllabus defines a course, it needs to be completed before the first class and should distinguish the new PBL format from the format of previous offerings of the course. Its contents provide a framework for discussing the issues in introducing PBL, while the course goals, noted previously, provide the basis for making decisions relating to these issues. Altman and Cashin (1992) identify the following seven major topics that should be in a syllabus: course information; instructor information; text, readings, and materials; course description and objectives; course calendar and schedule; course policies; and available support services. These will be discussed in turn with respect to decisions associated with getting started with PBL.

Course Information

This includes basic syllabus material, such as course title, course number, pre-requisites, credit hours, meeting time, and meeting place. Some of these items will be influenced by a change to a PBL format. For instance, when and where will the class meet? To provide longer time for discussion, it may be useful to have two 75-minute classes per week rather than three 50-minute classes. It may be worth considering nonstandard meeting times, such as 75 minutes on Monday and Friday to distribute time for out-of-class research if this is possible at your institution. The classroom itself is quite important. A room with tables where students can work comfortably in groups is preferable to a room with fixed seating in a tiered auditorium. A room with lots of blackboard space provides opportunities for effective communications within groups.

Instructor Information

As for every course, the syllabus should contain information about who the instructor is and where, how, and when he or she may be contacted. Not only is student communication with the instructor important in a PBL course, but other lines of communication are important and can be established ahead of time. E-mail newsgroups, chat rooms, and electronic class-mailing lists can be used to facilitate student-student and intergroup communication, which can be more important than in a typical class and may need to be structured ahead of time.

Instructor information in a syllabus might include a statement of teaching philosophy that relates to PBL. That information might also accompany a friendly e-mail message to the class during the week before the semester starts. Such a gesture can set a positive tone for the course and let the students know something about the course as well. If the syllabus is on a course website, the message can provide its URL. This also is a good time to get feedback from students that might be helpful in assigning them to groups. If the course involves teaching assistants or tutor-facilitators (Allen & White, 2000, and Chapter 8 of this book), that information can be included with information about the instructor.

Text, Readings, and Materials

Frequently, a PBL format changes the way instructors and students see and use textbooks. A decision that an instructor needs to make is whether to have a text, and if so, does a different text fit the PBL format better than texts used previously. For an advanced course built around problems in which students need to access multiple primary resources, a text may be unnecessary. For a course that uses a PBL format only part of the time to emphasize certain concepts during class time, a textbook is an important reference and may be selected for its encyclopedic character rather than its readability in independent study. Decisions on a textbook may be driven on whether the significant learning issues are (or are not) covered and whether this fits with the course goals.

Depending on the course goals, an instructor may provide supplementary readings in the library or eliminate them in courses where students need to find resources for themselves. With increased use of the Internet and the enormous variability in the quality of websites, some instructors choose to provide a list of Internet sites that provide reliable information. In another approach, instructors direct students to websites that provide guidance in evaluating other websites because students frequently equate an attractive layout with "good" informational quality. If one plans to make greater use of library and Internet resources, the availability to students also must be considered. Not all students have computers, and commuting students can be put at a disadvantage.

Course Description and Objectives

What is the purpose of the course? Where does it fit into the curriculum? How will students change as a result of taking the course? While many of the decisions identified so far appear in a syllabus as statements with little elaboration, the course description is the meat of a syllabus and requires a narrative, particularly if one plans to use PBL. For example, the course goals and learning objectives belong here. Students need to know what they are expected to do and why groups are important. Most certainly, a PBL format will lead to unfamiliar types of assignments, such as generating a concept map as a group. These may be introduced in a syllabus.

If the students entering the course have little or no experience with PBL, the syllabus is the place for the instructor to explain what PBL is. It also is a good place to explain why PBL fits in with the instructor's teaching philosophy and why it is important for student learning. Much of the resistance to PBL by students, particularly in the early weeks of a course, comes from the surprise of doing something unfamiliar and not knowing why the instructor is "doing this to them." As noted earlier, PBL relies on good communication, and it is the instructor's responsibility to discuss teaching philosophy in the syllabus and at the beginning and throughout a course.

Course Calendar and Schedule

The use of a PBL format implies that the instructor values group process and problem-solving abilities. Typical course examinations given during class time often do not incorporate such values. Consequently, a significant decision is whether or not to schedule out-of-class examinations with relaxed time constraints and incorporate group elements. For example, a three-hour evening examination permits successive individual and group parts (White, 1997). Such an arrangement extracts a cost because in most courses there will be a few students who have conflicting schedules. Furthermore, a room, perhaps the normal classroom, needs to be available and reserved. Many schools require that the dates and times of out-of-class examinations be printed in the registration booklet so that students can arrange their schedules accordingly when they register. This means that the decision for an out-of-class examination needs to be made and approved quite early.

One must decide how often to use a PBL format and incorporate that into the course schedule. Good PBL problems are open-ended and may take more time than anticipated. Students need sufficient time to research, discuss, and come to closure on a problem. Consequently, the schedule and instructor need to be flexible. One way to allow for changes during the semester is to title the schedule as "tentative."

Course Policies

PBL affects many course policies and thus requires decisions. Group progress and group dynamics depend strongly on full participation. Thus, absences and tardiness disrupt a PBL class in ways that would be unimportant in a lecture class. An instructor should have a firm attendance policy, which also is affirmed by group guidelines. In a lecture class, individual students can do quite well and not have to say one word in class during an entire semester. Such silence would undermine the PBL process. There are ways for introverted students to contribute significantly to group process. Ideally, the instructor's policies should be discussed and agreed to by all groups and appropriate consequences specified for noncompliance, for example, some groups may agree to exclude repeat offenders from group portions of examinations.

PBL also affects grading policies. What is the proper balance between individual and group work? How much will peer evaluation contribute to individual grades? How much are process skills valued, and how is that factored into a grade? What constitute criteria that distinguish one level of achievement from another?

Academic honesty creates a dilemma for some students in PBL classes. Throughout their academic career, teachers have discouraged collaboration with other students. Now the rules seem reversed. What constitutes academic dishonesty? What can be shared for credit? These issues need to be discussed and clearly defined in the course policies. Students need to know that they learn on their own and that there is individual accountability. Working in groups facilitates learning, but it is not a license to use the work of others as one's own.

Available Support Services

Students have access to a wide variety of academic support services. Some of these resources are especially useful for courses using a PBL format, and instructors may decide to set aside time to ensure that their students know about them and can use them. For example, a PBL course often requires students to identify and locate resources that they need. However, many students have only rudimentary skills in exploiting library resources and may need guidance. While they may be familiar with surfing the Internet, they may have little ability to distinguish authoritative information from the biased information available on a myriad of advocacy sites. In most disciplines, there are particular search strategies that are preferred to others. These may be laid out in a syllabus or on a course website. Given these needs, an instructor may arrange for a library tour or a presentation on web resources.

Getting Students Started with PBL
The First Week of Class

Despite all of the advanced preparation, a certain amount of apprehension and self-doubt accompanies the beginning of a first-time PBL class. What if something goes wrong? What if the students don't like it? Imagine a classroom full of students who have spent their entire education in lectures and are seated nicely in rows facing the front of the room. This course will be unfamiliar to them or, if not unfamiliar, something they may have found unpleasant. Will they buy into PBL?

There are many approaches and, as noted earlier, sending an e-mail message to the whole class a week before the semester starts can ease both student and instructor apprehensions about PBL. It is important, however, not to call PBL an *"experiment."* The students need to know what will be different and why, but they do not wish to be guinea pigs. The introduction could take the form of a lecture—but that may send the wrong message in a PBL course. A successful approach is to initiate group discussions that evolve into a whole-class discussion about the students' prior experiences with groups and why they liked or disliked those experiences. This demonstrates that discussion is expected and that student concerns are heard. In addition, an "ice breaker" exercise often shows in an experiential way what a lecture or discussion cannot. I have developed the following activity, *Stand and Deliver,* that provides a visceral appreciation of the importance of teacher-to-student, student-to-teacher, and student-to-student communication in learning.

Stand and Deliver

Much of what we do when we lecture is to describe things and create mental images with words. These words have discipline-specific meaning that students sometimes misinterpret or don't understand. The following group activity deals with verbal communication of images. The rules of this "game" are simple.

1. Teacher Selection. Within each group of four or five students, determine who has the birth date closest to today. That person will be the *teacher* for this activity.

2. Lesson Plan. Assemble all of the teachers in the hall outside the classroom and show them a simple geometric figure that they will have to describe orally to their group of "students." The figure should have about three simple components; for example, a square, a triangle, and a circle and of different sizes, in different positions, and overlapping in different ways so that the sizes, relationships, and orientations become important details to communicate.

3. The Lecture. The teachers return to their groups for two minutes while they describe, as accurately as they can, what they saw. The teachers *cannot use hand gestures,* and the students *cannot ask questions* of the teacher or talk among themselves during the "lecture." The students may take notes, but cannot draw pictures yet.

4. Teacher Conference. After the lecture, the teachers leave the room and can discuss the experience among themselves until step 7.

5. Individual Work. Without talking to each other, each student must draw, as closely as he or she can, a copy of the figure described by the teacher. The objective is to be as close to a carbon copy of the original drawing as possible. They have two minutes to do this.

6. Group Work. The members within each group compare their drawings and discuss the differences in an attempt to come to consensus. In five minutes, each group should have a revised consensus drawing to show to their teacher.

7. Teacher Assessment. The teachers return and see what their students have drawn. Groups then can discuss the exercise. At this time,

each group receives a photocopy of the original drawing to compare with their drawing.

8. Reflection. Among the questions groups might consider in discussing the implications are: Did everyone in your group draw the same picture? Did subsequent discussion improve the representation? Was the teacher happy with the results? What were your frustrations, if any? Can you make any conclusions?

This activity generates a lot of discussion and raises important questions about how we communicate and the importance of feedback. It also addresses what it means to teach and to learn. Given additional time, groups can discuss how such an assignment might be graded. Clearly, there will be many things going on during the first week of classes, and this is just one idea for getting started.

Keeping Going with PBL

For anyone getting started with PBL, the learning curve is steep. It may seem a bit overwhelming to have to deal with issues of group dynamics, educational psychology, and student learning skills in addition to the subject matter. However, practitioners need not be experts and one need not implement everything at once. The change in perspective that accompanies the adoption of a few PBL exercises in one course usually leads to more and to the transformation of other courses. It also leads to a revitalized interest in education. Once started, it is easy to keep going.

Author Biography

Harold B. White, III is Professor of Biochemistry in the Department of Chemistry and Biochemistry and Director of the Howard Hughes Medical Institute's Undergraduate Biological Sciences Education Program at the University of Delaware.

References

Allen, D. E., & White, H. B., III. (2000). Peer facilitators of in-class groups: Adapting problem-based learning to the undergraduate setting. In J. E. Miller, J. E. Groccia, & M. S. Miller (Eds.), *Student-assisted teaching: A guide to faculty-student teamwork.* Bolton, MA: Anker Publications.

Altman, H. B., & Cashin, W. E. (1992). *Writing a syllabus.* Idea Paper No. 27, Lawrence, KS: Kansas State University, Center for Faculty Evaluation and Development.

King, A. (1993). From sage on the stage to guide on the side. *College Teaching, 4* (1), 30–35.

McKeachie, W. J. (1986). *Teaching tips—A guidebook for the beginning college teacher.* Lexington, MA: D. C. Heath and Company.

White, H. B., III. (1995). Creating problems for PBL. *About Teaching 47.* (Distributed by the University of Delaware Center for Teaching Effectiveness, Newark, DE. Also posted at http://www.udel.edu/pbl/cte/jan95-chem.html)

White, H. B., III. (1996a). Dan tries problem-based learning: A case study. *To Improve the Academy, 15,* 75–91. (also posted at http://www.udel.edu/pbl/dancase3.html)

White, H. B., III. (1996b). Addressing content in problem-based courses: The learning issue matrix. *Biochemical Education, 24* (1): 41–45.

White, H. B., III. (1997). Untimed individual/group exams, problem-based learning. In S. Tobias and J. Raphael (Eds). *The hidden curriculum: Faculty-made tests in science. Part 2. Upper-division courses,* pp. 102–103. New York: Plenum Press.

Electronic Resources for Problem-based Learning

Biochemistry and Molecular Biology Education.
    http://www.elsevier.nl/inca/publications/store/6/2/1/2/4/5/
Cases Studies in Science. http://ublib.buffalo.edu/libraries/projects/cases/new.htm
PBL Clearinghouse. https://www.mis3.udel.edu/Pbl
UD PBL: Problem-Based Learning. http://www.udel.edu/pbl/

8

UNDERGRADUATE GROUP FACILITATORS TO MEET THE CHALLENGES OF MULTIPLE CLASSROOM GROUPS

Deborah E. Allen
and Harold B. White, III

Chapter Summary

Problem-based learning (PBL), which emphasizes individual initiative and collaborative classroom groups, may pose novel challenges to students who first encounter it. Undergraduate peer group facilitators help to ease this passive-to-active transition anxiety, and improve the quality of the PBL and group experience. This chapter describes an interdisciplinary program (which includes a university-wide course in Tutorial Methods of Instruction) for preparing undergraduates to function well in this peer group facilitator role.

Why Use Undergraduate Group Facilitators?

As we set out to develop undergraduate problem-based learning (PBL) courses (Allen, Duch, & Groh, 1996; White, 1996), we faced challenges that were similar to those confronted by the early adopters of PBL in the medical school setting. Not the least of these was the need to write problems that would be complex enough to encourage collaborative learning while remaining appropriate, in terms of content and skills objectives, to an undergraduate learning experience. Likewise (Engel, 1997), we had to overcome the initial skepticism of colleagues who viewed inadequate content coverage and lack of control over the direction of students' content learning as potentially serious barriers to implementation.

Implementation challenges more intrinsic to the undergraduate setting included insufficient resources to capture the prototype PBL model of a single content expert serving as a dedicated tutor-facilitator for a group of up to a dozen students. We also worried that the transition from the student passively learning from the teacher to students actively teaching each other (Felder, 1995) was going to be difficult for our students, particularly those fresh out of high school. In the traditional medical school model, the PBL tutor plays a central role in easing passive-to-active learning transitional anxiety, guiding and supporting the students as they "learn how to learn." In short, we had a host of concerns about how a single instructor could guide multiple groups through complex, multistage problems in this intensive manner, without seriously compromising the student-centered nature of the PBL process.

One solution to these concerns has been the use of undergraduate facilitators, who work with the faculty instructor to guide student groups through the PBL cycle as it unfolds in the classroom. Since its inception, use of the undergraduate group facilitator model has spread to courses of all sizes and descriptions on our campus (see Chapters 11, 12, 13, 15, 16, and 19 by Kitto & Griffiths; White; Hans; Cannon & Schell; Donham, Schmieg, & Allen; and Lieux, respectively, in this book). This prompted us to develop a program to support the facilitators' fledging efforts at teaching PBL style. To date (four years since its inception), this campuswide, multidisciplinary program has affected 12 courses, 85 group facilitators and over 1400 undergraduates. Many additional undergraduate and graduate students have served as group facilitators through programs offered in association with individual courses.

The peer facilitator program consists of four components: a preservice workshop, a course in Tutorial Methods of Instruction, discipline-specific mentoring sessions with individual PBL course instructors, and formal and informal review of facilitators' performance. These basic elements of the program are discussed more fully in later sections of this chapter, along with a sampling of how we run the preservice workshop and a typical Tutorial

Methods class session. An initial description of what we ask the undergraduate group facilitators to do will set the stage for this later explanation of how they learn to facilitate.

What Role Do Peer Group Facilitators Play in a PBL Classroom?

The "Dedicated" Facilitator Model

We originally modeled the general features of an undergraduate peer facilitator's role after that of the PBL "tutor" in the medical school setting (Barrows, 1988), with one major exception. We assumed that we could not expect undergraduates to match the content expertise of a seasoned faculty instructor. Even so, what remains in the job description for the functional facilitator in the absence of advanced content expertise (Mennin and McConnell, undated) is quite impressive. In the realm of content processing, it includes the ability to (1) use questions to probe the reasoning process; (2) guide or intervene to keep the discussion on track; (3) help students see connections; (4) help students tie together information; (5) lead students to examine available evidence when drawing conclusions; (6) set high yet reasonable standards; and (7) promote the use of appropriate resources. At the same time, the well-functioning facilitator monitors and influences the group dynamic by (1) showing interest in the group and in the subject; (2) involving all students; (3) supporting good interpersonal relationships; (4) helping the group to plot its course; and (5) modeling the process of giving and receiving feedback. Consideration of this daunting list of facilitator functions underscores why we choose not to throw undergraduates into the role without preparation and ongoing support.

In this earliest and most conventional of peer group facilitator models, each undergraduate dedicates his or her efforts to a single group for the duration of a course (the "dedicated" model), attending each classroom PBL session. Facilitators prepare for each session by reviewing related readings (provided by the course instructor), and they attend weekly course meetings and begin to engage in "reflective practice" by keeping logs of interactions with students and plans for improvement.

The "Floating" Facilitator Model

As faculty on our campus began to adapt PBL to a more diverse range of classroom settings, the role of the peer facilitator had to evolve and expand to be a useful strategy for group monitoring. For example, in large-enrollment courses, it is difficult for faculty to round up the requisite cadre of qualified undergraduate facilitators. To address this large-class dilemma, instructors ask undergraduate facilitators to monitor more than one group (typically from two to five), pulling from strategies used by faculty members who manage multiple groups in courses without undergraduate facilitators (the "roving" or "floating" facilitator model).

In addition, for these same or other courses, some university faculty use PBL models in which a smaller amount of class time (typically 30% or less) is spent on group activities, and/or use problems that don't require extensive out-of-class research (in some cases, problems that can be introduced and wrapped up in the same class period). For these one-session problems, group assignments commonly are due at the end of class.

The exceptional facilitator in this floating model has a finely honed ability to size up the current state of the group's progress and deliver an appropriate intervention (such as a question). This is often a more difficult role than that of the facilitator who can focus on one group. The one-session PBL problem model can also challenge facilitators to find ways to stimulate discussion in the face of a tendency for some groups to approach the problems with a "bottom-line" focus on completion of an assignment by the end of class.

Common Features of the Dedicated and Floating Facilitator Roles

A prominent feature of PBL is the overtly constructed and stated demarcation between what students know they know and what they don't know or are uncertain about. Students have learned to blur or camouflage this line for faculty, because awareness of knowledge gaps is rarely rewarded and often penalized. However, it is the starting point for discussion, and for generation of the new learning issues needed to make progress. To encourage students to voice uncertainties and reveal a lack of knowledge during group discussions, we don't ask the facilitators, who work so closely with them, to grade assignments or exams. In fulfillment of their role in modeling the giving and receiving of feedback, facilitators do evaluate their students' performance as PBL group members, typically twice per semester using predetermined criteria (see Allen & Duch, 1998; and Chapter 11 by Kitto and Griffiths in this book, for examples of these group evaluation forms and criteria). Students often voice a preference that peer facilitators, and not faculty instructors, perform this crucial aspect of ensuring accountability among group members. In addition, in some courses with an extensive writing component, facilitators serve as peer reviewers of students' first drafts.

Finally, facilitators aren't expected to meet with their groups outside of class, although some do by choice. However, they typically are required to be available by phone or e-mail between class sessions.

How Do Tutors Know What to Do?
Preservice Workshop
The group facilitation experience starts with a three-hour orientation workshop, offered at the beginning of each semester. The initial focus of this workshop is to introduce all facilitators to the PBL method and underlying philosophy. We discuss the anxieties that their students may have when first presented with (what for them may be) a new teaching and learning paradigm, then go on to formulate strategies to ease the transition to PBL. Facilitators also begin to air their anxieties as their first experience with guiding groups approaches, allowing us to address these concerns openly and directly. We conclude the workshop with some brainstorming about the roles and responsibilities of facilitators and of their perceptions about those of faculty PBL instructors to their facilitators. Because the facilitators play the difficult role of middleman in a multilayered teaching and learning scheme, we find that this helps them to think about how they will negotiate this role during the semester, remaining allies to two groups (faculty and students) who often do not speak the same classroom language.

Table 8.1 provides a schedule for a typical orientation workshop, along with the topical themes addressed and activities that support these themes.

Tutorial Methods of Instruction Course
A course designed to help develop and boost group facilitation skills, Tutorial Methods of Instruction (after the professional school PBL "tutor"), is at the core of the program. The course meets in fall and spring semesters in eight two-hour sessions, most of which occur in the first half of the semester, when the participants generally have a lighter workload in their other courses. Skills or topics listed in Table 8.2 are introduced in a progression that takes into account when they're most needed in the PBL classroom and our perceptions about the difficulty of the skill. The authors team teach the course, alternating the role of primary instructor each semester.

The format of all sessions is similar, resembling a faculty development workshop—preparatory reading of articles, short orientation lectures, and group or whole-class brainstorming sessions (initiated by questions, teaching cases, or pencil-and-paper exercises), followed by reflective processing. With

Table 8.1. Synopsis of the Topics, Strategies and Schedule for a Typical Preservice Workshop for Facilitators

Topical Theme	Activities That Support Topical Themes	Elapsed Time
Introductions	1. Round-robin self-introductions: name, major, course in which will serve as a facilitator, reasons for choosing to be one.	0–15 min
Introduction to Course	1. Distribution of synopsis of TMI syllabus, with URL to longer electronic version. 2. Minilecture overview of course objectives, course sessions, and instructors' expectations. 3. Introduction to important ground rules for the course (concerning ways to protect student confidentiality and for constructive feedback).	15–35 min
PBL Strategies and Underlying Philosophy	1. Minilecture overview of idealized PBL cycle and why instructors use the approach. 2. Distribution of sample PBL problem. 3. Formation of groups. 4. Questions posed for group discussion, followed by reporting out to whole class—"*In what ways does PBL and its objectives differ from and resemble teaching/learning strategies you have encountered in other courses?*" 5. Wrap up of whole-class discussion by instructor that leads to next topic.	35–75 min

Table 8.1. *Continued*

Topical Theme	Activities That Support Topical Themes	Elapsed Time
Student Expectations for a New Course	1. Questions for groups: "*What aspects of the first day of a course lead you to think it will be a positive experience? What aspects lead you to think it will not be a pleasant or beneficial one?*" 2. Report from groups and instructor-led discussion. 3. Question for groups: "*What first-day strategies would help set up a positive climate for learning in a PBL class?*" 4. Report and discussion, focusing on any mismatches between student expectations and what PBL will entail.	75–120 min (a 10–15 min break begins at about 90 min)
First Day Activities for Groups	1. Run through of sample group warm-up activity. 2. Brief brainstorming of new or recounting of former warm-up activities.	120–155 min
Roles and Responsibilities	1. Assignment for groups: "*List at least five roles and responsibilities for peer facilitators and faculty instructors in PBL courses.*" 2. Report and discussion, focusing on aligning facilitator and faculty perceptions.	155–175 min
Send-off	1. Introduction to next session topic. 2. Question for reflection (the first question for discussion in the next session).	175–180 min

Table 8.2. Session Topics for Tutorial Methods of Instruction, a Two-credit Course That Provides In-service Supervision and Support for Peer Tutors in PBL Courses

---

- Intellectual development of undergraduates
- How to involve all students in the group process
- Group dynamics and the behaviors that foster "good and bad" interactions
- Detecting and dealing with conflicts that arise when people work together
- Peer, self-, and group assessment
- Questioning techniques, and the role of questions in PBL
- Writing and learning from teaching case studies
- Reflective practice in teaching
- Ethical issues in teaching (for example, "How friendly should a tutor be with his group?")

---

each semester's experience, we have scaled down expectations in terms of prior processing of course readings and have allotted progressively more time for structured or informal reflections on facilitators' experiences since the last course meeting (by facilitator request). These reflections lead to brainstorming about strategies for resolution of any ongoing problems with group dysfunctions. Facilitators are encouraged to meet with the specific PBL course instructors to discuss problems in between Tutorial Methods sessions, particularly in instances in which a greater degree of confidentiality is needed than the Tutorial Methods sessions can guarantee.

We also run a "fish bowl" exercise in at least one of the sessions. In one type of fish bowl activity, we use a modification of a tutor training strategy introduced to us by PBL experts from the University of Mexico School of Medicine's Primary Care Curriculum. Some of the facilitators role-play a student group working on a PBL problem, another the group's facilitator, and the rest of the class sits and observes. A course instructor sits on the far sidelines and provides a running commentary on the facilitator's strategies to one of the observers, modeling the "rules" of constructive feedback. At the end of a role-playing session, the observer gives this verbal feedback to the individual who has played the facilitator role, adding observations of his or her own. Another role-playing session is then initiated, using the same or a new problem. This cycle continues for about four iterations, then a round-robin reflection on the process ends the class.

The last two sessions of the Tutorial Methods course are used for presentation and discussion of teaching cases that the facilitators write based on critical incidents in their experiences working with groups. We've collected over

100 of these teaching cases, which continue to inform us about facilitators' perceptions of the experience, thus guiding an ongoing evolution of the course. With permission, we've rewritten these to change the specific scenarios into ones invoking the same behavior in a different context, so they could serve as scripts for trigger tapes (enacted by student actors) that we've produced for use in the course and for general distribution.

A typical session on group dynamics begins with a questionnaire (Figure 8.1) that facilitators fill out individually. From among the list of situations frequently encountered, they must first identify those that they have observed in the group(s) they supervise. Then they must pick the one situation that they feel poses the greatest threat to the success of their group(s). Every year, the majority of students pick item 10, which relates to student satisfaction with a superficial understanding of topics. We then use an appropriate teaching case or trigger tape to initiate discussion on that or another topic of concern.

In designing this and other sessions, we have adapted some strategies used to inform new teachers in a more general context (Lewis, 1992). Those thinking of designing a course with similar goals to Tutorial Methods will also find that a manual produced to support near-peer instruction (The Workshop Project, 2000) provides useful ideas for adaptation as do chapters 6 and 7 of an on-line PBL text (Pross, 2000) on the role and characteristics of a PBL tutor.

Course-Specific Preparation

What transpires in the preparation sessions held for the PBL courses in which the facilitators actually work with student groups varies from course to course. In an example from an introductory biology course (the course, designed by Allen and Donham, is described in Chapter 16 of this book) the facilitators and course instructor meet weekly for an hour session. After an initial discussion of the previous week's course activities, facilitators lead a discussion of an upcoming problem on a rotating basis, having written and distributed a plan for how that problem could unfold. The plan includes timing issues (how to intertwine the group activities led by facilitators with whole class activities led by the course instructor), anticipated learning issues, potential conceptual pitfalls, tips for facilitator preparation in content background, and a stockpile of questions from which facilitators can draw when stumped about ways to stimulate discussion and dig for deeper understanding. At the start of the semester, facilitators are given a notebook containing all of the problems for the semester and several associated readings. While requiring the facilitators to search for these resources themselves may have pedagogical merit (and is consistent with the "PBL philosophy") we assume that this would be an imposition on their already oversubscribed schedules.

Consider each of the following situations. Check the boxes by those you recognize in the group you are now tutoring. Circle the one you think is most likely to interfere with the success of your group. Be prepared to talk about the information you have used to diagnose this as a "problem" situation. Think about ways to deal with the situation.

❏ Student who confidently presents information that is incorrect yet goes unchallenged by other group members.

❏ Student who misses class or regularly comes late to class and requires class time for the more conscientious members of the group to fill him or her in on what was missed.

❏ Unprepared student who routinely comes to class but doesn't contribute to group discussions or projects.

❏ Likeable, talkative student who is unaware that he (or she) frequently interrupts others and dominates discussion thereby preventing contributions by quieter members of the group.

❏ Student who readily understands the material but is not particularly interested in sharing that knowledge with other group members.

❏ Student who thinks problem-based learning is not a good way to learn and deliberately or unconsciously disrupts the process.

❏ Quiet student who has good thoughts to contribute but never seems to get the attention of other members of the group.

❏ Students whose friendship outside of class creates a subgroup that frequently breaks off from the main group in class discussion.

❏ Student who, due to illness or some other legitimate reason, misses a week or more of class.

❏ Group that gets along well and is satisfied with a superficial procedural understanding and doesn't seem to be aware of or interested in a deeper conceptual understanding.

❏ Student who has difficulty focusing on course material and frequently ends up discussing sports, the campus social scene, or the previous night's TV show.

❏ Student who ignores or puts down group members who have a different cultural background, racial background, or physical appearance.

❏ Student who doesn't listen to or seem to understand the points made by other group members.

❏ Group that can't make progress without assistance and shows signs of frustration (and perhaps resentment) when the tutor doesn't provide the information desired.

❏ Group in which a disparity in the abilities of members makes communication of concepts difficult.

❏ Student who directs all of her or his questions to the tutor (and instructor).

❏ Students who do all of the necessary work but do not seem to enjoy discussing problems and related concepts with one another.

FIGURE 8.1. "Common Group Situations that Tutors May Encounter," an exercise used in Tutorial Methods of Instruction to introduce issues of group dynamics and function

Formal and Informal Evaluation of Facilitator Performance

Twice a semester, facilitators in the Tutorial Methods course are evaluated by the students in the course they supervise. The evaluation forms typically use predetermined criteria resembling the behaviors and characteristics of the well-functioning facilitator listed in a previous section of this chapter. Ratings choices are accompanied and clarified with specific comments. Course instructors fill out a similar form and write a summary of student comments (preserving student confidentiality). In turn modeling the process of bidirectional feedback, some instructors initiate dialogues about their own and the facilitators' ongoing performance in the course-specific preparation meetings. Facilitators, likewise, are often encouraged to solicit verbal feedback from their groups on a routine basis, and strategies for doing this are offered in the Tutorial Methods of Instruction course.

Facilitator Selection Process

How Facilitators Are Recruited

Faculty identify and recruit prospective facilitators through casual or solicited word-of-mouth recommendations from faculty and former facilitators, distribution and posting of flyers, and by encouraging students in introductory level PBL courses to make contact later in their academic careers. Instructors in upper-level courses have a more limited pool of potential applicants, since they cannot expect to encounter quite as many students with exposure to the course in a previous semester or year. Another option for them (see Chapter 11 by Kitto and Griffiths in this book) has been to use true chronological age peers, often enrolled as honors section students in the courses in which they also serve as facilitators.

Selection criteria used by the faculty recruiters vary. Typically, those teaching in a small-class, Honors format have access to the most academically motivated and successful students and can be more selective (if these are criteria they value). In all cases, however, faculty look for facilitators with a good (but not necessarily excellent) academic record, some (but not necessarily total) "buy-in" for the PBL philosophy, indication of a high level of responsibility, and a personality that can best be described as "easy to work with" (but not necessarily an extroverted one).

Incentives for Participation

Students can receive two credits toward graduation for participation in the Tutorial Methods of Instruction course; others receive honors credit for serving as true peer facilitators in a course in which they are also enrolled as students. Many of the facilitators, including most of those enrolled in Tutorial Methods to date, in addition receive a small stipend ($300 for courses in which PBL sessions are less frequent, and $600 for full-time service) in recognition of time spent as a facilitator in the PBL classroom.

Indicators of Success of the Program

The Student Perspective

Students value the presence of undergraduate facilitators in their classrooms, as assessed through both qualitative and quantitative measures described previously (Allen & White, 1999; 2000). The average overall rating of facilitator performance on end-of-semester course evaluations is generally high (on average, 1.3–1.5 on a 5-point scale in which 1 is "excellent"), and students indicate agreement (usually strong agreement) with the statement that "my facilitator benefits my learning of the subject." Written comments on the bisemester facilitator evaluation forms are consistent with our expectations and goals for the program, particularly as they relate to helping students make an easier transition to a PBL classroom environment.

The Facilitator Perspective

Facilitators are equally positive about the experience, as reflected in both written and verbal evaluations. They report that it not only has personal rewards, but also helps them envision themselves in future teaching roles. Most agree that it has increased their understanding of their major subject, confirming our expectation that PBL group leadership could serve as a type of capstone experience (a final overview from the perspective of heightened content knowledge) that college faculty are being urged to provide by various higher education constituencies (Boyer Commission, 1998).

The Faculty Perspective

Faculty generally agree with students' appraisal of the skills their facilitators possess. We agree that facilitators generally do well at presenting a friendly and interested persona to their groups, modeling good interpersonal relationships, fostering even participation, providing information when needed (and conversely, knowing when to hold back), and keeping the group discussion on target. Student evaluations have also given us a wealth of information about skills that we need to assist facilitators with (in terms of the PBL strategies we use) and continue to target in both course-specific meetings and the Tutorial Methods of Instruction course. These include helping students identify and appraise the relevancy of learning resources, prioritize the importance of learning issues, and make connections between old and new problems. We have added another skill to this list based on our own perceptions; that is, many undergraduate facilitators tend to have a more directive questioning style. We have observed facilitators missing golden opportunities (from our viewpoint) for asking questions of a more open-ended nature and leaving superficial coverage of a learning issue unchallenged by the art of questioning. This may be an area in which experience, as well as content expertise, must be drawn upon by the well-functioning facilitator; alternatively, it may not be the most essential skill in all PBL models, particularly when time available for working through a problem is a limiting factor.

Overcoming the "Fifth Wheel" Syndrome

Faculty sharing their classrooms with undergraduate facilitators must be prepared at first to feel unneeded—the "fifth wheel" syndrome. A common finding with a student-centered PBL experience is that the faculty instructor who doesn't serve as a floating facilitator must continually struggle to find ways (that students will find valuable to their learning) to be scripted into the classroom play. The course-related chapters in this book provide a wealth of examples, including lecturing on a "need-to-know" basis for clarification of difficult concepts and coordinating whole-class activities that help students develop their ability to critically appraise resources, build conceptual frameworks, (concept mapping, flow charts, model building), and learn to dig deeper to build reasoned arguments (debates, jigsaw grouping).

Unresolved Issues and Future Directions

We are still struggling with how best to support students in the "floating" facilitator role, the one that is the most feasible for large enrollment courses. An unforeseen drawback to the Tutorial Methods of Instruction course is that it provides a forum for facilitators to compare notes. Some of the floating facilitators make comments that indicate that they would prefer the dedicated role, mostly because of the personal satisfaction (as expressed by the "dedicated" facilitators) that comes from building a relationship with the students in one group over the course of a semester. The good news is that this does not seem to seriously impair the benefit that the floating facilitators derive from the experiences that they do have.

True peers also seem to have a more difficult job than the near-peer facilitators; the facilitator often may have to deal with at least one group member who never gave up the notion that he or she should have been chosen to be the facilitator. Students who serve as the group facilitator in a concurrently meeting honors section often must struggle against conveying the impression that they have a favored or privileged status in the course, and instructors must be careful not to give these facilitators a content understanding edge (that will translate to a better grade) by holding separate preparatory sessions with this focus. The feeling of accomplishment, however, that these facilitators can have after a semester in this role seems to compensate for the moments of anguish their groups can create for them. We also think these facilitators will go on to make good workplace supervisors, particularly of other skilled professionals.

Our experience with undergraduate facilitators in many ways parallels the independent experience of others. Gosser and Roth (1998), for example, use undergraduate students as "workshop leaders" to assist groups of students. They too have developed a course to prepare students for their instructional role (The Workshop Project, 2000). Their course deals with many of the same topics found in Tutorial Methods of Instruction. There, as here, responsibility for teaching the interdisciplinary course does not clearly fall within a particular department; thus, faculty workloads must be negotiated.

Conclusion

In addition to providing the means for using problem-based instruction at the introductory level (where it can have the greatest impact in subsequent learning), the PBL peer group facilitator program provides a natural progression for attracting good students to teaching careers. It allows them to gain an overview of their chosen major as a capstone experience prior to graduation. For students in introductory PBL courses, these upperclass guides assist with the often difficult transition between the academic expectations of the high school versus college experience, particularly as they relate to the novel challenges of PBL. For faculty teaching PBL courses, the facilitators serve as far more than a practical solution to managing multiple groups, becoming our apprentices and allies in creating a community of scholars in the PBL classroom.

Authors' Biographies

Deborah E. Allen is Associate Professor and Undergraduate Programs Director in the Department of Biological Sciences and an affiliated faculty member of the University Honors Program at the University of Delaware.

Harold B. White, III is Professor of Biochemistry in the Department of Chemistry and Biochemistry and Director of the Howard Hughes Medical Institute's Undergraduate Biological Sciences Education Program at the University of Delaware.

References

Allen, D., & Duch, B. (1998). *Thinking towards solutions: Problem-based learning activities for general biology.* Philadelphia: Saunders College Publishing.

Allen, D. E., Duch, B. J. & Groh, S. E. (1996). The power of problem-based learning in teaching introductory science courses. In L. Wilkerson and W. H. Gijselaers (Eds.), *Bringing problem-based learning to higher education: Theory and practice.* (*New Directions in Teaching and Learning in Higher Education 68*, (43–52) San Francisco: Jossey-Bass.

Allen, D. E., & White, H. B. III. (1999). A few steps ahead on the same path: Using peer tutors in the cooperative learning classroom—A multilayered approach to teaching. *J. College Science Teaching 28*, 299–302.

Allen, D. E., & White, H. B. III. (2000). Peer facilitators of in-class groups: Adapting problem-based learning to the undergraduate setting. In J. E. Miller, J. E. Groccia, and M. S. Miller (Eds.), *Student-assisted teaching: A guide to faculty-student teamwork.* Bolton, MA: Anker Publications.

Barrows, H. S. (1988). *The tutorial process.* Springfield: Southern Illinois University School of Medicine.

Boyer Commission on Educating Undergraduates in the Research University. (1998). *Reinventing undergraduate education: A blueprint for America's research universities.* Princeton: Carnegie Foundation for the Advancement of Teaching.

Brookfield, S. D. (1995). *Becoming a critically reflective teacher.* San Francisco, CA: Jossey-Bass.

Engel, C. E. (1997). Not just a method but a way of learning. In D. Boud and G. Feletti (Eds.), *The challenge of problem-based learning.* London, England: Kogan Page, pp. 17–27.

Felder, R. M. (1995). We never said it would be easy. *Chemical Engineering Education 29*, 32–33.

Gosser, D. K., & Roth, V. (1998). The workshop chemistry project: Peer-led team learning. *Journal of Chemical Education 75*, 185–87.

Lewis, K. G., (Ed.). (1992). *Teaching pedagogy to teaching assistants: A handbook for 398T instructors*. Austin, TX: University of Texas at Austin.

Mennin, S. P., & McConnell, T. Undated document. *A guide to quality tutorials*. Albuquerque, NM: W.H.O. Collaborating Center for the Dissemination of Community-Oriented, Problem-Based Education and the University of New Mexico School of Medicine.

Pross, H. (2000). Introduction to problem-based learning at Queens. http://meds.queensu.ca/medicine/pbl/ (2000, June 30).

White, H. B., III. (1996). Addressing content in problem-based courses: The learning issue matrix. *Biochemical Education 24*, 41–45.

The Workshop Project. (2000). The workshop model: peer leadership and learning—A guidebook. http://www.sci.ccny.cuny.edu/~chemwksp/ulm.html (2000, June 30).

9

ASSESSMENT STRATEGIES IN A PROBLEM-BASED LEARNING COURSE

Barbara J. Duch and Susan E. Groh

Chapter Summary

Moving to a student-centered, cooperative-learning format of instruction requires rethinking how to assess student learning in such an environment. This chapter discusses many of the decisions faculty make concerning assessment when adopting problem-based techniques.

Introduction

For many instructors, the decision to move to a problem-based approach to teaching marks the culmination of a period of intensive research and fact-finding, discussion with other faculty, and reflection on one's goals and philosophies of teaching. Once the decision is made, however, a whole new set of issues and concerns arise that must be addressed. Paramount among these are questions centered on assessment: How will problem-based learning affect how well my students are learning? How will I *know* how well they're learning? Can I use my old methods of testing in a course that may be structured in a very different way? What happens now that students are working in groups—must they all be graded together?

Assessing student learning, however, is just one part of a successful assessment strategy. Other key components that should also be addressed include evaluating the course itself, asking students questions that will inform the instructor about what is working well in the course and what isn't. Faculty should also evaluate their role as an instructor, soliciting information from their students throughout the length of the course and documenting their own role from the instructor's viewpoint.

This chapter will address the assessment questions faced by many faculty who have incorporated problem-based instruction in undergraduate courses in a typical college or university that does not have a PBL track or program. Often, a problem-based practitioner may be the only faculty member in a department or one of only a few faculty in an institution to offer PBL instruction. Especially when an instructor is teaching a "prerequisite" course in a major, he or she may feel the need to justify his or her instructional decisions and document student learning to colleagues. Assessment issues that become relevant if an entire curriculum becomes problem-based are emphasized in Boud and Feletti (1997). Comparisons of student achievement in PBL vs. traditional tracks and evaluations of PBL programs are generally taken from the health professions literature (Albanese & Mitchell, 1993; Feletti, Saunders, & Smith, 1983; Newble & Jaeger, 1983; Norman, 1997; Vernon & Blake, 1993).

Assessment of Student Learning

A challenge that faces faculty members who are using problem-based instruction in undergraduate courses is how to assess accurately the extent to which their students have met the learning objectives of the course. Some would argue that faculty who use problem-based instruction should not limit their students' self-guided learning by documenting learning objectives for the course. However, except for some special programs or colleges, most undergraduate instructors are constrained to guide their students in learning a designated body of concepts and principles in approximately 14 weeks. Therefore, the authors of this chapter advocate writing learning objectives for students and assessing the extent to which students meet those objectives. Most faculty are generally comfortable in testing content, but if PBL instructors are expecting their students to be able to demonstrate that they can think critically, evaluate evidence, analyze information, and justify conclusions, they will need to think beyond standard testing practices, particularly in medium- to large-size classes. Many management issues arise when one thinks through the following questions:

- What products will students produce when they complete a problem? Will it be an individual product or a group one? How will it be graded?

- How can an instructor promote group learning but ensure that individual achievement is assessed?

- How can a problem-based scenario be used in an exam?

- Should group skills and communication skills be assessed? If so, how?

PBL practitioners may think of more questions related to assessment issues as they think about using a problem-based approach to their course.

First Things First: Learning Objectives

Decisions concerning the assessment of student learning in a PBL course should begin with an examination of the course's learning objectives. This is true for any type of course, but the learning objectives in a PBL course generally go beyond simple content mastery, so the connection between these and assessment bears further examination. It is important to list all learning objectives in a syllabus so students can see and understand the expectations of the instructor. Learning objectives should focus on broad concepts and skills rather than on the details of the course content, since listing them is not intended to limit student research and self-guided learning. The first step in thinking about assessing students' learning begins with asking two questions (Uno, 1999) that will guide one to find appropriate assessment tools.

1. What should students know, value, and be able to do by the end of the course?

2. What evidence will indicate that they have reached these goals?

What Should Students Know?   Content-oriented objectives are those concerned with the mastery of material specific to that course or discipline. Thinking about what students should know or be able to do in terms of content is not particularly hard. Instructors are accustomed both to setting these goals and assessing them in traditional ways. Testing content knowledge objectives through multiple choice and short-answer tests are common ways that faculty assess student learning. However, many times these methods do not help one to judge the extent to which students have developed higher-order thinking skills. In order to choose appropriate methods of assessment, faculty should be specific about what they want their students to know (content-based objectives). For example, Valerie Hans (see Chapter 13) in one of her criminal justice courses lists the following two objectives:

- Acquire knowledge and understanding about the criminal courts and how they function.

- Analyze and critically evaluate claims made in public policy debates about the court.

Among Deborah Allen's specific content objectives for her introductory biology students (see Chapter 16) are the following:

- Explain how CO_2 is used in photosynthesis.

- Diagram the role (including life histories and nutritional requirements) of marine phytoplankton in the marine food chain.

- Construct a concept map of the carbon cycle and its relationship to atmospheric CO_2 formation, burning of fossil fuels, photosynthesis, and respiration.

Notice that the first objectives of both instructors ask students to perform at Bloom's lower cognitive levels of understanding (knowledge and comprehension) (Bloom, 1956; and Chapter 5) and could be assessed using traditional testing methods. The remaining objectives require students to achieve higher or deeper levels of understanding (analysis, synthesis, and evaluation) and are more difficult to assess in a 50-minute test. Hans and Allen have each found alternative ways to evaluate whether students have met those learning objectives, as will be discussed.

A point worth emphasizing at this stage is that despite common usage, the term *assessment* is not limited to a formal system of comprehensive testing in order to make a judgment or establish grades. In addition to this type of "summative" process, assessment may also be "formative"—i.e., have the aim of providing feedback and suggestions for improvement in a more informal manner. Both types of assessment have a place in a problem-based learning format.

What Should Students Be Able to Do?   Many of the skills students need to develop are tied to content objectives, such as those previously discussed ("Analyze and evaluate . . . ," "Diagram the role . . . ," "Construct a concept map . . . "). In addition, there are other, more general "process"

skills that can be listed as learning objectives for students. Some of these objectives were mentioned in the Introduction of this book and can prove to be a motivating factor in why faculty choose to adopt problem-based instruction. They include the ability to do the following:

- Identify, find, and analyze information needed for solving a problem.

- Communicate ideas and concepts verbally and in writing.

- Collaborate productively in groups.

These objectives are not necessarily linked to specific content, but are applicable to any discipline; hence, their development is easily overlooked. Too often, it is assumed that students will acquire these skills and be able to bring them to bear as needed in content courses, without addressing the question of who is responsible for their development. As one can see with some of the higher-ordered thinking content objectives, process skills are not easily assessed in a traditional testing format. In many cases, assessing these objectives may involve formative methods.

What Do You Want Your Students to Value?   Many times teachers neglect to address this issue—with themselves and their students. In a problem-based course it may be desirable for students to recognize their own ability to learn independently, express confidence in their ability to work cooperatively with others, or express other attitudes that are important to the instructor. These "values" objectives should also be listed in the course syllabus and be assessed using methods that may or may not affect students' grades.

Connecting Assessment Strategies to Course Objectives

Once an instructor has listed all the content, process skills, and values objectives in the course syllabus, one needs to decide what assessment strategies will be used to evaluate whether students are meeting those objectives. Some objectives can be assessed using traditional means, such as exams, but others may require additional, sometimes innovative methods. (A wealth of information concerning techniques for classroom assessment may be found in the works of Angelo and Cross [1993] and Walvoord and Anderson [1998].) It is important to again emphasize that although the goal is to assess students' progress in meeting course objectives, some assessment may actually not involve grading. For example, one of Allen's objectives ("Construct a concept map . . . ") may be planned as a group activity, with each group reporting on their own concept map during classtime with no specific grade assigned.

Table 9.1. Sample Learning Objectives and Their Assessment

Learning Objective	Assessment Method
Explain how CO_2 is used in photosynthesis.	Exam—multiple choice, short answer, or homework assignment
Analyze and critically evaluate claims made in public policy debates about the court.	Group assignment, question on exam, or homework assignment
Identify, find, and analyze information.	Take-home group or individual exam, problem write-up or summary, and/or evaluation of individual effort within the group
Express confidence in ability to work with others.	End-of-course rating form

Table 9.1 uses the Allen's and Hans's course objectives shown earlier to demonstrate how learning objectives and assessment methods can be linked to help students understand how the instructor will evaluate whether they are meeting those course objectives.

If process skills are valued by an instructor, then efforts must be made both to provide training and practice in the development of such skills, and to signal their value by including them in an assessment plan. Does this mean that instructors must now generate two separate sets of tests and measures—one for content objectives and another for process skills? Not at all: in fact, we might turn this around and point out that the process of assessment provides a very natural opportunity to bring both content and process objectives together. Process skills can be demonstrated and assessed as an integral part of assessing content knowledge.

An example may illustrate this better. One of us (SEG) teaches a course in general chemistry to freshmen science majors. Among the most important learning objectives for this course is the development of strong critical thinking skills: the ability to analyze a situation, to evaluate observations and patterns in data in the light of fundamental principles of chemistry, to see the ramifications of such principles and use them to predict behavior, and so forth. The PBL and homework problems that students encounter in the course are designed to stimulate and develop critical thinking; since these are group situations, though, they do not provide the best opportunity to examine an individual's critical thinking skills.

For this reason, I decided to build assessment of critical thinking skills into the content exams by designing questions that would go beyond simple knowledge or comprehension, into the higher Bloom levels of thinking (application, analysis, evaluation and synthesis) (Bloom, 1956; and Chapter 5). Complex situations involving multiple concepts, based on the real world or some novel setting the students have not previously encountered, lend themselves to this: questions can be asked that require students to recognize the concepts involved (analysis), to use those concepts in answering the question (application), to judge the relative merits of different explanations, and/or to pull several ideas together to make predictions (synthesis).

One content area important in this course concerns the nature of solutions: in particular, how the behavior of a pure substance, such as water, is affected by the presence of some other material dissolved in it. Chemists recognize a group of "colligative" properties that change in the presence of a solute: compared to pure water, e.g., a solution of salt water will have a higher boiling point, a lower freezing point, less evaporation, etc. These effects are quantitative and can be calculated readily from a few pieces of information. While being able to calculate such changes can be useful, understanding why and how the changes occur in the first place is, to me, much more valuable. It requires thinking about the behavior of particles at the molecular level and seeing how that behavior manifests itself in these macroscopic properties. The analysis involved, based on relative rates of competing processes, is fairly sophisticated for these students and requires careful thought to understand the phenomenon.

Typical exam questions in this area test at the simple knowledge or comprehension levels, e.g., "Calculate the vapor pressure of a solution of 5.8 g of NaCl in 100 g of water at 25° C" or "Explain why a solution of NaCl will have a lower vapor pressure than pure water." The former is a classic "plug and chug" question. After carrying out one simple conversion of mass into moles, the student need only plug numbers into a simple equation to calculate the answer. The second question looks more complex. One would think that to explain this phenomenon would surely require some higher-order thinking. In this case, however, the question refers to the very situation that was analyzed in class when the concept was being studied. All a student really needs to do to answer this question is to memorize and recall the explanation developed in class.

An exam question that does require critical thinking while still giving the student a chance to display simpler levels of content knowledge deals with the following situation. Display cases in museums are used not only to keep valuable artifacts and documents from being handled, but also to maintain a constant atmosphere of controlled humidity around the materials to help preserve them. The problem states that the relative humidity within an enclosed (but not airtight) display case can be kept at a constant 75.3% by placing within it a saturated aqueous solution of NaCl, in contact with excess undissolved NaCl. The question posed is for the student to present a molecular level argument to explain how this constant level of humidity may be maintained, even when air saturated with water (100% humidity) enters the case.

To provide a thorough explanation of this practice requires more than a knowledge of the basic idea involved—that the presence of salt will produce a lower humidity (i.e., vapor pressure) in the atmosphere over the solution. Asking how this atmosphere can be maintained despite the addition of more humid air forces the student to recognize the dynamic nature of this equilibrium between liquid and gaseous water, and to think about how the perturbation will affect the final humidity. The concept of a saturated solution also comes into play in explaining the role of the excess salt: as water from the more humid atmosphere enters the case, it will ultimately dilute the saturated salt solution and cause the humidity to gradually increase in the absence of sufficient salt to keep the solution saturated. This question, then, builds in elements of analysis, application, and synthesis, while still providing an opportunity to assess comprehension of the core concept of solution vapor pressure.

This and similar essay questions are graded using a partial credit system. A list is made of the ideas that should show up in an exemplary answer, and a certain number of points are assigned to each. In this way, a student who states that the salt solution is responsible for the lower humidity in the case but is unable to go farther, still receives credit for that fundamental knowledge (here, 3 points out of 10). Similarly, a student who explains how the more humid air will perturb the vapor pressure equilibrium without recognizing the role of the excess salt (the most challenging "synthesis" part of the question) will still receive full marks (9 points out of 10) for getting to that stage.

Questions like this, then, provide a means for probing a student's ability to think critically within the context of a more traditional assessment method (exams)—one need not manufacture an artificial situation aimed only at assessing critical thinking. The extent to which such questions are included in exams is, of course, a matter of preference, in keeping with the instructional goals of the course. We consider it important to provide assessment at a variety of Bloom levels: students must have the opportunity to demonstrate basic knowledge and comprehension, as well as higher order skills. To provide an example of how this balance can be achieved, an analysis of the exam in which the humidity question appeared was carried out to determine how many points (out of 100) were allocated to items at different Bloom levels. To do this, the separate components of an exemplary answer to a question were classified by

Table 9.2. Breakdown of Exam Items by Bloom Level

Bloom Level	Number of Points	Total Points Possible by This Level	Corresponding Letter Grade
Knowledge	9	9	F
Comprehension	36	45	D–
Application	22	67	C+
Analysis	20	87	A–
Synthesis	9	96	A
Evaluation	4	100	A

Bloom level and the points awarded for specific levels in each question tallied. For example, of the 10 points allocated to the humidity question, 2 corresponded to comprehension, 3 to application, 4 to analysis, and 1 to synthesis. The results for the exam as a whole are shown in Table 9.2.

On this exam, a student who can go no further than demonstrating simple knowledge and comprehension can still pass, although barely. Being able to apply the concepts increases the score, but the biggest gain comes from the demonstration of analytical thinking, in keeping with the emphasis placed on the development of this skill in this particular course. Which areas an instructor might choose to emphasize will depend on the learning objectives for that course.

One can imagine similar strategies to assess learning with respect to other global skills as part of the assessment of content knowledge: using debates, written or oral reports to reveal both content and communication skills; evaluating how well a group is able to function in the preparation of a project; asking students about how they obtained information for a report; or posing a challenging search for some content-related material; and so on. Again, the point is that both content and process can be linked and evaluated together at assessment time.

Grading

Group learning is a central aspect of the learning experience in a PBL class, and instructors may want to think of ways to factor it into the total grade given to students. Some methods used by other faculty including the following:

- Give students one group problem on an exam, followed by the individual portion of the test. The group question may be given in class or as a take-home assignment. This is one method of planning an authentic PBL assessment by assigning a PBL problem similar to one that students have worked through in class.

- Grade group problem summaries.
- Use the ratings by group members of individual contributions to the group as a part of a participation grade.
- Grade group presentations.

Assessment of the Course

In addition to assessing student learning, it is important to think about ways to assess the course itself. Students are a wonderful source of information and can provide timely feedback that can help ensure that the problem-based experience is a positive one for students. Scheduling a feedback session two to three times during a semester gives students the opportunity to tell the faculty member what is working well in the course, and what should be changed to make the learning experience better. Some examples of items that can be used on a midsemester feedback form include the following:

1. How satisfied are you with this class so far this semester? (Circle one.)

1	2	3	4	5
Very Satisfied				Very Dissatisfied

2. What helps you learn in this class?
3. What hinders your learning?
4. What could you do to make this learning experience better for you?
5. What could the instructor do to make this class better for you?
6. What specific questions/content are still unclear to you?

After receiving the feedback from students, the instructor should be sure to respond to their comments in class. One can categorize the various suggested changes that students made, and then explain how he or she plans to alter the format of the course, or explain why he or she is not making changes.

At the end-of-semester evaluation, it is important to ask students questions related to group work and their confidence in finding and using resource materials in addition to more traditional questions and comments found on departmental or college course ratings forms. A list of suggested items may be found in the appendix of this chapter.

The students' point of view about the course is not the only one. The instructor also should assess what worked well in the course and how it could be improved. The following questions may be helpful to guide course reflection:

- Did the problems focus student learning on the course objectives?

- Which problems worked well, and which need to be improved?

- Were the problems suitable (i.e., of sufficient complexity) for groups to solve?

- Did the students demonstrate a deeper level of understanding about course content?

- Was the course structured appropriately for the size of class, level of students?

- Was the instructional role in the classroom satisfactory? Was the course sufficiently student-centered?

- What should be planned differently the next time? What should be kept the same?

- Did the groups function well? If not, what can be improved?

Conclusions

When faculty members move from a traditional to a problem-based learning environment, many instructional decisions need to be made, including how to assess students' learning in the course. If developing critical thinking skills, communication skills, research skills, and other lifelong learning skills are a priority for the instructor, then students should expect to be assessed on how well they are meeting those learning objectives in addition to the content objectives. Thinking about what to assess, as well as how to assess, can be a challenge to any PBL practitioner, since this exercise makes faculty grapple with what is important instructionally, and what is possible to accomplish in a limited amount of time. This reflection is essential in developing reasonable and fair assessments for students in problem-based classes.

Authors' Biographies

Barbara J. Duch is Associate Director of the Mathematics and Science Education Resource Center at the University of Delaware.

Susan E. Groh is Assistant Professor in the Department of Chemistry and Biochemistry and an affiliated faculty member of the University Honors Program at the University of Delaware.

References

Albanese, M., & Mitchell, S. (1993). Problem-based learning: A review of literature on its outcomes and implementation issues. *Academic Medicine 68*, 52–81.

Angelo, T. A., & Cross, K. P. (1993). *Classroom assessment techniques* (2nd. ed.). San Francisco: Jossey-Bass.

Bloom, B. S. (Ed.). (1956). *Taxonomy of educational objectives: The classification of educational goals.* New York: Longman.

Boud, D., & Feletti, G. (Eds.). (1997). *The challenge of problem-based learning* (2nd ed.). London: Kogan Page.

Feletti, G., Saunders, N., & Smith, A. (1983). Comprehensive assessment of final year medical students performance based on undergraduate programme objectives. *The Lancet,* 34–37.

Newble, D. I., & Jaeger, K. (1983). The effect of assessment and examinations on the learning of medical students, *Medical Education, 13,* 263–268.

Norman, G. R. (1997). Assessment in problem-based learning. In Boud, D. & Feletti, G. (Eds.), *The challenge of problem-based learning* (2nd ed.). London: Kogan Page.

Uno, G. (1999). *Handbook on teaching undergraduate science courses: A survival training manual.* Philadelphia: Saunders College Publishing.

Vernon, D. T. A., & Blake, R. L. (1993). Does problem-based learning work? A meta-analysis of evaluative research. *Academic Medicine, 68,* 550–563.

Walvoord, B. E., & Anderson, V. J. (1998). *Effective grading.* San Francisco: Jossey-Bass.

APPENDIX TO CHAPTER 9

The following are some suggested items that may be included on an end-of-course ratings form using the rating scale: A: strongly agree; B: agree; C: neither agree nor disagree; D: disagree; E: strongly disagree.

1. The course helped me learn to obtain information from a variety of sources.
2. I feel that I can apply the general principles I learned to other (your discipline) problems.
3. I am comfortable with working in groups.
4. I feel comfortable with asking for help from others in my group.
5. I feel that my group members listen to me when I present information.
6. I feel that my group members show respect for me and my learning style.
7. I feel comfortable sharing information with others.
8. As a result of this class, my ability to find, read and analyze information has improved.
9. I like the idea of evaluating myself and my group members.
10. I benefit from the whole-class wrap-up sessions after each problem.

PROBLEM-BASED LEARNING AND THE THREE Cs OF TECHNOLOGY

George H. Watson

Chapter Summary

Ready access to networked databases, on-line newspapers and journals, and other Internet resources has dramatically altered students' pursuit of information for problem-based learning. The availability of the Internet coupled with numerous channels of electronic communication empowers student groups to work more expeditiously and more proficiently. This chapter will highlight some examples of integrating creative uses of on-line resources with problem-based learning.

Introduction

Today, we have access to a broad array of electronic aids and gadgets to assist in our daily living and entertainment. The incursion of technology into our lives seems to be growing exponentially, much like the incredible sustained exponential growth in the power of these devices represented by Moore's law. Clearly, the world of today's undergraduate students is strikingly different from that experienced by their professors as undergraduates. The impact of technology on student lives is dramatic when compared to campus life during the college days of even our newest assistant professors, although not nearly as dramatic as for a typical tenured faculty member who may have entered college more than 20 years ago. To point out just a few changes seen in the last year or so, students now use instant messaging to chat online with their friends down the hall and then download their favorite MP3s over the Internet to play on their way to class. How has the rampant use of technology by our students affected their learning?

The technologies affecting instruction and student learning can be categorized as the three Cs: computation, communication, and collections. Comparing my own freshman experience and the current state of affairs in these three areas is illustrative as shown by the following reminiscences.

The power of students to calculate routinely and expeditiously in the classroom leapt markedly in the early 1970s. In the fall of 1973, I entered Lafayette College as a freshman physics major. That summer some of my high school graduation money had gone toward the purchase of a shiny yellow Pickett Model 3 Powerlog slide rule. Only later did I realize that scientific calculators were appearing on the scene, albeit at a steep price—$495 for an HP45. Numerical computations in freshman physics and chemistry were excruciating; however, this did not seem to be the case for those students fortunate enough to already own a calculator. I vividly recall that at the end of my first year, the students who were still using slide rules were given an additional 15 minutes on the final examination to compensate for the computational advantage afforded by the calculator, hardly adequate compensation in the opinions of the remaining slide rule practitioners. That summer, Commodore offered the first affordable portable scientific calculator, and the slide rule had virtually disappeared from campus by the fall of 1974.

Over the past two decades, the expanding power of first calculators and then personal computers has been phenomenal. Simple four-function calculators have given way to graphing calculators. The computing power on each new student's desktop typically has doubled over that available just two years prior. Laptops are beginning to accompany students to their classrooms. With the increased capability for computation, how has teaching and learning been affected in the modern classroom?

The ability of students to communicate routinely and expeditiously has steadily increased. In 1973, I would save up a pile of quarters so that I might phone my girlfriend back home once per week. Handwritten letters had to suffice on the remaining days. How things have changed in the communication sector! Today's student has access to a multiplicity of channels of communication: e-mail, voice mail, chatrooms, FAX, pagers, cell phones, and instant messaging. New classrooms are being wired to connect laptops to the Internet at each seat. With the increased capability for communication, how has teaching and learning been affected in the modern classroom?

Student access to information, collections—the final element of the three Cs, has also changed markedly over the past few decades. In 1973, I would venture into the college library and wade through drawer after drawer of index cards in the card catalog, hoping to find a resource that would be relevant to my assignment. If I were lucky, the book would be available upstairs in the library so that I might have access to the information it contained. With some training, I was able to find and retrieve relevant articles from journals in the stacks, although current periodicals were often missing or hidden in dark corners of the library. Today's student is fortunate but may take for granted that information is available in a readily searchable format and accessible online simultaneously to multiple users. Library holdings are cataloged on the Web, and networked databases abound. Most major newspapers publish online. Even the entire Encyclopedia Britannica is now available online! With the increasing access to the collections of information and human knowledge, how has teaching and learning been affected in the modern classroom?

Technology, its availability to students and its use by students has changed dramatically since our own experiences in college. Has our teaching changed dramatically from that we experienced as undergraduate students or do we continue to teach primarily as we were taught? Has our use of technology for teaching kept pace with advances in computation, communication, and collections? Problem-based learning challenges us to provide the best opportunities for our students to learn. An equally important challenge is for us to embrace the use of instructional technology for providing effective opportunities for our students to access and acquire information and to communicate with their peers and with us as they learn via problem-based learning (PBL). I share here some ideas and suggestions for bringing the three Cs of technology to PBL.

Websites to Organize a PBL Course

Clearly, the Internet and the worldwide web have made the most highly visible contribution to the three Cs in technology and education within the past decade. Thus, consideration of the interaction of technology and PBL should begin with a discussion of course websites. Most instructors, regardless of their pedagogical inclinations, see the merit of using Internet resources in their courses, and many are currently supplementing their courses with custom individualized websites. Significant attention has been directed to the creation and use of websites in teaching by numerous entities; resources too numerous to list are available for assisting and leading instructors in effective web design and implementation. Nevertheless, there are a number of features associated with using the Web in teaching that should be emphasized specific to PBL. Many of the following examples come from my science and technology course for nonscience majors known as SCEN103 Silicon, Circuits, and the Digital Revolution (see Ref. 1 for its URL).

The first few days of a PBL course are critical for the buy-in of the students and their ultimate success in the course. Students new to PBL must be oriented to the approach and be assured of a support system underlying the endeavor. Numerous PBL practitioners have written eloquently on the subject and have made their motivational material available online. With the author's permission, much of the PBL orientation in the course syllabus may be borrowed and incorporated in one's own website. Typically included is an introduction to PBL and problem solving; roles and responsibilities of students, peer tutors, and instructor; working in effectively in groups with sample ground rules and consequences; frequently asked questions about PBL; and forms for assessment of individual performance in groups. In my course syllabus (Ref. 2), I have borrowed liberally (and often verbatim) from the writings and syllabi of Deborah Allen, Barbara Duch, Susan Groh, and Elizabeth Lieux, all colleagues at the University of Delaware. You may visit their course websites by referring to sample syllabi at the UD PBL website (Ref. 3).

Organization of groups is also facilitated by a course website. Group listings of individual names, e-mail addresses, links to personal homepages, and photos are useful for getting the permanent groups started. A list of group names and mailto: hyperlink tags including all e-mail addresses for the group is a good way to facilitate communication with the entire group. Often you may wish to communicate with the entire group when an individual from a group inquires regarding an assigned problem—most e-mail software packages permit creation of local group aliases that are helpful for group discussion.

A number of Internet- and web-based approaches are available to facilitate conversations and problem solving among members of a group. Newsgroups and bulletin boards served in this capacity soon after instructors began using the Internet for teaching, but these tools suffered from limited features and poor ease of use. Web-based group facilitation took a leap forward a few years ago when such companies as eGroups.com began providing free access to tools for creating chat rooms, sharing files, coordinating calendars, posting messages, and coordinating small groups. The latest, greatest tools for electronically organizing small groups of students are provided by so-called course management systems, such as WebCT, the CMS currently used at the University of Delaware. Among the many features provided by WebCT for organizing a course website, discussion groups rank high on my list. Discussion groups may be created for selected students and set to either private (just the group) or public (the entire class) depending on the objectives of the instructor. In either case, it is advisable for the instructor to be a member of each group, thus providing the ability to monitor the progress of groups at work if desired. Topics for discussion may be created, opened for discussion, locked when complete, and archived for future review. Also, course management systems are easing the burden of administering collaborative webspaces.

Most students enjoy seeing their images online. Digital cameras are a convenient way to capture an image of a group working during class and post it to the website after simple image editing. This is an excellent way to facilitate learning student names early in the semester, considered by many to be an essential ingredient of an active learning environment. (A student roster with faces accompanying names also helps recall student names in subsequent semesters as you pass familiar faces while crossing campus.) If group images are being displayed on the roster page, use of thumbnail images of about 25% of the original size is prudent to avoid undesirable delays in downloading the page. Hyperlinks to larger image files may be made from the thumbnail sketches. Alternatively, group identity can be initiated by way of interesting or amusing group names. In SCEN103, student groups were asked to select a small technology company (microcap) publicly traded on the stock market. In this course, the company icons associated with each group were added to the group roster page for visual interest (see Ref 4 for this example). An example of a group roster based on thumbnail images of groups may be found at Ref. 5. One word of caution—although most students seem to enjoy seeing their images appear online, an occasional student will feel uncomfortable or object; it is a good idea to secure student permission before publishing their images and e-mail addresses on your course website.

Project-based learning provides many of the same benefits as problem-based learning. Projects combined with web delivery of the final project can be an enticing and rewarding way to disseminate project outcomes to the remainder of the class near the end of the semester. Students are eager to create their own web documents with multimedia elements; of course, some are less skilled than others, and the collaborative aspect of a web-based group project builds on the strengths and diminishes weaknesses of the individuals involved. In SCEN103, students research a current topic of scientific or technological relevance to the course using the same methods of finding and evaluating resources and synthesizing contributions from multiple individuals into a coherent whole as they execute in solving PBL problems. This aspect of the course has been well received by students (see Ref. 6 for an archive of student projects).

Integrating Online Resources with PBL

Before the advent of the Web, students engaged in PBL would typically resolve their learning issues by relying on material in their textbooks or supplemental resources found at the library. Today, students routinely turn to the Internet for supplemental course resources—if not to the website of the course, then off to the worldwide web. As educators, we recognize that the Web is full of misinformation, biased representation, and even flat-out lies. However, this provides an opportunity to work with students to develop their critical thinking skills in the context of evaluating on-line resources. Critical thinking skills are also exercised in the process of executing web searches effectively. Thus, finding and evaluating the broad array of resources needed for resolving learning issues in the PBL classroom helps develop the critical habits of mind and the ability to "learn to learn" that is such an important part of PBL. There are numerous resources available online to assist students in searching the Web effectively and evaluating on-line resources (see "Getting Started" at the ITUE website at Ref. 7).

Although not directly related to PBL, the so-called Internet Challenge is a valuable and fun way to model for students how to search effectively and evaluate critically. Early in the semester, I encourage student groups to pose to me two or three questions that have known definitive answers. I then spend the weekend (or longer!) searching the Web, documenting the steps I take and how I evaluate the site as authoritative. During the following class, I review the process and outcomes of each search (see Ref. 8 for examples accumulated over the years). Following this discussion, the students participate in the Reverse Internet Challenge, where they test their own abilities to find answers to questions that I pose each group so that I see how well they have learned their lessons.

If finding and evaluating resources is not a significant objective for a course, the instructor may instead post relevant URLs for problem assignments. This can be conveniently done via a web page associated with each problem; many versions of e-mail software now also support embedded URLs in e-mail messages that may simply be visited by clicking. Bear in mind that burrowing deep into websites to provide references for students may be counterproductive for their learning in the PBL setting. More general, high-level sites can serve as appropriate starting points for their investigations if there is a concern that students will waste time searching the Web futilely or finding inappropriate resources. Also, high-level URLs are less likely to change; listing numerous resources by web page deep inside a website begs for numerous broken links after a year or so.

Many libraries now provide a wealth of information through networked databases, rich repositories of data and information that students may access for their investigations. A sampling of the on-line databases at the University of Delaware include the following:

- *Lexis-Nexis Academic Universe:* Full-text information from newspapers, the legal literature, and other sources on a variety of topics

- *Web of Science:* Citations, abstracts, and cited references to material published in thousands of scholarly journals in all subject areas

- *Expanded Academic ASAP:* Citations, with abstracts, from scholarly and general interest periodicals; includes some articles in full text

- *Business and Company Resource Center:* company profiles, company brand information, rankings, investment reports, company histories, chronologies, and periodicals

- *CINAHL (Nursing and Allied Health Literature):* Citations, with abstracts, to articles in journals relating to nursing and allied health disciplines

- *MEDLINE (Cambridge Scientific Abstracts):* Citations and abstracts to journal articles relating to all aspects of medicine, nursing, dentistry, veterinary science, and the preclinical sciences

- *Britannica Online:* Electronic version of the Encyclopedia Britannica

More specific databases may be available for a discipline, and arrangements can be made with publishers to get copies of CD-ROMs for students' use. As an example, Prof. James Magee uses the MicroCase Analysis System with great success for student exploration of statistical correlations as part of his problems in the University of Delaware course on American government.

Setting a PBL problem in a current context is an excellent way to generate student interest in the problem. Newspaper articles that catch our attention often serve as the basis for new problems or for updates of existing problems. The on-line availability of major newspapers, as well as many regional papers, facilitates a wider variety of perspectives on current events. Problem writing may be improved by turning to regional papers for the extensive local coverage of an event that receives moderate attention in a national newspaper. Students may similarly be directed to on-line newspapers as resources for solving problems. In a University of Delaware course on African politics, Prof. Gretchen

Bauer has her students regularly read their choice of on-line African newspaper; the variety of newspapers that can be selected is clearly much greater than is typically available in a university library. Among many good directories of on-line newspapers, I often refer to Yahoo Newspaper by Region (Ref. 9) or E&P Media Links (Ref. 10).

PBL Clearinghouse

The Web is also an excellent venue for sharing problems designed for PBL courses. Sample problems and curricular materials are beginning to appear on a variety of websites. Searching online with

+"PBL" + problem + <name of your discipline>

may turn up suitable problems—or maybe not! At the University of Delaware, we have decided that the time is right for an electronic clearinghouse of PBL problems. At the time this chapter is being written, the production version is in final testing; by the time this book is being read, the clearinghouse should have been announced for general use to PBL educators.

One goal of the PBL clearinghouse is to make available field-tested problems in all disciplines. Problems are submitted online to an editorial panel for peer review. Supporting material, such as Format of Delivery, Student Learning Objective, Student and Instructor Resources, Author's Teaching Notes, Assessment Strategies, and Solution Notes, are associated with each problem. Problems published in the clearinghouse are electronically searchable by keyword, discipline, or author. Through the peer review process, the clearinghouse aims to elevate the creative and scholarly aspects of problem writing to a more readily recognizable and rewarding level. In addition, the clearinghouse will publish articles and tutorials to support its mission to demonstrate and disseminate PBL as a superior teaching methodology. In short, we hope that the PBL on-line clearinghouse will become a "one-stop shop" for educators looking for PBL materials and resources.

Summary

The use of technology in teaching does not guarantee successful outcomes any more than the application of any other tool at our disposal. In fact, indiscriminate use of technology for its own sake can often get in the way of meeting course objectives. However, technology marches onward, and new solutions to old problems continue to materialize. The impact of PBL on student learning and student attitudes can be enhanced through appropriate use of technology. Computation, communication, and collections are essential elements of the problem-solving process and are at the heart of successful implementation of problem-based learning.

Author Biography

George Watson is Professor in the Department of Physics and Astronomy at the University of Delaware.

Website References

1. http://www.physics.udel.edu/~watson/scen103/
2. http://www.physics.udel.edu/~watson/scen103/colloq2000/syllabus.html
3. http://www.udel.edu/pbl/
4. http://www.physics.udel.edu/~watson/scen103/colloq2000/groups/
5. http://www.physics.udel.edu/~watson/phys345/fall1998/rosterexample/
6. http://www.physics.udel.edu/~watson/scen103/projects/
7. http://www.udel.edu/itue/
8. http://www.udel.edu/inst/I-challenge/
9. http://dir.yahoo.com/News_and_Media/Newspapers/By_Region/
10. http://emedia1.mediainfo.com/emedia/

PART THREE

CASE STUDIES IN PBL FROM DIFFERENT DISCIPLINES

Part Three presents case studies from instructors in a number of disciplines who have incorporated problem-based learning into their courses. Featuring courses in areas ranging from agriculture to teacher education, these studies highlight specific contextual considerations and the instructional strategies developed to address those in transforming each of these courses into a PBL format.

11

THE EVOLUTION OF PROBLEM-BASED LEARNING IN A BIOTECHNOLOGY COURSE

Sherry L. Kitto and Lesa G. Griffiths

Chapter Summary

"Biotechnology: Science and Socioeconomic Issues," a sophomore-level course, has used problem-based learning (PBL) exercises in combination with traditional lectures since 1993. The PBL component of the course has evolved continually, including reducing the size of the groups of students, training and using honors students as group facilitators, reassessment of peer evaluation procedures, redistribution of the PBL exercises more evenly throughout the semester, use of an interactive course web page, and requiring the use of technology for group presentations.

Introduction

"Biotechnology: Science and Socioeconomic Issues" is a multidisciplinary course and, as such, is listed in three departments within the College of Agriculture and Natural Resources: Animal and Food Sciences, Food and Resource Economics, and Plant and Soil Sciences. PBL was introduced in 1993 to address growing concerns about how the agricultural sciences are taught. The objective of the course is to enhance the ability of both science and nonscience majors to make informed decisions on biotechnology related issues in agriculture. From its inception in 1989, abstract concepts and principles were presented, but real examples and applications in agriculture were not always offered. For many years, instructors could only speculate on potential applications of biotechnology in agriculture. As products began to make their way to the marketplace, the PBL exercises made it possible for us to introduce the students to real-world problems using topics associated with agricultural biotechnology. The PBL exercises allow the students to not only learn about what biotechnology is and the associated controversies, but to develop a sense of confidence in expressing their own personal opinions related to current events.

The course was divided into four quarters, with the last quarter being reserved for the PBL exercises. The first three quarters introduced the science, applications, and socioeconomic issues associated with agricultural biotechnology. When we first started using PBL, we felt that the students needed to have a knowledge base prior to working through the PBL exercises. Challenges associated with this paradigm included building group rapport and collegiality in a short time frame, the final four weeks of the semester. We also now know that a knowledge base is not necessary prior to working through a PBL exercise. Part of the purpose of the exercises is for students to gain knowledge. Currently, the course is divided into the same three content "parts"; however, the PBL exercises are distributed evenly throughout the semester. So, while the students still do three PBL exercises, they begin group work on day two of the course.

Model

In the beginning, we taught the course in a traditional classroom, and the chairs were moved each class period we did a group exercise. Students did not have assigned seats. The class was divided into three groups because we had three instructors in the class and each facilitated a group. Advantages to this design were the pacing of the exercises and ensuring that the expectations for the exercise (e.g., making sure the students understand a well-designed experiment) were consistent. The main drawback to this was the large size of the groups—up to 13 students; based on reports from fellow PBL-users, this group size was too big.

To circumvent this problem, we added an honors section to the course with the objective of teaching the honors students to be peer facilitators for the group work. Now the number of registered honor students determines the number of groups. Although we have had as many as nine groups, each is facilitated by an honors student and each group has only four to five members who sit together as a unit during all classes. The class is taught in a PBL classroom, in which seats are arranged at hexagon-shaped tables. In these small groups, each person has a role, making the work more equitably divided.

Initially, while students were assigned to sit as a group, they did not do group work for a number of weeks. Now, in an effort to build team spirit as soon as possible, we assign students to groups on day one and schedule a sharing exercise for the second day of class. We have found that the sooner the students start to work together as a group, the sooner they are willing to share, trust, and evolve into a confident, dynamic group. This is especially important for the more introverted students. A first-day homework assignment has the students complete the Kiersey Temperament Sorter via the Web. On the second day, students come prepared to share and discuss their temperament with their group. We also have them take home a Kolb Learning Style Inventory. The purpose of these two exercises is to get the group members talking about and appreciating the diversity within each group. We want the students to understand that people learn in different ways and that people have differing strengths. It is beneficial to the group as a whole if students can identify early on group members' strengths. One side benefit is the new knowledge that each student takes away concerning himself or herself.

As of 1999, each group has a notebook. The notebook contains information and ground rules for the group. Also, this was the first year groups were expected to complete a contract containing a brief outline of what group members should discuss in reference to the contract, such as what roles members may play in the group (discussion leader, recorder, reporter, materials provider, presenter, technology expert), and the consequences for being a nonparticipator. Each group wrote ground rules that included the consequences for not following those rules, and then each group member signed the sheet agreeing to what had been written. Other information in the notebook covers teams and leaders; problem solving; spotting and sorting through group problems; assessment; and directions for using the digital camera, PowerPoint, and Excel.

Use of Peer Facilitators

The course has two sections: a regular section and an honors section. The honors section meets an extra hour per week, during which time they are introduced to the concepts of group work and how to facilitate group work. We discuss their role in the group and how to be an effective tutor/facilitator. It is not uncommon, for example, for students to question the "power" of their peer facilitators or to expect their content-driven questions to be answered by the peer facilitators. We let the peer facilitators know that it is not their job to answer content/knowledge questions; rather, it is the group's responsibility to do library or Web searches for answers.

Honors students work closely with the instructors as they facilitate the PBL class sessions. Early on, we had the honors students read through a book that explained the concepts involved with active learning and the roles of peer facilitators. We have found that the honors students prefer to learn facilitation firsthand "by doing" rather than by reading how-to publications. While we still read and discuss the same basic information presented in the books, it is done in a more informal manner. Each student reads one chapter and presents an overview of the major concepts. The honors students also work through a classroom PBL exercise so they have a "real" PBL experience similar to what the in-class groups will experience.

Two instructors are present during each of the PBL exercise days. The instructors serve as technology troubleshooters and as resources for the peer facilitators. The instructors roam the room and keep an ear open with regard to whether groups are on track or not. The honors students meet weekly with instructors and honors peers to discuss their in-class group progress. We use these sessions to discuss conflict resolution and as group help/venting sessions. Brainstorming through problems or challenges helps to reduce anxiety about what is expected of them. We regularly update our course library on team building, teamwork, and tutors; how to facilitate coming to reasonable consensus; how to gather information; how to stimulate group functions; and how to stay on task. The instructors make sure that the honors students are guiding their groups toward an appropriate goal.

The PBL Exercises

The instructors developed the first PBL exercises used in the course based on what was being discussed in the popular press. As of 1996, the honors students develop the new PBL exercises. The honors students, with guidance from the instructors, choose new PBL-exercise ideas by reading through files put together expressly for this purpose. Honors students work in self-selected teams to choose an idea for the development of a PBL exercise. Once an idea is accepted, the honors students spend two weeks conceptualizing the exercise as a whole, collecting resources and information, and creating the PBL exercise. It is understood that development of a PBL exercise is a multiclass meeting project, requiring time outside of class. Ideas and concepts are shared and critiqued during class time by the other honors students and the instructors. In some ways, the honors students are more in tune with what their peers consider "good" exercise ideas. PBL exercises developed by the honors students are no less thought provoking or sophisticated than those developed by the instructors.

Exercise authorship stays with the students. The honors students have developed some excellent exercises. Once a class has used a PBL exercise, the exercise may be modified. We view the exercises as dynamic so they are constantly modified, updated, and improved based on student (regular and honors) use and experience. At midterm the students evaluate the class and suggest revisions to improve the class and PBL exercises. After each PBL exercise, the honors students are asked for ways to improve the exercise for future use.

Students can earn bonus points by handing in popular press articles, cartoons, or web addresses related to agricultural biotechnology. Appropriate websites are added to the class web page. Biotechnology related cartoons are worth a double bonus. These items (we have received as many as 247 in a semester) are kept in a master file and serve as a source both of ideas for future PBL exercises and as a miniresource library for exercises being used in class.

The PBL exercises vary in objective and length. Three class days are devoted to the first and the third PBL exercises. Initially, the exercises were broken up into four or five pieces that were handed out piecemeal as the groups progressed through the exercise. The students, especially the facilitators, did not like this format and requested that we combine all of the pieces into a single unit and label them as day one or day two. We have used this single-unit paradigm for the past two years and agree that it is a smoother process for us; we don't have to photocopy a bunch of pieces and pass them out piecemeal, and students have a clearer idea of what they are working toward. In this way, they better understand the objective of the case. Each exercise is handed out in a previous class period so that students have time to read and understand their assignment. This way they can spend time during the first PBL class meeting working on the questions and understanding what their objective is (e.g., write an ad jingle or design an experiment). The students have a lower frustration level when they know why they are answering a series of preliminary questions. Some groups work faster than others at different points in an exercise. On these two PBL exercises, two in-class days are spent learning and gathering material; the third day is reserved for group presentations. Ability to organize class time to access information in the provided files and via the Internet and library can reduce the out-of-class time meetings.

The second PBL exercise is really a series of three minicases that are completed during one class period. Minicases are one paragraph long. Students have five minutes to come to consensus on a controversial topic. Minicases often consist of more than one part, with subsequent parts introduced after consensus has been reached on earlier parts. Each successive part introduces a more controversial aspect to the minicase. The purpose of the minicases is for the students to understand the dynamics involved with reaching consensus and the importance of time limits.

There is definitely an improvement in how the groups work as units over the semester. Most of the students have not experienced PBL prior to our class, so the first exercise is a real learning experience. None of our PBL exercises has a "right" answer. Groups are expected to reach consensus and develop a reflective presentation. Presentations for the first and third exercises are followed by a brief question-and-answer period. Students who ask questions get bonus points. The ability of a group to respond to questions is considered during grading. The students' answers to questions are not always correct, and this is revealed at the end of the presentation. In the past, creative groups have placed "canned" questioners in the audience.

Using Technology

Presentation requirements have evolved with the rest of the course. Initially, students gave traditional presentations relying on costumed skits, the printed page, posters, and 3-D artwork. Now students are required to use a laptop computer and digital camera in their presentations. We have found that students need clear directions for use of technology, as well as time limits. It is difficult for them to summarize their work into a five-minute presentation. While the creativity exhibited in the presentations has always been superb, quality presentations have not been the norm, especially presentations for the first PBL exercise. The groups learn by watching their peer groups' presentations. While the first presentations are never really bad, the third presentations are always very good. The presentations create a competitive spirit, and the students prepare for them in a very professional manner. The instructors evaluate the presentations.

A USDA Challenge Grant allowed us to purchase three laptop computers that we bring to class during the PBL exercises. The computers were introduced to the class four years ago. Our course Web page has a number of information links that the students can access during class time. Student acceptance of the computers and willingness to use them during class time have improved over the years. Although many think that everyone has great technology knowledge, there are always a few students who are technophobes. The number of technophobes has become fewer each year. We spend part of one class period with the groups working on a nongraded, impromptu assignment using the offerings on our web page. This allows for a more nonthreatening learning environment. The downside of the computers is system crashes.

We have now made it mandatory for the groups to use computer technology (e.g., PowerPoint) for the first presentation and a digital camera for the third presentation. There are grumbles, but it is obvious that the techno-confidence of the group members has increased tremendously by the third presentation. Each group has at least one really technology-literate student who teaches the rest of the group.

A new challenge since the addition of the technology requirement for the presentations is time management. Early in the course history, each group just got up and gave their presentation, but now each presentation needs to be booted up, and this takes time. Therefore, we now have a much stricter time requirement for the presentations.

Outcomes

Assessment of the course includes traditional exams and the PBL exercises. Each successive PBL exercise is worth a greater percentage of the total grade, so that students have the opportunity to become familiar with the PBL process.

One of the most difficult aspects of PBL is assessment of the group exercises. Our assessment instruments have evolved from more complex to less complex. Prior to the use of student peer facilitators, each student was given the opportunity to provide a self-evaluation and an evaluation of the contribution of each member of their group. The third and last component of the assessment is the instructor's component. Students were provided with an assessment form (Allen & Duch, 1998) identifying eight different aspects of group work, such as, "comes prepared," "completes assignments," and "answers questions in a way that promotes group understanding." Students wrote their name and the names of each group member across the top of the form and scored each group member in each of the eight categories reflecting the contributions each student made. Each student also rated him or herself on the same scale. We found that students did not seriously consider the different roles a person might play in a group. Rather than scoring individuals higher for some tasks and lower on others, the students scored students somewhat uniformly and highly for *all* the categories.

As instructors, we found it difficult to keep track of the contributions of individuals in large groups, and when we added the honors section, we began to use peer tutors in smaller groups. The peer tutors became the fourth input for group assessment (peer, self, tutor, and instructor). We adapted a peer assessment form (Allen & Duch, 1998) that used a different ratings scale and listed other items such as "contributes relevant information," and "good listener, respects other's opinions." At the same time, we adapted a similar assessment form (with categories of possible group roles and contributions) for the peer tutors (Allen & White, 2000). The tutors were asked to evaluate each group member using the group form, and each group member was asked to evaluate the tutor using the tutor form. The peer tutors provided more meaningful assessment information, and although the grades were still high, there was a range.

In order to get students to provide a more meaningful assessment of group work, we added one line to the form, asking students to provide an overall numerical grade (based on 100%) for each member of their group. It was interesting that students did not seem to consider the total of the 10 categories as being indicative of the numerical grade they should assign each member. The numerical grades provided us with more range, but we were not sure how to handle differences between the two scores. We were left with hours of calculations and felt there was still significant grade inflation.

Because students seemed willing to provide a more realistic grade when asked to assign their peers a numerical score, we decided to experiment with a simplified assessment form that directed the students to consider the manner in which each group member participated and contributed, and then to simply provide an overall numerical score (Figure 11.1). The same form and format was used for assessment of each group's peer tutor. Students were also told that they must justify uniformly high scores. We have used the new assessment form for two years now. Although we still experience some grade inflation, students are providing us with a range of grades. It takes us considerably less time to summarize and calculate the grades than it did when we had 50 pieces of information (10 categories × 5 group members) for each student. Students are required to turn in a completed assessment form during the class period following completion of each PBL exercise.

ANSC PLSC FREC 270   GROUP_____
Biotechnology: Science   CASE STUDY_____
  and Socioeconomic Issues

Case Study Assessment of Individual Performance

Evaluation Scale. Use the following scale to numerically score each of your group
members: 77–79 (C+); 80–82 (B–); 83–86 (B); 90–93 (A–); 94–96 (A); 97–100 (A+).

Evaluation of Group Members. When evaluating the other members of your group,
consider the following: Did the person attend all class meetings, come prepared for the
discussion, and contribute to the group's discussion? Did the person ask relevant
questions and respond to the questions of others? Was the person willing to do any
work outside of class and bring relevant information back to the group for discussion?
Was the person a good listener who respected the opinions of others? Did the person
contribute to overall organization and group consensus?

Names of Group Members. Put your name on the first line   **Numerical Score**
for your self-evaluation.

1. My name is_____   _____
2. _____   _____
3. _____   _____
4. _____   _____
5. _____   _____
6. _____   _____
7. _____   _____

Comments:

Evaluation of Peer Tutor Group Member. When evaluating the peer tutor of your
group, consider the following: Did the person show active interest in all group members
by listening and responding to student concerns and/or problems? Did the person
facilitate use of the web page to interact with the distance members of the group? Did
the person help identify relevant issues, guide and intervene to keep the group on
track, and provide information when the group got bogged down? Did the person pose
questions back to the group rather than answer questions? Did the person help the
group refine their presentation? Did the person help the group come to consensus?

Name of Peer Tutor.   **Numerical Score**
1. _____   _____

Comments:

FIGURE 11.1.   Assessment instrument used from 1998 to 1999

Authors' Biography

Sherry L. Kitto is Professor in the Department of Plant and Soil Sciences.

Lesa G. Griffiths is Associate Professor in the Department of Animal and Food Science, and Associate Dean of the College of Agriculture and Natural Resources at the University of Delaware.

References

Allen, D. E., & Duch, B. J. (1998). *Thinking towards solutions: Problem-based learning activities for general biology.* New York: Harcourt Brace, 153–154.

Allen, D. E., & White, H. B., III (2000). Peer facilitators of in-class groups: Adapting problem-based learning to the undergraduate setting. In J. E. Miller, J. E. Groccia, & M. S. Miller (Eds.), *Student-assisted teaching: A guide to faculty-student teamwork.* Bolton, MA: Anker Publications.

12

A PBL COURSE THAT USES RESEARCH ARTICLES AS PROBLEMS

Harold B. White, III

Chapter Summary

Introduction to Biochemistry, a problem-based learning (PBL) course for sophomore majors, uses a series of connected research articles as problems and is a useful template for courses in other disciplines. In addition to providing students with a historical perspective on their discipline, the approach addresses many issues and skills relating to the conduct of research that normally are not treated in textbook-based survey courses.

Introduction

I am absolutely convinced that science is vastly more stimulating to the imagination than are the classics, but the products of this stimulus do not normally see the light of day because scientific men as a class are devoid of any perception of literary form.

—J. B. S. Haldane, 1968

While students in English classes read the works of renowned authors, playwrights, and poets, students in the sciences rarely read the classic articles of their discipline. Rather, they read textbooks that condense, conceptualize, and summarize major scientific discoveries. Much is gained by that approach, but much is also lost—the context, the controversy, the uncertainty, the mistakes, the excitement, the interpretation of results, the design of experiments, the personalities, the creativity, the motivation, and the history. So removed are some textbooks from the practice of science that they convey the impression that science is a collection of facts and concepts rather than a powerful way to cultivate curiosity and learn about the natural world. Courses based on the primary literature attempt to recapture that which is frequently lost in textbooks.

The campus atmosphere of the late 1960s tolerated bold departures from standard pedagogy. When faced with teaching a section of introductory biology for nonmajors, Herman T. Epstein (at Brandeis University) reasoned that these students would learn more and be better served if he abandoned the survey approach and changed the focus of the course to *what biologists do* (Epstein, 1970; 1972). His students devoted the whole semester to reading and understanding a series of about eight research articles, culminating with one he had authored. While Epstein made no attempt to cover biology, the conceptual breadth required to understand most research articles permitted his students to learn quite a lot of sophisticated biology within a context that sustained their interest. At the time, Epstein provided a model for research scientists at a number of universities to become involved in introductory science courses (Epstein, 1972). However, the approach waned along with the activism of the era, and few institutions, notably Hampshire College (Woodhull-McNeal, 1989; McNeal and Murrain, 1994), still structure introductory biology courses around research articles.

Ironically, Epstein's nonmajors probably acquired a better understanding of the nature of science than did their biology-major peers who had taken an intensive fact-filled survey course. Recognizing this deficiency in the formal education of majors, the University of Delaware included an introductory course (Introduction to Biochemistry) modeled on Epstein's as a requirement in their new biochemistry curriculum (White, 1992). First taught in 1989 with 10 students in an informal lecture-discussion format, the course focused on hemoglobin and sickle cell anemia using a series of 10 articles spanning nearly a century. By treating the articles as problems, the course shifted smoothly into a student-oriented problem-based learning (PBL) format in 1993 (White, 1996a, 2000a). Three years later, peer tutor-facilitators were added (Allen and White, 1999; 2000). While retaining Epstein's emphasis on research articles and the motivation and activities of scientists, this course has evolved into a distinctive and effective PBL course that serves 20 to 35 students.

Model

Much of our educational system seems designed to discourage any attempt at finding things out for oneself, but makes learning things others have found out, or think they have, the major goal.
—Anne Roe, 1953

Goals

Because Introduction to Biochemistry is not a survey course, its content goals depend significantly on the set of articles selected as problems (White, 1996a). Thus, the content goals can vary somewhat from year to year. The articles (problems) are vehicles for the more important process goals (Table 12.1) that do not vary and could be achieved with a completely different set of articles. Although stated in the context of the discipline, these process goals transcend the discipline and address the goals of general education (Boyer Commission, 1998).

It is indeed rare for a scientific paper to remain central to current concerns several decades after its publication; in general, papers decay like last winter's leaves or this summer's pop songs, and scientists instead cite the latest review paper.
—Edward Ahrens, 1992

Selecting Articles as Problems

While each year the periodical literature generates thousands of articles, of which many could serve as problems, classic articles provide the best scaffolding for a problem-based course based on the primary literature. Classic articles punctuate and shape the history of every discipline. They often represent conceptual advances or paradigm shifts that resolved long-standing controversies. Typically, the authors are revered in the field. Instructors often know this culturally important information but students rarely do. By using classic articles, students not only learn major disciplinary concepts, they get a perspective on history, and in a sense, meet the giants in the field. How many biology students (or faculty) have read Watson and Crick's short description of the DNA double helix?

Earlier versions of Introduction to Biochemistry explored different themes, such as "Vitamin C and the Common Cold" and "Insulin and Diabetes." While they each used entirely different sets of articles than the current theme of "Hemoglobin and Sickle Cell Anemia," they had essentially the same goals noted in Table 12.1. Regardless of the theme, students read at most

Table 12.1. Instructional Goals for Students in Introduction to Biochemistry

1. Become intellectually independent learners.
2. Cultivate curiosity in the molecular processes that underlie observable phenomena.
3. Recognize and confront areas of personal ignorance.
4. Review and apply principles from other disciplines in a biochemical context.
5. Stimulate interest in undergraduate research.
6. Improve problem-solving skills.
7. Create, understand, and value abstract biochemical models.
8. See biochemistry in relevant historical and societal contexts.
9. Discover and use the resources of the library and the Internet.
10. Gain confidence in the ability to read and understand scientific articles.
11. Experience the powers (and pitfalls) of collaborative work.
12. Appreciate the importance of clear oral and written communication.
13. Learn to organize logical arguments based on evidence.

10 articles in historical sequence so that the progression and timing of advances emerge. Nobel Prize winners and prominent scientists appear among the authors of almost every article.

Far more classic articles exist within each subdisciplinary area than can be read in a semester. Consequently, one must use the course goals to provide additional bases for selection. In the case of Introduction to Biochemistry, sophomores will have taken a variety of prerequisite courses that may seem irrelevant to them. One of the goals of the course (no. 4 in Table 12.1) addresses the relevance of biology, chemistry, physics, and mathematics to biochemistry. Thus, the articles in the course need to reveal how these disciplines relate to biochemistry. A *learning issue matrix* (White, 1996a) enables an instructor to see how well a set of articles meets a course's goals. The matrix lists important course goals as column headings and articles as row headings. The elements of the matrix display the contribution of each article toward course goals (e.g., concepts from prerequisite courses) and reveals where emphasis is weak or strong. Clearly, an instructor has great latitude and can tailor the content of a course with a judicious selection of articles.

There is no form of prose more difficult to understand and more tedious to read than the average scientific paper.
—*Francis Crick, 1995*

Managing Student Anxiety

Few students subscribe to or regularly read the primary literature in their discipline. Often their first encounter with a technical article is like reading a foreign language and generates similar anxiety. Many words and concepts appear without explanation. Initially, they do not understand and often lack the resource skills to make sense of an article (McNeal, 2000). The problem-based learning approach is ideal for this situation because it requires students to define what they do not understand or are unsure of so that they may seek the needed information elsewhere. While a dictionary may be sufficient to get started, textbooks, the Internet, library resources, and other people soon become valued resources. The fact that students work in groups and can pool their findings and share their frustrations, provides considerable support. Nevertheless, they need to be properly prepared for this new experience because at first many will have trouble accepting that the teacher, who understands the article, won't simply describe it to them (White, 1996b, 2000a).

To establish the necessary study habits and resource skills takes time. Thus, the first article/problem may take more time than subsequent articles. In Introduction to Biochemistry, students spend three weeks or almost a quarter of a semester on the first article (White, 2000b). Students also need this time to establish functioning groups (White, Chapter 7 of this book). They gain confidence and discover the strengths and weaknesses of their colleagues. By the end of the course, most students do not expect to understand an article on first reading, but they have the experience and confidence to know that with some effort they can understand it. That self-knowledge proves helpful to students in subsequent courses, where they may need to read the primary literature, but have to do it on their own.

Tutor-Facilitators

The experience and maturity of students significantly influences how an instructor manages a PBL course of this type. In introductory courses with students who are not familiar with the PBL process, there are considerable in-class demands on an instructor to address student questions and keep multiple groups on task. This requires more structure and frequent opportunities for the whole class to deal with issues. For experienced students in upper-level classes, such close supervision is less important. My experience suggests that 25 students and five groups in an introductory course are manageable. However, tutor-facilitators significantly accelerate the process and improve the experience for students and the instructor for introductory

PBL courses with larger enrollments (Allen & White, 2000). Typically, these facilitators are students who have taken the course before, done reasonably well (B or better), and have good social skills.

> *Only by understanding the difficulties encountered in trying to do what now seems simple can a student appreciate the hurdles which must be surmounted in modern experiments of which we, for the most part, hear only the conclusions.*
> —*James Bryant Conant, 1946*

Assignments

Assignments in a PBL class need to be challenging and reflect the goals of the course. In order to engage students collaboratively and induce more than superficial understanding, assignments must go beyond and be more complex than typical end-of-the-chapter problems. Using articles as problems provides the opportunity for some unique assignments that involve a mix of group involvement and individual accountability (White, 2001). For example, older articles often lack an abstract. Students as a group can read what an abstract should include (e.g., Day, 1983), discuss this in the context of a particular article, and then write abstracts individually.

In general, writing assignments do not work well as group assignments because it is difficult to involve several people simultaneously. Alternatively, assignments that involve visualization work well as group assessment strategies— for example, generating a group concept map or constructing a figure or model appropriate for an article. Another type of assignment asks students to play the role of an investigator who has read the article and must propose a line of investigation that elaborates or tests ideas in the article. Each group can present its ideas to the class.

Examinations

One overriding principle guides the construction of midterm and final examinations in Introduction to Biochemistry—namely, that examinations must reflect the course goals. Consequently, there are individual and group parts to each examination, with the individual part constituting 75% (White, 1997). Students may bring notes, their course reader, a textbook, and any course handouts. Because thinking takes time and the length of normal class periods often discourages challenging questions, the examinations are longer and scheduled in the evening. The individual part comes first and takes about two hours. Typically, the last and particularly difficult question on the individual part serves as the question for the group part of the examination.

Given that problem-solving and conceptual understanding pervade the course, these features figure prominently in the examinations. Sometimes 50% or more of an examination will ask students to relate what they know or have learned to new situations. For example, students may be asked to read and comment on abstracts from the recent literature or interpret data from a paper they have not read. Such examinations are rare in introductory courses, and they generate considerable anxiety. Students recognize that they cannot study in the usual way (e.g., cram facts) for such an examination and must concentrate on concepts in preparation for the unknown. To prepare students, the syllabus clearly lays out the nature of the examinations and students can obtain copies of old examinations on the course website (White, 2000b).

While questions involving facts and calculations appear occasionally, most questions require a narrative or a diagram. The headaches generated by assigning grades after evaluating well-written flawed responses along with poorly constructed valid ones and everything in between, tempts one to revert to multiple-choice examinations. However, such ordeals reveal the importance of subjective examinations in the sciences for conveying the value of good writing skills and logical thinking ability. Because the level of difficulty of these examinations varies from year to year, it is impossible to establish numerical cutoff values for different grades. The average grade is a B, and students rarely fail the course.

Outcomes

Assessment

On the first day of class, all students complete an initial anonymous questionnaire on which they report their experience and reaction to student groups in problem-based courses, their attitudes toward science, and their prior knowledge of the subject matter of the course. Among other things, they reveal whether they have sold their textbooks from prerequisite courses and what newspapers and magazines they subscribe to or read regularly. At the midterm, there are formative peer-self-group-course evaluations, evaluation of tutors by students, and evaluation of students by tutors. These three evaluations are repeated at the end of the course and contribute up to 5% of a student's grade. In addition, all students complete a summative anonymous course evaluation that includes questions on attitudes and course goals. These data, representing

95% of the students who have taken the course over the past six years, along with daily attendance data and the instructor's annual reflective evaluation, provide a multiyear record to assess changes in the course.

The introduction of upper-class tutor-facilitators in 1996 had a noticeable and persistent effect on the course (Allen & White, 2000). Attendance, which always was near or above 90%, improved even further to better than 94%. Coincident with the increase in attendance was a greater than 20% increase in the number of hours students reported they spent on the class. Almost every student disagrees with the statement, "My group would have done fine without a tutor."

A significant number of students have difficulty accepting the daily responsibilities imposed by problem-based learning. Often these are good students who are not accustomed to working in cooperative groups and feel the academic rules have been changed. They often suggest that the course have more lectures. Tutors-facilitators, who in many cases are converted skeptics, can use their experience to involve recalcitrant students and get groups to function where an instructor would lack credibility. On a scale of 1 (excellent) to 5 (poor), students' average rating of the course is 2.02 in the five years since first using tutor-facilitators.

Compared to their other science courses, students report that Introduction to Biochemistry requires more library research skill, more writing, a greater amount of collaboration with classmates, more use of oral communication skills, and more conceptualization. When asked to reflect on the course after a year or two, many students say that learning how to read a scientific article was the most important thing they learned.

Given that students entering Introduction to Biochemistry have little and often mistaken knowledge about hemoglobin and sickle cell anemia, there is no doubt that they learn a lot about these topics in the course. Nevertheless, if content knowledge were the major goal of the course, there would be more efficient ways for students to learn the material. The course uses content as a vehicle to sharpen various skills students will need eventually to learn on their own and that are not emphasized in most of the other courses they take.

Suggestions for Adoption

Introduction to Biochemistry has an extensive website that provides a template for adoption or adaptation (White, 2000b). While the course serves majors, its origin comes from a nonmajor's biology course (Epstein, 1970).

The PBL format works well with up to 35 students in facilitator-led groups of four or five. In principle, any discipline with an extensive primary literature could use the model. Because few curricula include such a course, enrollments may have to rely on satisfying certain general education requirements.

Author Biography

Harold B. White, III is Professor of Biochemistry in the Department of Chemistry and Biochemistry and Director of the Howard Hughes Medical Institute's Undergraduate Biological Sciences Education Program at the University of Delaware.

References

Allen, D. E., & White, H. B, III. (1999). A few steps ahead on the same path: Using peer tutors in the cooperative learning classroom—A multilayered approach to teaching. *J. College Science Teaching, 28,* 299–302.

Allen, D. E., & White, H. B., III. (2000). Peer facilitators of in-class groups: Adapting problem-based learning to the undergraduate setting. In J. E. Miller, J. E. Groccia, & M. S. Miller (Eds.), *Student-assisted teaching: A guide to faculty-student teamwork.* Bolton, MA: Anker Publications.

Boyer Commission. (1998). *Reinventing undergraduate education: A blueprint for America's research universities.* Washington, DC: Carnegie Foundation. Available online at http://notes.cc.sunysb.edu/Pres/boyer.nsf.

Day, R. (1983). *How to write and publish a scientific paper.* Philadelphia, PA: ISI Press.

Epstein, H. T. (1970). *A strategy for education.* New York, NY: Oxford University Press.

Epstein, H. T. (1972). An experiment in education. *Nature, 235,* 203–205.

McNeal, A. (2000). How to read a scientific research paper. http://helios.hampshire.edu/~apmNS/RESOURCES/HOW_READ.html (2000, June 20).

McNeal, A. P., & Murrain, M. (1994). Drugs in the nervous system—A course in learning to learn science. *College Teaching, 42* (2), 47–50.

White, H. B., III. (1992). Introduction to Biochemistry: A different approach. *Biochemical Education, 20* (1), 22–23.

White, H. B., III. (1996a). Addressing content in problem-based courses: The learning issue matrix. *Biochemical Education, 24* (1), 41–45.

White, H. B., III. (1996b). Dan tries problem-based learning: A case study. *To Improve the Academy, 15,* 75–91.

White, H. B., III. (1997). Untimed individual/group exams, problem-based learning, In S. Tobias and J. Raphael (Eds.), *The hidden curriculum: Faculty-made tests in science. Part 2. Upper-division courses*, pp. 102–103. New York, NY: Plenum Press.

White, H. B., III. (2000a). Confronting undergraduate dualism with problem-based learning. In P. C Taylor, P. J. Gilmer, & K. G. Tobin (Eds.), *Transforming undergraduate science teaching: Social constructivist perspectives*. Philadelphia, PA: Lang Publishers, University of Pennsylvania.

White, H. B., III. (2000b). Homepage for CHEM-342, Introduction to Biochemistry, Spring 2000. http://www.udel.edu/chem/white/teaching/CHEM342.htm (2000, June 20).

White, H. B., III. (2001). Research articles as problems for problem-based learning: Stokes' 1864 spectroscopic study of the "redox" behavior of hemoglobin. *Journal of College Science Teaching*, accepted for publication.

Woodhull-McNeal, A. (1989). Teaching science as inquiry: A course example. *College Teaching, 37* (1), 3–7.

13

INTEGRATING ACTIVE LEARNING AND THE USE OF TECHNOLOGY IN LEGAL STUDIES COURSES

Valerie P. Hans

Chapter Summary

This chapter describes the integration of active learning principles and the use of technology in an undergraduate course on the criminal courts. The project requires students to participate in teams in a plea bargaining exercise, in which they research relevant law on the Web and negotiate with others to resolve a hypothetical case.

Introduction

Snapping after years of abuse, a battered child kills his sleeping father. As his defense attorney, should you employ the hotly debated "battered child defense" to reduce or excuse the child's criminal culpability? As a prosecutor, you handle the case of a college student who drove while drunk and caused a serious automobile accident, killing a passenger in the other car. Is it more appropriate to charge the student with vehicular homicide, manslaughter, or even murder?

These are some of the questions my students are confronting firsthand in problem-based learning (PBL) exercises I have created for my legal studies courses. Courses in legal studies, criminology, and criminal justice, which examine the operation of law and legal systems, are a superb arena for the use of PBL. Employing actual and hypothetical court cases presents an opportunity to convey the ethical and empirical issues inherent in many court cases in a way that is very engaging to students. Active participation is also a superb way to teach students how to use technology and on-line resources to obtain information about law. There has been an explosion of law-related material on the Internet, providing a rich resource for faculty and students interested in learning about law and legal institutions (Greek & Henry, 1997). Students must learn to navigate these resources to resolve PBL problems. The use of law-related PBL problems, then, can be a highly motivating way to integrate active learning and the use of technology in college teaching.

Background: Getting Started with PBL and Technology in Teaching

In teaching courses on the courts and legal studies for two decades, I periodically used exercises and activities that called for students to take the role of legal system actors, such as judges or jurors, or to conduct their own surveys and experiments on course topics. I used these activities more frequently in my smaller seminar classes. The large class that I teach regularly, a course about the purposes and functioning of the criminal courts, consisted almost exclusively of "stand and deliver" lectures. This was very consistent with the lecture-based emphasis of the other introductory courses in my department.

I had become increasingly concerned about the large lecture class. The course is required for Criminal Justice majors and fulfills a college social science requirement, so the students in the class vary dramatically in their preexisting knowledge about the courts. Nevertheless, from my perspective, much of the course material can be intrinsically interesting no matter what a student's background. The ethical and moral dilemmas of defense attorneys and prosecutors, the challenges facing judges and jurors who try to do justice, and the empirical realities of how the courts operate have succeeded in attracting many viewers to legal news stories and CourtTV, as well as fictionalized legal dramas on television and the movies (Hans & Dee, 1991). Despite the potentially interesting subject matter, attendance in my lecture class on the courts was low, and student performance on exams was mediocre.

Participation as a Fellow in the University of Delaware's Institute for Transforming Undergraduate Education (ITUE) in 1998 offered me the opportunity to refashion the course. The ITUE workshop demonstrated how active learning approaches could be used to improve student understanding in a range of courses, including large lecture classes. The workshop organizers structured the Institute so that all of the Fellows had time set aside to identify a topic for a problem, sketch out the problem, work on staging, present a draft of the problem to other Fellows and organizers, and receive feedback. I chose to develop a plea bargaining exercise to use in my lecture class on the courts (Hans, 1999b).

The Plea Bargaining Exercise: Combining Active Learning and Technology

ITUE organizer Barbara Duch gives a valuable piece of advice to novices developing their first PBL problem: select a central topic that is always covered in the course (Duch, Chapter 5 of this book). The issue of plea bargaining easily meets that qualification for a courts class. It is arguably the most important phenomenon in criminal case processing. Plea bargaining, which refers to the negotiation procedure whereby the defense attorney and the prosecutor agree to resolve the case with a guilty plea rather than a trial, is the method by which the majority of criminal cases are concluded (Neubauer, 1999). Many legal actors, including judges, prosecutors, and defense attorneys, claim that the system would be overwhelmed if most cases were tried rather than resolved through plea bargaining, yet the practice is controversial. The very term *bargain* suggests to some critics that criminal defendants benefit from the practice and that the outcomes are more lenient than they deserve (McCoy, 1993). In some jurisdictions, it has been outlawed (Rubinstein & White, 1979). In recent years, legislatures have affected plea bargaining by passing minimum mandatory sentences for crimes. Nevertheless, resolving a case through plea bargaining reduces uncertainty and holds other incentives for both the prosecution and the defense.

In prior years, I conveyed the complexities of the plea bargaining process through lecturing about the phenomenon and presenting the findings of empirical research. In contrast, the PBL problem takes an active approach, presenting a hypothetical case to students, allowing them to select roles, and having them negotiate with one another in small groups to arrive at a resolution in a specific case. The plea bargaining exercise gives my students a firsthand look at the attractions and challenges of negotiating a guilty plea, covering some of the same material as the lecture approach but in a more dynamic way.

Two weeks during the semester are set aside for the problem. Students are assigned to four-person groups in advance and meet in their groups during class time over the two-week period. After initial group-building activities, such as identifying the pleasures and pitfalls of group work and setting up group rules (Allen & Duch, 1998; Michaelsen, 1997–1998), students read the description of a fatal accident:

> [After drinking at a local watering hole], Sam Sad . . . began to drive to his Newark home. However, according to several witnesses, at the intersection of Routes 896 and 4, he ran a red left turn light and hit head-on a car coming the other direction. Madeleine Mad was driving the car, with her husband Mark in the passenger seat. Mark, who was not wearing his seat belt, was thrown through the front window and was killed by the head-on collision. Madeleine, who was three months pregnant at the time of the accident, was injured despite the fact that she was wearing a seat belt. She suffered a concussion and broken arm; furthermore, the day following the accident she began bleeding and had a miscarriage. (Hans, 1999a)

Students learn that Sam Sad's blood alcohol level was .23, exceeding the legal limit, and that he was arrested by the police. They have an initial group discussion, identifying some of the legal and evidentiary issues in the case and assessing what they will need to learn to negotiate a resolution to the case. These small-group discussions are followed by a whole-class report, to ensure that all students are aware of the full range of issues implicated in the case.

In the second stage of the problem, students select roles and engage in the essential background research necessary to resolve the case. Students choose their own roles in the negotiation. Each group must include a student representing the victim, the prosecutor, the defendant, and the defense attorney. The roles are described in such a way as to highlight typical problems and issues in criminal case resolution. For example, to emphasize the cost borne by families of the incarcerated, the defendant is a young man who is the sole support of his wife and two small children so that imprisonment will dramatically affect his family. The surviving victim joins Mothers Against Drunk Driving (MADD), to illustrate the role of interest groups in litigation.

The four-person groups divide into two teams for the background research and negotiation stages. The prosecutor and victim comprise the prosecution team, while the defense lawyer and defendant collaborate to research and present the defense perspective. They first discuss their interests and priorities in the negotiation and determine what they will need to know to negotiate effectively. The prosecution teams then research Delaware state law and sentencing guidelines, which are available online, and propose an initial set of charges to the defense team. The charging process is complex, since the accident and its consequences could well be charged in several different ways. In addition to selecting an appropriate initial charge for the passenger's death, the prosecution team has to undertake legal research about whether or not the death of a fetus can be charged against the defendant. During this time, the defense team is examining case law, information on rehabilitation, and treatment programs for drunk driving, to use as counteroffers and bargaining points in the negotiation. Students use law-related websites and library resources to put together charges, counteroffers, and arguments.

During several class periods, the group members negotiate together until they come up with a resolution of the case that is acceptable to all of them. To assist them in negotiation, I assign *Getting to Yes* (Fisher & Ury, 1991), the well-known negotiation text. I also set aside class time for group members to outline and write a group paper that summarizes their negotiation. The paper includes a discussion of the priorities of each group member, the initial charge, the progress of the negotiation, and the outcome agreed upon by the group. There is also an evaluative component. In line with the approach of *Getting to Yes* to attempt solutions that best meet the participants' goals, students analyze the degree to which their group outcome maximizes (or detracts from) each party's interests.

Outcomes

Over the two years I have employed the plea bargaining negotiation, student reactions have been generally favorable. Feedback from students is obtained through anonymous evaluations of the pros and cons of the plea bargaining exercise shortly after it is concluded, as well as in final course evaluations. The majority of students (ranging from 60 to 70%, depending on the class) agree that the plea negotiation is a valuable learning experience. Students report that the negotiation problem improves their ability to use the Web and other resources to find information about criminal law, expands their substantive knowledge of criminal law and plea bargaining, and gives them good experience in cooperative teamwork. In the most recent evaluation, for example, 71% of the students said that their ability to use the Web to locate criminal law information had improved; 79% agreed that their knowledge of criminal law had expanded; 75% said that their knowledge of the plea negotiation process had increased; and 65% stated that the exercise had provided them with a good experience in cooperative teamwork. Student comments about the positive aspects of the negotiation include: "I liked applying the negotiation process to a real problem. It made me better understand the process and the law, while making it fun"; the "in-depth group collaboration," "the actual negotiation between the prosecution team and defense team because research is just gaining knowledge but negotiating is gaining experience." Thus, opportunities to cooperate and participate actively with others are cited as aspects of the negotiation that are most helpful in learning.

Students also identify aspects of the negotiation exercise that interfere with learning. The chief culprits appear to be other students who don't contribute their fair share, are absent, and whose schedules don't allow out-of-class meetings. For example, "group members not showing up or doing their work, " and the fact that is it "too hard to get the whole group together," are listed as serious problems by some group members. Some students note the potential unfairness that "someone's grade can be greatly affected by a group member not doing their part." Consistent with the students' comments, my teaching assistants and I did observe that in some groups, certain participants did not contribute their fair share. A peer evaluation form distributed at the end of the assignment allowed students to provide input on the contributions of group members, which were taken into account in assigning credit. However, students were perhaps overly generous to one another in their ratings, and only the most extreme failures to participate were penalized by group members.

The book *Getting to Yes* has both fans and critics among my students; for some it "helps to know the negotiation process and make it more organized" and "helps me learn how to use common sense in negotiating," while others recommend dropping the book requirement, seeing it as a waste of time.

From my vantage point, the plea negotiation produces greater involvement and more and better work from the majority of my students. Class attendance improves, although one can count on the fact that there will always be some students who miss the in-class group activities and interfere with their group's progress. In my course, two weeks of class time is set aside for the assignment (in the evaluations, some students requested more time). Even so, students spend very significant amounts of time outside of class doing library and web research and writing the final group paper. The vast majority of the negotiating groups are able to arrive at a legally justifiable outcome. Indeed, the most common plea recommended by groups is the outcome that Delaware legal experts say would be the most likely outcome if the case were to occur in the real world.

The quality of the group papers has been exceptionally high. For example, the most recent time I used the plea negotiation, the paper grades were 16 As, 9 Bs, and 2 Cs. Many papers reflect a sophisticated understanding of the links between law on the books and law as applied to individual cases, and an appreciation of the different perspectives of the prosecutor, defense attorney, defendant, and victim in negotiating a case outcome. The power differential between prosecution and defense hits home, as does the impact of minimum mandatory sentences on case negotiation. Judging by the papers, the exercise successfully moves students beyond Bloom's cognitive levels of knowledge and comprehension of plea bargaining (what my students would probably have gained through the lecturing approach) to application, analysis, and evaluation levels (Bloom et al., 1956).

Adoption

There are some good reasons, then, to employ law-related PBL exercises in classes in criminal justice and legal studies. Giving students a chance to resolve a case themselves can be an engaging way to communicate the factors that influence plea bargaining.

All the same, the difficulties of employing an intensive problem-based learning experience like this one in a large class should not be underestimated. Even with the help of a PBL-savvy teaching assistant and undergraduate teaching assistants who have done the problem themselves in a prior class, I find it difficult to monitor the progress of 25 to 30 groups and to be able to intervene in problem groups in a timely fashion. Using law-related PBL exercises in smaller (25–40 person) classes, I have discovered that it is more feasible to speak to every group in each session to observe their development of the problems and to provide guidance. Absenteeism is lower and is also easier to spot! One alternative is the use of undergraduate peer tutors (Allen & White, 1999), who receive training in PBL and are assigned to one group or a small number of groups during a semester. The peer tutor approach allows an instructor in a large class using PBL to keep apprised of each group's progress and to intervene when necessary.

Another factor that should be considered is the instructor's time. The planning and supervising of the student plea negotiation groups takes much more time than giving a set of lectures on the topic. The assignment asks for student input about the progress of the negotiation, which needs prompt response, and there are the papers to mark! An instructor could adjust the assignment to conform to the amount of time available. For example, the instructor could prepare a response sheet with specific questions for groups to answer when they completed the negotiation, rather than requiring each group to write a paper. Depending on class size, class presentations might be another alternative to the group paper for reporting the results of the negotiation. Whatever method is employed, my experience indicates that getting students actively involved in negotiating a court case outcome increases their motivation and the intellectual quality of their work.

Author Biography

Valerie P. Hans is Professor of Sociology and Criminal Justice at the University of Delaware.

References

Allen, D., & Duch, B. (1998). *Thinking toward solutions: Problem-based learning activities for general biology.* Philadelphia, PA: Saunders College Publishing.

Allen, D. E., & White, H. B, III. (1999). A few steps ahead on the same path: Using peer tutors in the cooperative learning classroom—A multilayered approach to teaching. *J. College Science Teaching, 28,* 299–302.

Bloom, B. et. al. (Eds.). (1956). *Taxonomy of educational objectives.* New York, NY: Longmans, Green.

Fisher, R., & Ury, W., with Patton, B. (1991). *Getting to yes: Negotiating agreement without giving in.* New York, NY: Penguin Books.

Greek, C., & Henry, D. B. (1997). Criminal justice resources on the Internet. *Journal of Criminal Justice Education, 8,* 91–99.

Hans, V. P. (1999a). Crime and punishment: Case negotiation in the criminal justice system. PBL Problem for CRJU202: Problems of the Criminal Judiciary, Fall 1999. http://www.udel.edu/soc/vhans/negotiation.html (2000, September 15).

Hans, V. P. (1999b). Plea bargaining: Active learning in a course on the courts. *About Teaching,* Fall. Newark, DE: Distributed by the Center for Teaching Effectiveness, University of Delaware. (Also available online at http://www.udel.edu/cte/aboutteach/fall99/hans.html.)

Hans, V. P., & Dee, J. L. (1991). Media coverage of law: Its impact on juries and the public. *American Behavioral Scientist, 35,* 136–149.

McCoy, C. (1993). *Politics and plea bargaining: Victims' rights in California.* Philadelphia, PA: University of Pennsylvania Press.

Michaelsen, L. K. (1997–1998). Three keys to using learning groups effectively. *Essays on Teaching Excellence, 9* (5). Valdosta, GA: POD Network.

Neubauer, D. W. (1999). *America's courts and the criminal justice system.* Belmont, CA: Wadsworth.

Rubenstein, M. L., & White, T. J. (1979). Alaska's ban on plea bargaining. *Law & Society Review, 13,* 367–383.

14

PROBLEM-BASED LEARNING IN LARGE AND VERY LARGE CLASSES

Harry L. Shipman and Barbara J. Duch

Chapter Summary

When an instructor uses problem-based learning (PBL) in a large class, some changes need to be made in the method to accommodate the changed teaching situation. The first part of this paper will describe some ways we have used PBL in large and very large classes. In general, the class and course require more structure than smaller classes. The second part of this paper is a preliminary report on a study of the implementation of PBL in two identical classes, a large class of 120 students and a very large class of 240 students. We found that the method did succeed in both classes. However, the experiences of both students and instructors were better in the smaller class.

Introduction

Many students in colleges and universities in the United States find themselves in very large classrooms, attempting to learn whatever it is that they are supposed to learn. Class size is really not considered to be a teaching issue. Classes of 4 coexist with classes of 400 and sometimes, depending on the institution, even larger. These courses are taught in the same departments, in the same major fields of study, and sometimes by the same professors. For many administrative purposes, one course is the same as another, no matter what the enrollment. In some large universities, the largest lecture halls are only slightly smaller than Rome's Colosseum, with the professor a tiny figure who is barely visible, and sometimes not even audible, from the back row.

In precollege education, the issue of class size takes center stage in some rather noisy debates among parents, teachers, administrators, and politicians about teaching practice. Parents complain bitterly when their children are placed in classes which are "too large," meaning more than 25 students in many cases. The State of California is spending $1.5 billion every year in an effort to reduce class sizes in some of its primary schools to fewer than 20 students (Bracey, 1999). In college, however, there is no such public debate. Our educational system functions as if human beings can suddenly become adapted to large lecture rooms at the age of 18.

Existing research on class size does show a larger effect of class size on teaching effectiveness for younger students than for older students. A number of studies (e.g., Finn & Achilles, 1999; Zahorik, 1999; and a nice review by Grissmer, 1999) have shown that in elementary school, students in smaller classes do learn better. At the college level, a large number of studies of teaching effectiveness have shown mixed results. The results of a very early study by Edmondson and Mulder (1924) showed that student performance on simple cognitive tasks was not significantly different when the class size was changed from 43 to 109. However, when more complex cognitive tasks, such as critical thinking and real-world problem solving, are studied, research favors smaller classes, but the effects are relatively small (Kulik & Kulik, 1989). Research on samples of college students in a large university has shown that some college students report a high comfort level with the anonymity of larger classes (Wulff, Nyquist, & Abbott 1989). A brief but excellent review of the research is provided in McKeachie's classic work (McKeachie 1994, pp. 198–202).

The research on the effectiveness of teaching in large classes has practical consequences. Many enlightened and informed administrators are aware that research in college classes shows small or no benefits from small classes. So faculty who advocate for smaller classes are challenged to make a case for them. One reasoned response is that much of the research is based on the lecture paradigm. We are not aware of any studies of the effects of class size on teaching effectiveness where an inquiry-based mode of instruction such as PBL is used as the basic teaching method. Consequently, we conducted the study reported in the second part of this chapter.

This paper will not venture into the causes of the traditions that make large lectures such a significant presence on college and university campuses. Rather, we accept these conditions as reality for much of higher education in many parts of the world. A reform like problem-based learning must work in large classes if it is to have a significant impact on American higher education. If it can only work in medical schools and in small, liberal arts colleges, such as Swarthmore (where the largest classroom on campus seats 40 students), its impact is limited. The primary focus of this chapter is "What happens when an instructor implements PBL in progressively larger classes?"

Barriers to the Implementation of PBL in a Large Classroom

Both authors have experienced PBL, in some form, in large and small classes. One of us (HS) probably has had the most extreme conditions in either direction, with using PBL in classes as small as 4 and as large as 340. We have team-taught classes ranging in size from 8 to 240.

In a small class, we can give groups a problem to work on and let the individual groups essentially take their own directions toward a solution. As long as the class size is less than about 25, it is possible for one instructor to keep in touch with what each group is doing and take appropriate action if the group ends up going in a direction that the instructor knows is unproductive. When the authors of this paper team-taught a physical science course to eight students, most of whom were in-service teachers, we observed two different groups of four students go off in completely different directions in solving a problem relating to the science of color. We provided each group with appropriate guidance, and both groups developed an appropriate understanding of the topic. In fact, the members of the two groups appreciated the different paths that each had taken.

The principal change that takes place as the class gets larger is that an instructor is not able to keep in touch with what is going on in all of the groups. For example, in an interdisciplinary, team-taught class on Science and Religion, a class of 50 students was divided into permanent groups, and both instructors (HS and Jeff Jordan, a philosophy professor) roved around the room, facilitating discussions within the groups. The first year this course was taught, one group at the front of the room always seemed seriously engaged in quite animated discussion. One student observed on a midsemester evaluation that what was going on in the group was that an atheist and a theist were vigorously arguing and that the other group members were not participating in the discussion. Actual classroom observation showed that the student was correct. While the instructor could, and did, intervene in order to try to include all members in group discussions, the pattern had been set. Unless one of the two instructors devoted his class time exclusively to that one group, it would be slightly dysfunctional. Final student evaluations of group performance confirmed that the functioning of this group was less than optimal.

Several strategies can be employed to adapt a small-class PBL technique to a large-class situation and are discussed in more detail in Chapters 4 and 8 of this text. Instructors can do the following:

- Find help, bringing peer tutors, graduate TAs, or other individuals into the classroom so that more individuals can monitor groups.

- Add more structure to the PBL teaching style, so groups are less likely to get off track.

- Use more minilectures to minimize the instructors' need to know what is going on in each group.

Find Help

Many Delaware instructors using large-class PBL have a number of additional individuals in the classroom, either undergraduate peer tutors or graduate teaching assistants. These additional individuals can circulate around the room, monitoring many more groups than is possible for a single instructor. Undergraduate peer tutors are described elsewhere in this volume by Allen and White. The authors' experience so far has primarily been with graduate teaching assistants (TAs), who may or may not be able to be helpful depending on the specifics of the teaching situation.

Graduate TAs can be helpful if they have had some experience with inquiry learning techniques, have an opportunity to get to know individual students in the class, and clearly understand that group facilitation in the large class is part of their job. One of us (BD) taught a physical science class in the spring of 2000 where the majority of laboratory and discussion section teaching was done by two graduate TAs. Each of these individuals taught lab and discussion sections to the same set of 48 students and so was able to get to know them. Both of these individuals had better than average communications skills. The course was set up in such a way that the TAs were able to anticipate what was going on in the larger class. However, when TAs simply come into the large class to deal with students and learning situations they don't know so well, their help has been less useful.

Add Structure

Flexibility in a PBL setting diminishes as the size of the class grows. When dealing with 250 students, or even 120, our experience based on classroom observation shows that the group discussion time needs to be limited to no more than 15 minutes at a time. Students should also be made accountable for the results of their discussions by knowing that they will be reporting them verbally or in writing. Giving groups overhead transparencies and pens at the beginning of discussion is a good method for having many groups share their ideas with the whole class. More detail on adding structure to large PBL classes can be found in Chapter 4.

Use More Minilectures

We have found that one way of adding structure is to intersperse group discussion time with minilectures based on the results of issues that arise during group discussion time. After students identify their learning issues and have done some research on them, the instructor can base a minilecture on some central ideas that are critical to understanding those concepts. In a sense, the instructor can use minilectures to do the same guidance and probing that a tutor or facilitator would do in a small group.

Facilitating the Transition to PBL

As was the case nationally, much of the PBL innovation at Delaware and in the authors' own careers started with smaller classes. One of the chief barriers to introducing PBL in large classes is that instructors are concerned with what will happen if things go wrong in a major way. This concern is repeatedly raised by participants in the PBL workshops that we have offered, both on campus and elsewhere in the country. It was crucially important for one of us (HS) to create an opportunity where he could teach a small class to try out PBL before it was tried in a large class.

Another way for faculty who habitually teach large classes to become adapted to PBL is to have them begin with some easier techniques that permit students to work in small groups, even in a class where the dominant pedagogical mode is still the lecture. Angelo and Cross (1993) describe a number of such techniques. We have found that think-pair-share and the minute paper are the easiest to adapt to larger class settings.

The presence, at the University of Delaware, of a substantial group of faculty who have adopted and adapted PBL in their own large classes has provided some consistent mutual support and encouragement to many of us. Simply knowing that someone who teaches more than a hundred students has been able to get out of lecture mode can help faculty members surmount some of the barriers. Someone else's success can encourage faculty to try inquiry-learning techniques like PBL. In the early days (the early 1990s), there were only a few Delaware faculty who had used PBL in large classes. Now, in 2000, there are at least a dozen. It is often not even necessary to visit someone else's classes to benefit from their experience (though classroom visits can help). A few encouraging words in a short conversation can make a big difference.

PBL in a Large and a Very Large Class

In the spring semester of 1999, the two authors of this chapter studied the implementation of PBL in two identical sections of the same course. The course was a physical science course, offered to general audiences, including a significant component of elementary teacher education majors, who were using the course as one of their three required science courses. Discipline areas covered included physics, chemistry, and astronomy. One class section, which we refer to as the "large class," enrolled 120 students. The other class section, the "very large class," enrolled 240 students. The two classes were taught on the same day, with a 15-minute break in between the two, making it easier to offer the same instructional experience in both classes. Both sessions of the class were taught in the same room, an auditorium-style classroom originally built in 1962 with fixed, forward-facing seats, raked upward toward the back with only two aisles running toward the front of the room to provide student (and teacher) access to the seats. This is not the kind of room that is usually thought of as being conducive to group work.

The classes were taught with the PBL paradigm, based on the philosophy of constructivism (Posner, Strike, Hewson, & Gerzog, 1982; Strike & Posner, 1992; Duit & Treagust, 1998). The teaching practices are generally congruent with recommendations of national bodies (National Academy of Sciences, 1997). A webpage describing the way this course was offered can be found at http://www/udel.edu/physics/scen102/. The 1999 offering of the course was the one we studied.

In classes of this size, it is possible to gather an extremely large amount of data. The authors both kept journals and were in class almost every day, even when the other instructor was leading the class. We preserved all student artifacts, including the written reports of student groups. Occasionally, the class was monitored by independent observers, and we used data that they gathered. The data that played the greatest role in the present paper were journals of students and professors, a midsemester course evaluation (which was independently analyzed by Gabriele Bauer of the University's Center for Teaching Effectiveness), interviews with focus groups conducted by Bauer and Beth Jones of West Virginia University, and an end-of-semester evaluation conducted on the IDEA system, a nationally validated and normed course evaluation instrument.

The Success of PBL in Both Large and Very Large Classes

Does PBL work in large classes? In summary, the answer is yes. A variety of ways of ascertaining students' ability to learn in groups shows that for the majority of students, their experience in solving problems in small groups significantly helped their learning and also prepared them for their working lives. Only a small minority of students in both classes did not find that their group worked for them. Student performance on examinations and in the class as a whole was good.

According to students' self-assessments, as validated by other measures, most students could learn successfully in groups. In an evaluation at the midpoint of the semester, students were asked in an open-ended question, "what aspects of this course contribute most to your learning?" In both the large and very large classes, group work was the second most often cited aspect of the course, with only classroom demonstrations mentioned more often. Data from the focus group interviews indicate that "a majority of students feel very strongly that they can learn actively" (Bauer & Jones, 2000).

Independent assessments of group performance validate the students' self-reports. In a classroom observation conducted early in the semester, where groups were monitored for 3 minutes and the observer recorded student behavior, 43 of a sample of 55 randomly selected students (78%) spoke to others in the group, 8 students (15%) did not speak but were attentive to group discussion, and only 4 students (7%) were inattentive to the group work.

At the end of the semester, students were asked to send the instructor a "reflective journal" in which they summarized their experiences in this course, highlighting the significant ones (whether they were positive or negative). A few extracts from these student journals capture the flavor of student reactions:

> The item that I found the most helping and therapeutic was the fact that we had groups. It was great to be able to have help on hand at all times, not only from the professors but also from my peers. I don't know if my group was an exception or not, but we have all become extremely close. Not only do we spend time together in class, but we spend time together outside of class now as friends too. (Female elementary teacher education major, large class)

> I found it very interesting to work with the other students in my group, in order to figure out a common problem. By combining all of our thoughts, we were able to figure out what was on the bottom of

the cube, without looking at it. Some of the reasons proposed by my group members fascinated me. (Female business major, large class)

Being in groups helped me to understand what problems and strengths groups can have. I can use what I learned by trying to get along in groups and tell my students difficulties and strategies that worked for our group work. (Female elementary teacher education major, very large class)

A minority of students did not respond positively to group work. In midsemester and final course evaluations, their comments called for "more lectures," "more explanations," and "less group work." Some of these students went so far as to completely tune out of group discussions during the large class. In some cases, with some encouragement from professors and TAs, students eventually would blend into the group. One of the four students who conspicuously ignored his group during the observation made early in the semester was credited by his group as being a full participant at the semester's end. A journal comment from one of these students captures the concerns that several expressed in different ways:

My group did hardly anything for me. There was a lack of interest in the group and hardly any participation except for when we needed participation points. I tried to spur conversation and get people thinking, but I got hardly any response. There was only one girl in my group who actually tried. The other two just sat there and stared out into nothing. (Male English secondary education major, very large class)

How many students did not buy in to the concept of group work? Depending on the way we answer this question and the intensity of student disengagement, the percentage ranges from 5% to just under 25%. A small minority of students—by any measures, less than 10%—had serious problems with group work. We asked students to assess the extent to which their peers contributed to group work. Only 20 students in both sections (5.5%) were credited by their fellow students with less than full participation. The students' reports are consistent with two classroom observations which showed 7% of students not interacting with their groups.

A larger percentage of students reported on evaluations that group work was not their preferred learning style. On the midsemester evaluation, 21.4% of 219 respondents explicitly asked for less group work in response to an open-ended question. Of 283 respondents on the final evaluation, 24.3% answered that the statement "I can learn the important concepts in class with group learning" was either "definitely false" or "more false than true." Fragmentary data on long-term trends at the University of Delaware indicate that the percentage who do not prefer group work has significantly decreased in the past five years. We do not have the data to determine how many of the students who self-report an inclination against groups really have troubles learning in groups. We can both think of examples of students who contributed reasonably well to their groups yet told us that they really would prefer it if we lectured more, or exclusively.

We regret that our use of group work and our explicit efforts to persuade students that they will need group skills in their later careers only succeeded with 75–95% of our students rather than 100%. However, we are still convinced that PBL and its use of collaborative groups are good ideas. Even students who have difficulty with groups can learn from the experience. HS had one experience with a student, "Brett" (a pseudonym), who had tremendous difficulties with his group in the physical science course. His groupmates were extremely upset when he was half an hour late to a major group presentation. His TA reported that "no two of the students in that group could work with the third." One semester later, Brett took another course with HS that incorporated permanent groups. He had a completely different—and much more positive—experience the second time around. His groupmates credited him with full participation, and classroom observation revealed a smoothly functioning group. We are pleased that Brett was able to learn how to work in groups in college rather than in a much less forgiving setting—on the job.

Student performance on examinations confirms the previously discussed, more subjective, data that shows that our use of PBL was a success. We used a number of questions that had been used in previous years with the class, which one of us (HS) has taught since 1989. Student performance in the study year of 1999 was consistent with performance in previous years, including the 1989 time period when the course was largely lecture-based. We used some questions from the Force Concept Inventory test. We cannot directly compare the performance of our general-audience students with average math skills (i.e., struggling with fractions and algebra) who studied motion for three weeks in a course with the performance of scientists and engineers who studied force and motion for a full semester in a calculus-based course. However, our students did substantially exceed our expectations. The number of Ds (10), Fs (1), and withdrawals (12) is a very small fraction of the 360 students in both sections of our course. There were no significant differences in the performance of a sample of students from each section on examinations, even when we matched a sample from each section using sex, major, and year in school.

Greater Success of PBL in the Smaller of the Two Classes

One purpose of our division of our physical science class into a class of 240 and a class of 120 was to investigate the effects of class size on student learning. In summary, while PBL worked in both the large and very large classes, from the viewpoint of both students and instructors, it worked better in the large class of 120 students than in the very large class of 240 students.

One of the most important objectives of a science class for general audiences lies in the affective domain—in the area of developing a better attitude toward the subject, as well as a greater understanding of it. Thus, the fact that we had comparable exam scores in the two classes only tells part of the story. Our future elementary teachers are more likely to spend their time and energy teaching science if they actually like the subject. The other students in our class, who include business leaders and politicians, are more likely to express their interest in science in their later lives through their entertainment selections and tax dollars if their college courses have fostered a positive interest in science.

A variety of measures of students' activities in their groups indicate more positive attitudes in the large class of 120 than in the very large class of 240. Twenty-six out of 81 respondents in the large class to the midsemester course evaluation (32%) mentioned group work as being something that contributed most to their learning. Only 33 out of 150 respondents (22%) in the very large class made similar mentions of group work. Other measures of student satisfaction with group work, such as their success on their "Big Projects" or student-designed, long-term independent laboratory investigations, also indicate greater engagement in the large class than in the very large class.

The most statistically significant of these measures come from an end-of-semester course evaluation conducted using the IDEA system. This course evaluation instrument, in development at Kansas State University for nearly 30 years and with most of the questions stable since 1975, has been nationally normed and validated with more than 100,000 student responses. Cashin (1995), Cashin and Downey (1992), and Sixbury and Cashin (1995) provide background on this system of course evaluation and support the validity of using it.

Table 14.1 lists the 5 of the 10 rating dimensions of the IDEA system where there were statistically significant differences between student ratings in the large class of 120 and the very large class of 240. Evaluations were administered on the same day by the department's laboratory coordinator, with neither instructor present when students filled out the evaluation. We

Table 14.1. Differences in Measures of Teaching Effectiveness

Criterion	Very Large Class Score	Large Class Score	Significance Level (Number of Standard Deviations; Adjusted Data)	Significance Level (from a T-test; Unadjusted Data)
Improved student attitude toward subject	40	46	4.7 _	$p < 0.02$
Overall excellence of teacher	47	51	3.1 _	$p < 0.04$
Overall excellence of course	41	50	7.1 _	$p < 0.006$
Learning fundamental principles, generalizations, or theories	37	46	5.5 _	$p < 0.0006$
Acquiring an interest in learning more by asking my own questions and seeking answers	38	44	4.7 _	$p < 0.02$
All 10 items reported by the IDEA system	52.3	49.7	6.5 _	

Because these data are reported by the IDEA center as T-scores, which all have a standard deviation of 10, the standard deviations of the mean are identical (0.73 for the large class, with $N=92$, and 1.04 for the very large class, with $N=185$). The first five items in this table report only those criteria where the difference between the large class and very large class is statistically significant and where the difference is consistent with and without IDEA's adjustments. The IDEA system adjusts the data for the effects of class size, student desire to take the course no matter who taught it, and other student motivational influences, based on their experience.

The last two columns report the significance of the data. The fourth column uses the language and methods of the physical sciences and reports the difference between the IDEA-adjusted means in units of standard deviations of the mean. The usual criterion of significance depends on the investigator but is generally 2 or 3 standard deviations (2–3 _). The fifth column uses the language and methods of science education researchers to report the difference between the *unadjusted* data, using student's two-tailed T-test. For a description of the IDEA system, see http://www.idea.ksu.edu or Cashin and Downey (1992).

find it particularly interesting that the difference between the two classes persists even when the IDEA system corrects its ratings for the effects of class size, using an algorithm developed from all of the classes in its database (the majority of which are lecture-based). We also find it interesting that two of the dimensions on which there is a difference ("Improved Student Attitude Towards Subject" and "Acquiring an Interest in Learning More. . .") are primarily from the affective domain.

Implications

At the current stage of data analysis, it is not possible to determine exactly why PBL was more effective with a group of 120 than with a group of 240. However, we can offer a number of observations. We could give the students in the class of 120 considerably more individual attention than those in the class of 240. In the spring of 1999, the room could hold exactly 283 students, which meant that conditions in the class of 240 were quite crowded. The impact of teaching the large class on the instructors' time was considerably less than is the case with the very large class.

A class of 120 students sounds like a large class and is a large class, but when students work in groups of 4, there are 30 student groups, and it is possible for an individual instructor to give each group some attention at least occasionally. When groups are asked to report to the large class, it is occasionally possible to get students to speak in front of the large group without feeling intimidated. Our experience in the spring of 2000, when each of us taught a class of 120, was that we could learn many if not all students' names and, indeed, could treat them as individuals. We can deal more easily with individual groups and be more attentive to their needs. Our perceptions are quite consistent with the data reported for smaller classes and earlier grade levels by Zahorik (1999).

From an administrative perspective, the issue is not just how large an individual class is, but how many students a particular instructor is responsible for during a given semester. During the study year (1999), the two of us were collectively responsible for 360 students, and one of us had some administrative responsibility for the laboratory for the entire course of 480 students. In the spring of 2000, each of us was only responsible for one class of 120, with one of us having some responsibility for the course laboratory (which again enrolled 480 students). We both found that when we only had 120 students to deal with in one semester we could give them considerably more attention.

Another issue is room capacity. In the class of 120, we left several rows of seats vacant so that we could be in conversation with every single group in the room. While we intended to leave a few vacant rows in the class of 240, we had to fill up those vacant rows; thus, we could not gain access to some student groups. In addition, groups that were assigned seats in the back of the room could not move if they wished. In the class of 120, we called our seat assignments for groups "initial assignments" and permitted groups to move where they wanted. (In HS's class of 120 in the same room in the spring of 2000, about one-third of groups moved from their initial positions). In the class of 240, we were not able to move students. The effects of the room size and crowded conditions appeared in one student journal:

> I was placed in the back of the room. Usually in large lecture classes it is to my advantage to sit in the front where I can participate and interact with the professor more. I found that even though I spoke to you and Dr. Duch, [it was] to no avail[;] I could not be moved. I found the back to be distracting and as a result my learning was not to the fullest. I think that group work on the whole is a noble idea but not in the lecture hall setting.

Our last observation about class size involves our reaction as instructors. All college instructors are used to putting in overtime, and we are no exception. However, keeping track of the group assignments as students added and dropped the course simply consumed the attention of one of us (HS) for the first three weeks of the semester. Fortunately, BD was leading the class during that time. During the semester, we had to intervene to help manage a few groups, all of which were in the very large class. At the end of the study semester (spring 1999) neither of us was willing to manage permanent groups in a class of 240. The following fall, when HS had a class of 280 (taught in a different, larger room), he used casual groups, in order to avoid the management problems of dealing with permanent groups. He did use permanent groups in his other classes that academic year, which had enrollments of 30 and 120. BD has used permanent groups in her classes, which had enrollments of 120 or less.

Teaching is a sufficiently subtle and complex process that we do not believe it is possible, on the basis of the present study, to say (for example) that it is always all right to use PBL in a class of 120 and always not all right to use it in a class of 240. Indeed, one of us has used PBL in a class of 280 since this class was taught, but with casual groups rather than permanent groups. However, we do believe that the present study suggests that class size makes a difference when inquiry-learning techniques, such as PBL, are implemented. The research literature indicates less of a difference when a class is taught primarily by lectures.

As a recommendation for both further studies and administrative practices, we believe it is particularly important to pay attention to class size when the size goes beyond 100 students. Another significant variable is the total number of students a faculty member is responsible for in all of that instructor's courses. It is also important to consider the size of the room that a particular class is taught in, compared with the number of students in the class. PBL teaching techniques can benefit from extra space so that students can move around.

This research has been supported by NSF grants DUE-95-53787, DUE-97-52285, and by the Pew Charitable Trusts. We thank Gabriele Bauer, Beth Jones, and Judi Provencal for their observations of this class at various times in the spring of 1999 and Duane Pontius for his encouragement.

Authors' Biographies

Harry L. Shipman is the Annie Jump Cannon Professor of Astronomy, in the Department of Physics and Astronomy at the University of Delaware.

Barbara J. Duch is Associate Director of the Mathematics and Science Education Resource Center at the University of Delaware.

References

Angelo, T., & Cross, K. P. (1993). *Classroom assessment techniques* (2nd ed.). San Francisco: Jossey-Bass.

Bauer, G., & Jones, E. (2000). Summary of major findings from student focus groups on problem-based learning (PBL) experiences. Internal University of Delaware Report.

Bracey, G. W. (1999). The ninth Bracey report on the condition of public education. *Phi Delta Kappan, 81*(1), 147–148, 150–160, 162–168.

Cashin, W. E. (1995). Student ratings of teaching: The research revisited. IDEA Report No. 32. Manhattan, KS: Instructional Development and Educational Assessment Center.

Cashin, W. E., & Downey, R. G. (1992). Using global student ratings for summative evaluation. *Journal of Educational Psychology, 84,* 563–572.

Duit, R., & Treagust, D. (1998). Learning in science: From behaviorism towards social constructivism and beyond. In B. J. Fraser and K. Tobin (Eds.), *International Handbook of Science Education* (pp. 3–26). Boston: Kluwer.

Edmondson, J. B., & Mulder, F. J. (1924). Size of class as a factor in university instruction. *Journal of Educational Research, 9,* 1–12.

Finn, J. D., & Achilles, C. M. (1999). Tennessee's class size study: findings, implications, and misconceptions. *Educational Evaluation and Policy Analysis, 21* (2), 97–109.

Grissmer, D. (1999). Class size effects: Assessing the evidence, its policy implications, and future research agenda. *Educational Evaluation and Policy Analysis, 21* (2), 231–248.

Kulik, J. A., & Kulik, C.-L. C. (1989). Meta-analysis in education. *International Journal of Educational Research, 13,* 221–340.

McKeachie, W. (1994). *Teaching tips: Strategies, research, and theory for college and university teachers.* Lexington, MA: Heath.

National Academy of Sciences. (1997). *Science teaching reconsidered: A handbook.* Washington, DC: Author.

Posner, G. J., Strike, K. A., Hewson, P. W., & Gerzog, W. A. (1982). Accommodation of a scientific conception: Toward a theory of conceptual change. *Science Education, 66* (2), 211–227.

Sixbury, G. R., & Cashin, W. E. (1995). Description of database for the IDEA diagnostic form. Technical Report No. 9 Manhattan, KS: Instructional Development and Educational Assessment Center.

Strike, K. A., & Posner, G. J. (1992). A revisionist theory of conceptual change. In R. Duschl and R. Hamilton (Eds.), *Philosophy of Science, Cognitive Theory, and Educational Theory and Practice* (pp. 147–176). Albany, NY: SUNY Press.

Wulff, D. H., Nyquist, J. D., & Abbott, R. D. (1989). Students' perceptions of large classes. In M. G. Weimer (Ed.), *Teaching large classes well:* Vol. 32. *New directions for teaching and learning* (pp. 17–30). San Francisco: Jossey-Bass.

Zahorik, J. A. (1999). Reducing class size leads to individualized instruction. *Educational Leadership, 57* (1), 50–53.

15

PROBLEM-BASED LEARNING: PREPARING NURSES FOR PRACTICE

Christine A. Cannon
and Kathleen A. Schell

Chapter Summary

Nurses in practice today are challenged by a variety of problematic situations in providing healthcare. Nursing education must integrate problem-based learning (PBL) strategies that prepare students to approach and manage these real-life situations—ultimately, resulting in the safe, effective, and efficient delivery of care.

Introduction

To prepare students to step into professional practice, nursing educators focus on the most common roles and responsibilities assumed by nurses in practice. Preparation includes a foundation in the arts needed for caring in an expanding and increasingly diverse world, and in the many sciences upon which rational and systematic care is based. In addition, learning how to approach common situations, how to make decisions, and solve problems related to practice is critical. Application of knowledge occurs in a variety of practice settings from the classroom and lab to in-patient and community settings. The use of real-life problems is essential for preparing students for practice—making a strong case for the use of problem-based learning throughout the curriculum. This chapter describes the rationale for integrating PBL within nursing curricula, a brief review of the nursing literature describing the use of PBL, and the implementation of a PBL model at the University of Delaware's Department of Nursing.

The Case for PBL
Problem Solving in Practice

The rationale for integrating PBL into nursing curricula is obvious when one considers the most common practice responsibilities. For example, nurses use the scientific, problem-solving method known as the nursing process during care delivery in many settings. Steps in this process include: (a) the collection of history and physical assessment data through systematic questioning, inspection, palpation, percussion, and auscultation, (b) the prescription and/or review of laboratory and diagnostic test results, (c) collaborative planning based on the information gathered, (d) the delivery of coordinated care in which the client and family participate, and (e) the evaluation of responses to interventions to refine the plan of care. Each of these steps involves activities requiring thinking approaches that can be developed through PBL. For example, acknowledging first impressions, comparing data with norms, making hunches, and clustering data are steps in reasoning required for daily clinical assessment and evaluation. These thinking processes lead to continuing focused inquiry and problem solving essential for efficient and effective care (Rubenfeld & Scheffer, 1999). Based on qualitative analysis of observations and semistructured interviews of 80 novice and expert staff nurses, Taylor (1997) found that one thinking process, referred to as diagnostic reasoning, is a problem-solving strategy used while providing care. However, novice nurses infrequently implement this strategy. She suggests that PBL in undergraduate courses will improve problem-solving abilities in practice. PBL also promotes students' ability to collaborate and to participate in shared decision making, essential skills in health care (Amos & White, 1998; Bentley & Nugent, 1996). Critical thinking, communication, collaboration, and creativity required for care must be practiced throughout the educational experience.

Changes and Challenges

Dramatic changes in health care have created many new challenges that require the critical thinking skills that are so much a part of PBL. Today, nurses practice their professions in homes, communities, and over the Internet, as well as in the more traditional settings of hospitals, clinics and physician offices. The economic changes in health care delivery continue to challenge providers and recipients of care. Medical advances and economic mandates have contributed to shortened hospitalizations for clients with acute illnesses or trauma and for those undergoing surgery—leaving little time for psychosocial support and educational preparation. The consumer-focused health care system with active participation of health care recipients at all levels—from the provision of physical care to involvement with end-of-life decisions—is changing the advocate and educator roles of nurses. Creativity, flexibility, and the ability to apply practice knowledge and skills to changing contexts, new situations, and more involved recipients of health care require the use of logical, analytical, and problem-solving skills that characterize PBL (Catalano, 1996).

Nurses identify and approach an abundance of issues and problems affecting the profession. In 1999, during the American Nurses' Association convention, delegates discussed a number of global issues including the following: (a) the impact of Medicare payment systems on nursing practice, (b) rising incidence of occupational injuries and illnesses that face health care workers, (c) the need for engineering controls to prevent needle stick injuries and exposure to blood-borne diseases, (d) the preservation of privacy and confidentiality, (e) the use of genetic information, as well as (f) nursing's responsibilities related to the use of weapons and in mass casualty incidences (American Nurses' Association, 1999). Any of these issues representing problems being addressed in today's health care arena would make excellent examples for PBL activities.

The Practice-Education Gap

To strengthen the case for integrating PBL in nursing curricula, it must be remembered that those in nursing practice have long criticized those in nursing education for distancing students from the real world of health care. Traditional teaching strategies do not produce the desired outcomes of critical thinking, independent decision making, and autonomy that are needed by today's graduates (Bentley & Nugent, 1996; Biley & Smith, 1998; Heliker, 1994). Moreover, Creedy, Horsfall, and Hand (1992) claim that although graduates of traditional Australian baccalaureate nursing programs possessed analytical skills, they lacked the ability to synthesize information and place it in social context. The survival of educational programs is dependent on preparing students to practice in today's challenging health care environment. It is impossible to provide the breadth of knowledge that students will need to practice. Rather, relevant and meaningful information must be selectively chosen to reflect real-life situations (Horsburgh, Lynes, & Oliver, 1984). Knowledge acquired must be retained and applied to practice (Andrews & Jones, 1996; Bentley & Nugent, 1996; Heliker, 1994). PBL links theory with practice (Creedy et al., 1992; Frost, 1996).

Problem-based Learning in Nursing Education

Problem-based learning in nursing education was first described in the literature of the 1980s and was primarily used in Australia and New Zealand (Creedy et al., 1992; Horsburgh et al., 1984; Little & Ryan, 1987). This approach is slowly gaining acceptance in the United States, but it continues to be considered innovative in nursing (Heliker, 1994). PBL has been incorporated in undergraduate, baccalaureate for the registered nurse, and graduate nursing programs. It has been used in an interdisciplinary course for medical students and nurse practitioner students (Frost, 1996). Biley and Smith (1998), Creedy et al., (1992), Heliker (1994) and Tanner (1990) describe the theoretical underpinnings of PBL.

Incorporation of PBL in the Nursing Curriculum

PBL may be the primary teaching-learning approach used in a nursing program (Alavi, 1995; Little & Ryan, 1987), or it may be combined with other strategies (Andrews & Jones, 1996). For example, Helicker (1994) suggests that PBL discussion groups focusing on actual clinical situations could follow minilectures. Generally, students work on a PBL case for several class sessions (Bentley & Nugent, 1996; Garbett, 1996; King, Sebastian, Stanhope, & Hickman, 1997).

PBL has been applied to courses focusing on health and life changes (Alavi, 1995); adult health nursing (Garbett, 1996), nursing management of patients with pathophysiological problems (Horsburgh et al., 1984), "health breakdown" (Alavi, 1995; Little & Ryan, 1987), pharmacology-nutrition (Helicker, 1994), home health (Bentley & Nugent, 1996) and community health (Frost, 1996; King et al., 1997). PBL is effective in facilitating clinical postconferences for senior-level nursing students (Bentley & Nugent, 1996). In a baccalaureate program for registered nurses, PBL has been used to validate the students' current knowledge base and level of experience in several specialty areas, such as critical care, obstetrics, pediatrics, and psychiatry (Amos & White, 1998). PBL has also been incorporated into a preceptorship to facilitate the transition from student to graduate nurse during the first 6 to 12 months of professional practice (Crowe, 1994).

Implementation and Evaluation of PBL

The mechanics of PBL vary among nursing programs. Students may work in groups of between 4 and 10 (Amos & White, 1998; Biley & Smith, 1998; Little & Ryan, 1987). However, Alavi (1995) describes groups of 20 students who eventually work in smaller subgroups to gather information. Typically, the problems or situations are based on actual clinical cases (Alavi, 1995; Bentley & Nugent, 1996; Garbett, 1996; Little & Ryan, 1987). In fact, Alavi (1995) describes how faculty used information on patients admitted to a local Emergency Department during one shift to create a "learning package" that spanned the semester. Open-ended questions, guidelines, audiotapes, and videotapes may assist the students to explore the problem (Alavi, 1995; Bentley & Nugent, 1996; Frost, 1996; Horsburgh et al., 1984; King et al., 1997).

Anecdotally, PBL receives positive feedback from nursing students and faculty. Improvement in critical thinking, creative thinking, learning how to learn, teamwork, and research skills has been reported (Amos & White, 1998; Bentley & Nugent, 1996; King et al., 1997). Although PBL was challenging and a lot of work, students experienced personal growth as their self-esteem and professionalism increased (Amos & White, 1996). However, students may experience difficulty adjusting to faculty who do not simply provide knowledge and may need time to develop skills in self-directed learning (Little & Ryan, 1987). They may feel overwhelmed with this less traditional thinking process and may be anxious that they will not be able to pass final licensure examinations (Garbett, 1996). Upon program completion, students find PBL empowering and informative and are more confident in their problem-solving skills.

Andrews and Jones (1996) conducted a case study of the phenomenon of the problem-solving process among 11 senior-level baccalaureate students participating in the adult branch component of a course. The researchers observed six 3-hour PBL learning sessions, provided debriefing sessions for students, and then reflected on the previous events. Several concerns were expressed. For example, instructors often predetermine problem identification so that students may be weaker in recognizing problems. In turn, this may hinder application of classroom concepts to the clinical setting. They found that students were more competent at handling concrete problems than abstract problems. Furthermore, students were able to collect large volumes of information but did not consistently attain the depth of understanding desired. Because a variety of teaching methods were used in the course, identification of the direct outcomes of PBL was not possible.

Biley & Smith (1998) recommend that nurse educators cautiously adopt PBL because much of the supportive outcome research is found in medical literature, the research focuses on isolated variables, and the articles submitted are written from a pro-PBL stance. Evaluative research in the nursing discipline is essential for nurse educators to confidently embrace PBL in the curriculum.

Integration of PBL Methods Throughout the Nursing Curricula at the University of Delaware

Supported by the multiplicity of problems found in health care practice today and the opportunities within nursing education to learn problem solving in various settings, PBL methods need to be fully integrated throughout the curricula of basic and graduate programs. Concurrent with new curriculum development of the baccalaureate in the science of nursing program at the University of Delaware, PBL methods are gradually being integrated into didactic and clinical courses as faculty are searching for the most effective ways to prepare tomorrow's nurses. This complementary methodology is one of many used to foster learning, contributing to the achievement of course objectives and program outcomes.

Students begin the nursing courses with the advantage of exposure to PBL experiences in the science courses. The nursing content in each course builds on knowledge, skills, and attitudes developed in the preceding courses, conducive to developing problems that are addressed over more than one course. For example, prepared with information related to blood coagulation, cardiovascular functioning, and the immune response in injury from a course in human physiology, students are actively involved in learning about the etiologies, structural and functional alterations, and their associated clinical manifestations related to hemorrhage in a sophomore-level nursing course, Pathophysiological Concepts. A case study in which a teenager suffers massive trauma and proceeds into hypovolemic shock is analyzed by small groups of two to five students using PBL. In the junior-level Pathophysiology course, the same case study is reintroduced with PBL focused on complications that develop from shock related to blood loss, such as prerenal failure. Nursing care planning related to the case example is integrated within the medical-surgical courses at a time when students may have clinical opportunities to care for accident victims. In addition, the psychosocial issues for the teen and his family; the medication regimen; and related professional, safety, legal, ethical, and cultural issues, such as exposure to contaminated blood, use of safety helmets, end-of-life decisions, and organ transplantation may be discussed within additional courses. Extending problems over several courses guides learning from the understanding of basic concepts to managing complex situations of increasing depth and breadth. As knowledge of course content is acquired in a stepwise fashion, it makes sense to build systematic problem solving in the same manner.

This section will highlight the specific strategies used in sophomore-, junior-, and senior-level courses by the chapter authors. In the search for active learner involvement and the need to focus on how to approach problems, the authors describe strategies, including PATH charting, discussion section and small group analysis of simple to complex case studies, and the integration of case studies within large group lectures.

PATH Charting

The active learning strategy called PATH charting was developed to guide nursing students in their first nursing course, Pathophysiological Concepts. In this three-credit didactic course of 90 to 140 students, PATH charting was taught to help students think about assigned readings in ways that increase understanding and retention of the most important content. This technique used by students in preparation for class, by teachers during class, and in small groups in the process of analyzing case studies, actively engages students in categorizing, condensing, and connecting disease and injury-related information in ways meaningful to them. Causal links are made within and between disease etiologies, structural and functional physiological alterations, and clinical manifestations for a selected disorder. The process of PATH charting requires learner interest, motivation to learn "how to think," and an understanding of basic physiological concepts. It involves a series of steps including (1) the collection of information about the disorder (often from the course textbook); (2) the categorization of information in 3 columns—*etiologies* that include internal or external causes, risk factors, and precipitating factors; *structural and functional alterations* at the cellular, tissue, organ, and system levels presented in a flow diagram chronologically starting with initial changes and progressing to include complications and/or resolution; (3) the connection (with arrows) of column 2 alterations with associated *clinical manifestations*—groupings of signs, symptoms, and lab and diagnostic test findings. The product of the PATH charting process is a concise, informational chart with *paths* of interrelated cause-effect *path*ophysiological content.

In addition to the usefulness of PATH charting in preparing for PBL case studies, students have cited its helpfulness in reviewing for course and licensure exams, in learning focused history-taking and physical assessment, as well for planning and implementing client and family education. On evaluation, students reported an evolving sense of confidence and competence in organizing new and managing complex information, ease in visualizing a mental picture of pathophysiological relationships, preparation for more advanced conceptualization required for practice, and increased understanding, recall, and retention of content. Many students described their increased ability to systematically approach learning about health alterations (Cannon, 1998).

Case Study Discussion Section

Weekly case study discussion sections of one hour were added to the junior-level Pathophysiology course several years ago with the intention of gaining greater student participation following a weekly two-hour lecture instead of offering three hours of lecture. Lecture content, textbook and research reading assignments, and PATH charting prepare students to analyze 25 to 30 case studies during the course's discussion sections of 15 to 20 students each. The case studies are included in the course workbook along with related lecture content. Lecture content is organized by alterations that affect each system, so a case study on a person with Cushing disease is scheduled during the week that common endocrine disorders are presented. Specific case study topics are not discussed in lectures. Two to three case studies are reviewed at each weekly discussion.

Each student selects two case studies, partnering with another student for the first case and presenting the second case independently. The presenters are responsible for developing four to five questions for each class member to answer prior to coming to class and creating ways to involve class members in the discussion of the case study. Some of the most interesting presentations have involved role play (patient, family, nurse), video clips and X rays or scans of actual cases, human organ or tissue specimens, brief interviews of students with the disorder under discussion, gaming to test knowledge, and the inclusion of food tied in with the case (miniature peanut butter cups representing Ghon's foci in tuberculosis and minidonuts for herniated disks). In preparation for the case review, the presenters develop a PATH chart distributed to class members and a brief reference list that includes at least one research study related to the case study topic. Class members are required to review the cases to be presented and highlight key information related to the etiologies, risk factors, and precipitating factors found in the client's chief complaint and medical history in the initial section of the case. In the Course of Illness section, subjective (symptoms) and objective (signs, lab and test results) data are identified, and the underlying basis for their occurrence is hypothesized. The changes representing the resolution or progression of illness are noted. Students are asked to know the definitions of unfamiliar terms and descriptions of tests and treatments before coming to class.

Six pop quizzes during the semester and student participation in class provide evaluation data related to preparedness. Sixty percent of the course final exam tests subject matter from the case study discussions. Student presenters are graded on their ability to involve the class, their own preparation and organization of presentation, use of audiovisual aids, as well as the quality and quantity of references, the identification of a good research study publication, and the development of a comprehensive PATH chart and class preparation questions. Students evaluate the case study discussion activities as part of the course and instructor evaluations.

Small Group PBL in the Large Classroom

More recently, case studies were introduced in the sophomore-level course, Pathophysiology Concepts. At the end of three lectures, 30 to 40 minutes are left in the 75-minute lectures to break the class of over 100 students into over 20 small groups to begin the systematic analyses of three uncomplicated case studies associated with the lecture content. The case studies are divided into meaningful segments with questions for discussion and research attached to each segment. The goal of using this approach is to develop logical thinking processes for team analysis of real-life situations and problems. Questions focus on the definition of terms used; comparisons of assessment data, such as blood pressure, pulse, common lab results with normal values, the development of client questions based on the hunches made from preliminary data provided, as well as the formulation of hypotheses about the underlying pathophysiological alterations. As the questions in each segment are answered, the groups are given feedback from the teacher or teaching assistant, who provides the next segment of data with questions. Within the small groups, each member is given an assignment for the next class during which 30 minutes is provided at the beginning of the class to exchange information and complete the remaining questions. All work of the group is submitted for grading simply using a scale of 0 (no evidence of participation) to 2 (good evidence of participation). At the end of the course, the zero to six points are divided by two and added as percent points to the final course grade.

Overall, student evaluations of this method were favorable. The main problem was teacher availability to such a large number of small groups meeting in two large rooms. At times, it was difficult to control discussions unrelated to the case studies.

Integration of PBL Within Senior-Level Lecture Courses

Didactic class time offers another opportunity to promote questioning and decision making. For example, in a senior-level nursing course, Restorative Nursing Practice II, with an approximate enrollment of 100 to 130 students each semester, more complex disease processes, such as shock and neurotrauma and their interdisciplinary management, are presented through analysis of case studies presented in PowerPoint lecture format. In the large group, students are asked to analyze data and propose their actions. They are given partial data and are asked to determine what other information they would like to have to gain a thorough understanding of the patient's picture. The instructor validates answers and provides summaries of essential concepts in subsequent PowerPoint slides. Once or twice during class, students are asked to work in pairs to identify nursing diagnoses, expected outcomes, and evidence of the attainment of goals. Then pairs volunteer their ideas in a larger class discussion.

In a critical care elective course, four to five classes are devoted to students working in groups of three or four to analyze case studies. Students are required to bring textbooks and at least a few recent journal articles on a general topic that is given to them a week before the actual group work. The topics presented through the case study may have been addressed in various ways in previous courses but are not part of a formal class during the current course. Therefore, students tap previously obtained knowledge, as well as current literature and textbooks to analyze the cases. The instructor provides some resources for the groups and distributes the case, one page at a time, to be certain that the group is focused and working together. Once the group understands and is satisfied with the answers to the questions for that page, the next page is distributed. Student roles of leader, recorder, and group process analyzer are determined among the group and rotated each case study. The instructor facilitates the learning process by providing guidance if students are "off-track," assisting with the group process and offering positive feedback. A one- to two-page group process summary is submitted with the answers to the case study. A group grade is assigned to the case study, and group members evaluate each other's preparedness and contributions to the work.

Lab and Clinical Practicums

Intended outcomes of clinical teaching in nursing programs include knowledge, problem solving, critical thinking, decision making, psychomotor skills, interpersonal skills, organizational skills, professional socialization, and cultural competence (Gaberson & Oermann, 1999). Clinical teaching occurs in practice labs and in the actual patient care setting.

Throughout the curriculum, learning labs provide PBL opportunities to prepare students for clinical practice. In addition to the mannequins, models, and equipment used in clinical practice, the nursing labs contain an array of multimedia learning resources. Often, problems are scenarios incorporating assessment of situations, hands-on practice of psychomotor skills, and the development of communication skills needed before going into the clinical setting. Sources for problems include computer programs, interactional videodiscs, videotapes, audiotapes, and CD-ROMS, as well as the Internet and nursing textbooks. Through interaction with faculty and/or use of technology-based simulations, students solve patient care problems in a safe environment.

Skills gained in the nursing labs are then transferred to the practice setting. Students are assigned to or may select a variety of patients during clinical rotations in actual acute care or long-term care settings. Prior to and during clinical shifts, students are required to review patients' charts to collect data revealed in histories, physical exams, lab values, diagnostic results, and interdisciplinary progress notes. Data are also collected through interaction with other health care personnel, such as staff nurses, physicians, and physical and respiratory therapists. Patients and their significant others are key sources of data, while their health situations become the problems around which learning continues. Analysis of this information provides students with direction in understanding treatment plans and in planning their own nursing interventions. Hands-on care by students provides some of the best problem-solving opportunities, as students strive to provide textbook care amidst the nuances of reality. Clinical faculty, as well as staff nurse preceptors, encourage critical thinking as they ask students to select the most pertinent data, identify and explain relationships among data, plan care, and evaluate appropriateness and effectiveness of care. Written assignments are also mechanisms to assess students' understanding of data and their relationships and how this information directs patient care.

Students also problem solve in the community setting. They may be assigned to coordinate health education activities, such as trauma prevention in an elementary school, stroke risk screening among university staff, or prevention of osteoporosis in a senior center. They interact with the agencies' personnel to determine scheduling, location, and appropriateness of teaching materials and methods, and evaluation of activities. Health problems and goals included within Healthy People 2000 and 2010 often focus community coursework. Newspaper articles describing public health threats, such as increasing antibiotic resistance, global increases in tuberculosis and HIV infections, or issues of accessibility to care and economic constraints facing the care of specific populations, such as the elderly, provide many good examples for developing PBL projects.

Gradually, PBL is being incorporated throughout the BSN curriculum, not as a separate entity, but as one of several effective methodologies critical to the preparation of students as safe, responsible practitioners of nursing. With increasing integration of PBL within the curriculum, faculty are learning how to use PBL to their own and their students' advantage.

Authors' Biographies

Christine A. Cannon, Ph.D., R.N. is an Associate Professor at the University of Delaware.

Kathleen A. Schell, M.S., R.N. is an Instructor of Nursing at the University of Delaware.

References

Alavi, C. (1995). *Problem-based learning in a health sciences curriculum.* London: Routledge.

American Nurses' Association (1999, June). Agenda items presented at the Annual *American Nurses' Association Convention.* Washington, DC.

Amos, E., & White, M. J. (1998). Teaching tools: Problem-based learning. *Nurse Educator, 23,* 11–14.

Andrews, M., & Jones, P. R. (1996). Problem-based learning in an undergraduate nursing programme: A case study. *Journal of Advanced Nursing, 23,* 357–365.

Bentley, G. W., & Nugent, K. E. (1996). Problem-based learning in a home health course. *Nursing Connections, 9,* 29–39.

Biley, F. C., & Smith, K. L. (1998). Exploring the potential of problem-based learning in nurse education. *Nurse Education Today, 18,* 353–361.

Cannon, C. A. (1998). Path charting: A process and product for linking pathophysiological concepts. *Journal of Nursing Education, 37* (6): 257–259.

Catalano, J. T. (1996). *Contemporary professional nursing.* Philadelphia: F. A. Davis.

Creedy, D., Horsfall, J., & Hand, B. (1992). Problem-based learning in nurse education: An Australian view. *Journal of Advanced Nursing, 17,* 727–733.

Crowe, M. (1994). Problem-based learning: A new model for graduate transition in nursing. *Contemporary Nurse, 3,* 105–109.

Frost, M. (1996). An analysis of the scope and value of problem-based learning in the education of health care professionals. *Journal of Advanced Nursing, 24,* 1047–1053.

Gaberson, K. B., & Oermann, M. H. (1999). *Clinical teaching strategies in nursing.* New York, NY: Springer.

Garbett, R. (1996). Problem power . . . problem-based learning. *Nursing Times, 92* (1), 20–21.

Heliker, D. (1994). Meeting the challenge of the curriculum revolution: Problem-based learning in nursing education. *Journal of Nursing Education, 33,* 45–47.

Horsburgh, M., Lynes, L., & Oliver, L. (1984). Problem based learning: An educational strategy. *New Zealand Nursing Journal, 77,* 6–8.

King, M. G., Sebastian, J. G., Stanhope, M. K., & Hickman, M. J. (1997). Using problem-based learning to prepare advanced practice community health nurses for the 21st century. *Family & Community Health, 20,* 29–39.

Little, P., & Ryan, G. (1987). Educational change through problem-based learning. *Australian Journal of Advanced Nursing, 5,* 31–35.

Rubenfeld, M. G., & Scheffer, B. K. (1999). *Critical thinking in nursing: An interactive approach.* Philadelphia: Lippincott.

Tanner, C. A. (1990). Reflections on the curriculum revolution. *Journal of Nursing Education, 29,* 295–299.

Taylor, C. (1997). Problem solving in clinical nursing practice. *Journal of Advanced Nursing, 26,* 329–336.

16

THE LARGE AND THE SMALL OF IT

A Case Study of Introductory Biology Courses

Richard S. Donham, Florence I. Schmieg, and Deborah E. Allen

Chapter Summary

Problem-based learning (PBL) is used in both small and medium-large sections of a two-semester Introductory Biology sequence. Our experience suggests that while class size affects the instructor's choice of classroom management strategies, students value PBL and working in groups in both settings.

Introduction

> *. . . careful inspection of methods which are permanently successful in formal education . . . will reveal that they . . . give pupils something to do, not something to learn; and the doing is of such a nature as to demand thinking, or the intentional noting of connections; learning naturally results.*
>
> —*John Dewey, 1916*

The enhancement of learning by students "doing," as described by Dewey, is at the heart of most of the efforts to improve classroom experience, including use of PBL. With PBL, learning occurs as students move naturally from a tangible, engaging scenario to an increased understanding, and in the process gain experience with abstractions, generalization, and logical reasoning. It gives students personal experience with these sophisticated elements of understanding. It incorporates recommendations for effective teaching contained in science education reform documents, e.g., *Science for All Americans* (AAAS, 1989) and *From Analysis to Action* (NRC, 1996). Learning occurs best in context, by engaging students in authentic questions and by involving students in inquiry. PBL not only provides for content development, but also gives students practice in applying knowledge to real-world issues. The instructor can use problems to serve as tangible and accessible entry points leading to student development of abstraction abilities and reasoning skills.

Adoption of undergraduate PBL in the Department of Biological Sciences at the University of Delaware began in 1993. At the present time, courses available to science majors or nonmajors number at up to 12 per year, with a total impact on up to 700 students per year. In some courses, parallel offerings of PBL and lecture-based sections by the same or alternate instructors occur, which is the case for the biology sections described in this chapter.

In this chapter, we discuss our experience with the use of PBL in Introductory Biology, a multisection, high-enrollment, two-semester sequence taken mostly by freshman science majors. Most of the other instructors teaching the course use lectures as the primary pedagogical method. All sections adopt a syllabus with common objectives for content understanding. Our purpose here is to contrast the decisions made by the instructors for the best ways to use PBL in a small section (about 20–30 students) of Honors students with that of a medium-large section (65–80) of general students. Although there are some accommodations for class size, there are also some common features in both.

Model
How PBL Works: Common Features

Instructors in both the small and larger enrollment sections introduce PBL early in the semester to get a head start on building student acceptance. Students not previously exposed to such a student-centered learning paradigm have legitimate questions and concerns about the method. We find it useful, within the context of the course syllabus, to discuss our skills objectives for the students. The list includes skills and qualities often cited by employers as being important for success on the job, important for success in professional schools, and important for students to continue learning beyond the undergraduate setting. Practice in these skills is provided by PBL, and early acknowledgment of these goals helps us to point out the potential value of the PBL method to students.

PBL problems support student learning in the content objectives in both sized sections; similarly, other features of a good problem are the same in both the large and small classes (see Chapter 5 in this volume). We like to start with an engaging scenario described on a single page. This first page problem scenario concludes with two or three divergent questions that lead students to identify what they already know or may need to know, but do not direct them to a solution. The pattern of activity and learning initiated by the problems follows a similar general sequence, as summarized in Table 16.1.

At the second class period of a PBL problem, students report the results of their investigations to their groups. Freshmen frequently report frustration with their initial efforts. We, therefore, find a class discussion of what worked for some students to be an effective way to insert guidance that eases frustration, and this is an appropriate strategy regardless of section enrollment size. For example, particularly at the start of the semester, we lead discussions of Internet search strategies, including ways of evaluating reliability of information on the Web. This is part of a more general (and ongoing throughout the semester) discussion of appropriate and productive resources for researching problems.

In both small and larger enrollment sections, instructors informally monitor the student presentations of learning issues and the attendant discussions. If needed, minilectures are inserted on the spot to address general student misunderstandings about significant issues. In general, the extent of instructor facilitation during the PBL cycle is a decision made by considering personal preference, the prior biology background of the students, the time point in the semester, and the nature of the problem. If, for example, groups are asking "off-target questions" that lead group activity away from the content that we as instructors wish them to engage, the temptation is to provide directive questions that, in effect, tell the students what to research. It is sometimes difficult for us, because of our content concerns, to keep in mind that thinking about the problem is as important as coming up with the right answer. Too much direction may short-circuit the thinking process and compromise our skills objectives; too little direction in a freshman course may result in nonproductive student frustration.

The iterative process of problem reading and discussion, development of learning issues, research outside of class, exchange of information and group

Table 16.1. Sequence of Classroom PBL Activities: General and Common Features of Both Small and Larger Sections of Introductory Biology

Class Period	Student Activities and Responsibilities	Instructor Roles and Responsibilities
Session 1 Page 1 of problem	Students read, discuss problem	Preface remarks on problem
	List/discuss prior knowledge that relates to problem	Observe group discussions Facilitate (if necessary) development/prioritization
	Develop, prioritize learning issues	Monitor group functioning-sharing of responsibilities, tasks, participation in discussions, respect for other's opinions
	Assign research responsibilities	
	Out-of-Class Individual Research	
Session 2	Reporting on learning issues to group members with discussion—develop new learning issues?	Observe group discussions, minilectures as necessary to facilitate, focus student inquiry Facilitate new learning issue development (if necessary)
Page 2 of Problem	Application of prior knowledge to new material, develop new understanding, learning issues	
	Assign new research responsibilities based on newly developed learning issues	
	Out-of-Class Individual Research	
Session 3	Reporting on learning to group members with discussion.	Minilectures or lead class discussions toward resolution or understanding of problem/learning objectives
Distribute materials associated with assessment of learning	Resolution of problem—development of group product for assessment.	Assessment of group and individual achievement

discussion, and development of new understanding with new questions continues, as necessary (Table 16.1). Often a problem will conclude with a second or third stage, which provides some resolution of earlier stages, although not necessarily clear answers. By the time students arrive at the final stage of the problem, they are beginning to work on the product required, such as a position paper, a recommendation for a congressional subcommittee or an NSF panel, a dialogue or debate, a short essay, or a concept map. Final wrap-up by the instructor often includes a minilecture to help students see how specific content objectives relate to "the big picture" and to draw connections with other problems.

How PBL Unfolds in Honors Introductory Biology

In the small-class Honors sections, instruction is entirely through the use of six to eight problems that require two to five 75-minute class periods each to complete. These problems were aligned with the content objectives we had for the course (see Table 16.2 for a list of the problems and the general topics covered—please note that these topics are not statements of content objectives).

Group function is monitored by the use of peer facilitators (see Chapter 8 in this volume), so assignment of rotating individual roles (accuracy coach, recorder, reporter, etc.) is not as crucial as it might otherwise be without the peer facilitators. Each day, the instructors preview the problem-related activity at the beginning of the class, including any reporting of points and goals for the day. The peer facilitators' responsibility is to help the groups move themselves toward those expectations. The instructors leave time in class for students to complete group assignments, particularly complex ones. Exams are entirely short answer and essay in format (as they might be for a more traditional small class); some questions require students to apply their content knowledge to analysis of new (but much shorter and less complex) problems.

How PBL Unfolds in Large Sections of Introductory Biology

The instructor of the medium-large enrollment section (FS) uses three PBL problems in combination with lectures; PBL occupies about one-third of the available 50-minute class periods. Class time is carefully structured to accommodate class size and the attendant splintering of instructor attention between student groups. After the students receive the first problem, they are allowed about 30 minutes to discuss learning issues and to allocate responsibility for researching these issues. Midway during this period, the instructor may call the class together and ask individual groups to report on their learning issues,

Table 16.2. Sequence of PBL Problems for Honors Introductory Biology (First Semester) with the General Topics (Not Statements of Content Objectives) That Were Introduced by the Problems

Problem Title[1]	General Topics Introduced by Problem
Don Tries to Culture Fish Cells	Osmosis and osmoregulation; composition of body fluids; requirements of life at the cellular level, structural features of eukaryotic cells
The Geritol Solution	The global carbon cycle; photosynthesis; biological productivity; the energy cycle; marine ecosystem and food webs
Jimmy Harris	Central metabolic pathways; enzymes; oxidation/reduction reactions; structure and function of proteins; mechanisms of genetic inheritance
Kryptonite in His Pocket? (by Richard Donham)	Central metabolic pathways; cellular energy sources; cell structure and function
When Twins Marry Twins	Meiosis and sexual reproduction; mechanisms of genetic inheritance
To Be Tested or Not to Be Tested (by Linda Dion)	Mechanisms of inheritance; review of metabolism and cellular energy sources; DNA structure and function; how to sequence and localize genes
Anna or Anastasia?	DNA structure and function; DNA fingerprinting; inheritance of mitochondrial genes; forensic analysis; how good science is done; societal views of science
A Problem with Pore Behavior	Active transport; cellular processing of proteins; modern diagnostic methods for genetic diseases; introduction to population genetics

[1]Problems authored by Deborah Allen, or as noted beneath the individual titles. All problems are from Allen and Duch (1998).

thus generating a list of common learning issues for the entire class. For these students, an entire week is allowed for the individual research before the in-class PBL cycle resumes.

When groups reconvene to present their information, each student is required to submit a summary (with citations of references) of his or her research to the instructor for grading. On the final day of a problem, groups are chosen at random to present their ideas and solutions to the problem, and the instructor conducts a wrap-up discussion of the problem content. This discussion helps students make connections between previous and future lecture material and the context in which it is relevant to the real world.

Managing and Monitoring Groups

Careful management of groups is crucial to success in PBL (see Chapter 6 in this volume). In both small and large classes, groups of four to six students each are formed as soon as possible in the semester, usually after the student drop-add flurry has subsided. We follow the evidence suggesting the advantages of creating heterogeneous groups. In the smaller-enrollment course, the instructors use information, such as students' majors, interests, and home addresses to select groups. In the medium-large section, the instructor prefers to have all members of each group in the same laboratory section, thus providing them an opportunity to meet together outside of the classroom.

One of the most difficult problems in using PBL comes from monitoring groups and their learning. Small classes better allow the instructor to keep student groups on task, motivated, and otherwise working productively, particularly if peer facilitators are used. In any case, instructors walk around the classroom to listen to student discussions but try to resist the temptation to lead the group discussions or to answer questions directly. Too much instructor input may result in students relying more and more on the instructor for the understanding that they are in the process of learning to uncover themselves.

We move around the class to look for physical and verbal signs of group dysfunction. In the larger class, these signs must be more overt to be noticeable by the instructor, so the incorporation of formal mechanisms for monitoring groups into the course design is even more essential.

Several of these formal mechanisms are used in the larger class to keep students on task. As mentioned previously, students are expected to submit summaries of their individual research, which are graded. Some questions on the content examinations are derived from the problems for this same purpose and to promote individual accountability for learning.

In both sections, anonymous peer evaluations that count toward the grade are used. In the small class, these are filled out twice per semester (see Allen & Duch, 1998 for a sample evaluation form) and contribute to 10% of the final grade. In the larger section, evaluations are filled out at the end of each of the three problems; uniformly low evaluations are used to remove group points from a student's grade. In both sections, students draft ground rules for their groups' operation. These rules can be subsequently referred to as a reminder of the agreement that each group member made to be good group citizens.

While peer group facilitators (discussed in more depth in Chapter 8) may not be available in many circumstances, in our experience the use of upper-class biology majors as peer facilitators for freshmen promotes good group function, group cohesiveness, in-depth learning, and student satisfaction with this transitional experience. Well-coached peer facilitators keep the group activity on task, push students beyond their self-satisfaction level of inquiry, help to balance student participation, and promote respect for others' opinions and contributions. A good peer facilitator becomes, for incoming freshmen, a model for success and, as a result, can be a powerful advocate for the method and for general satisfaction in the course.

Assignments for Assessing Student Learning

Chapter 9 by Barbara Duch and Susan Groh in this volume discusses the major issues associated with assessment and PBL. One of the surest ways to disappointment as an instructor is to fail to link instruction to assessment; if problems do not support content objectives and the learning required for success on exams, students quickly learn to disdain the significance of the problems. Furthermore, if students are expected to collaborate in the development of understanding, then assessment of group products should be part of the grade (but not to the extent that individual accountability is compromised). In the small-enrollment course, for example, group work contributes to approximately 25% of the students' final grade in the course; in the large-enrollment section about 30% of the grade is derived from PBL (some of this comes from questions on the hourly content exams that are presented in a separate section of the exam).

Group products can be somewhat novel as compared to traditional assessment tools but the best are probably characterized by being enhanced by student collaboration. As an example, we have used concept maps for group assessment during or at the end of a problem. For example, The Geritol Solution is a problem written by Deborah Allen (1993) that has been used in Honors Introductory Biology for six years. An early version is available at the University of Delaware PBL website (http://www.udel.edu/pbl/) or also, slightly revised, in Allen and Duch (1998). The problem begins with a scenario about John Martin, a marine biologist who hypothesized that low iron content of certain areas of the ocean limits productivity. He proposed that seeding the water with iron might, therefore, help combat global warming. Several large-scale experiments (Iron Ex) have since been conducted to test various aspects of these assumptions. The problem evolves to engage student's thinking about the flow of energy through the biosphere, carbon and nutrient cycling, marine ecosystems, and the photosynthetic reactions. Near the end of the problem sequence, we ask groups to construct complementary concept maps. This in-class activity (the assignment handout is shown in the appendix for chapter16) culminates in oral presentations by each group of the thinking reflected in the concept map. The maps are submitted for instructor evaluation but are used primarily as formative feedback on student understanding of the connections between major concepts in biology. In larger classes, concept maps can be drawn and submitted on overhead transparencies; the instructor can then select and show representative maps to the whole class to provide feedback, thus alleviating the necessity to do extensive grading and written comments.

In the small-enrollment course, we also use dialogues (information about their use is provided by Herreid, undated document on the National Center for Case Study Teaching in Science website) and position papers as group assignments. Group problem assessments can serve as effective formative assessments, allowing the instructor to evaluate student understanding of underlying concepts. If misconceptions or superficiality is suggested, there is time for remediation.

Outcomes

For small sections of Honors Introductory Biology, student reactions are overwhelmingly positive to the thoughtful use of PBL. End-of-course evaluations from 120 students indicate that students value working in groups, having a peer facilitator, the process of applying concepts to problems, and if given a choice, they would take another PBL course (Table 16.3). Responses of students to end-of-course questions in the larger sections also have been quite favorable. When asked if they would have liked less, more, or the same amount of PBL, 85% reported more or the same (35% would have liked more). Students reported that they saw the greatest amount of improvement in team skills, ability to use resources to solve problems, and upon their ability to see real-world applications of the material covered in the course. They report an average amount of improvement in their content knowledge.

Table 16.3. What Students Say: End-of-Course Ratings for the Small-Enrollment Section of Introductory Biology

Ratings Question	Mean Score[1]
The following aspects of the course were beneficial to my learning of biology:	
Working in groups	1.38
Working with a peer tutor	1.36
Application of concepts to problems	1.35
Lectures	2.70
If given the choice, I would take another class designed like this one.	1.50

[1]Responses are on the following scale: 1—strongly agree to >5—strongly disagree. Numbers are the average of 120 students over several years.

If there is a critical undertone to an individual response to free-range questions on the end-of-semester evaluations, student complaints often fall into one of these areas: there were not enough lectures (but, we have also heard the opposite) or that their group did not function well.

A common comment by students is that they think learning is more in-depth and connected to the "real world." They often complain that they work harder in their PBL courses than other similar courses. Interestingly, however, this is largely from the choice they make not to let their group down. They sometimes complain that instructor guidance is insufficient. Students almost always report that the group is among the most valuable aspects of their experience. They often bond so tightly with their other group members that at the end of the first semester they plead to keep their group together in the second semester!

Suggestions for Adoption

For individuals interested in trying PBL in an introductory course setting, we have the following suggestions for implementation, whether in a small- or large-enrollment section:

1. Use problems early and often enough to make problem assignments a significant part of the course grade.

2. Have problems support major course objectives, not just minor or trivial ones.

3. Have assessment aligned with problem activities.

4. Make both individual effort and group participation count in the grading.

5. Give the groups something to do that is challenging enough that they will see obvious benefits in collaboration.

6. Give students an opportunity to reflect on what may be a new classroom experience (through both informal and formal means), and respond to their input. Align these course evaluations to the PBL method.

Conclusion

One of the satisfactions that we as instructors have from PBL is that we get to know our students better than we do with a traditional lecture class. By removing ourselves from the center of classroom action, we get to observe and listen to students during every class. This allows us insight into the structure of their understanding of biology and gives them experience in doing what we all know is the most effective way to learn a topic—teaching it. This creates a classroom situation in which "learning naturally results."

Authors' Biographies

Richard S. Donham is Associate Policy Scientist in the Mathematics & Science Education Resource Center at the University of Delaware and has a adjunct appointment as a faculty member in the Department of Biological Sciences.

Florence I. Schmeig is Assistant Professor of Biological Sciences at the University of Delaware and an affiliated faculty member of the University Honors Program.

Deborah E. Allen is Associate Professor and Undergraduate Programs Director in the Department of Biological Sciences, and an affiliated faculty member of the University Honors Program at the University of Delaware.

References

Allen, D. E. (1993). *The Geritol Solution.* University of Delaware Problem-Based Learning Website. http://www.udel.edu/pbl/ (2000, Sept. 26).

Allen, D. E., & Duch, B. J. (1998). *Thinking toward solutions: Problem-based learning activities for general biology.* Philadelphia, PA: Saunders College Publishing.

American Association for the Advancement of Science. (1989). *Science for all Americans.* Washington, DC: Author

Dewey, J. (1916). *Democracy and education.* New York, NY: Macmillan, p. 181.

Herreid, C. F. (Undated). *Dialogues as case studies.* National Center for Case Study Teaching in Science. http://ublib.buffalo.edu/libraries/projects/cases/dialogues.html (2000, Sept. 26).

National Research Council. (1996). *From analysis to action: Undergraduate education in science, mathematics, engineering, and technology.* Washington, DC: National Academy Press.

APPENDIX TO CHAPTER 16

DIRECTIONS FOR GROUP ASSIGNMENT ON DEVELOPING A CONCEPT MAP FOR THE GERITOL SOLUTION

Introduction to Concept Mapping
A Tool for Learning, Organizing, and Retaining Concepts

Construct a concept map with one of the following titles (to be handed in by the beginning of the next class):

The Light-Dependent Reactions of Photosynthesis

The Light-Independent Reactions of Photosynthesis

The Global Carbon Cycle and The Geritol Solution

The Flow of Energy Through the Biosphere

A concept map demonstrates meaningful relationships between concepts through the use of propositions. A concept is a noun or mental image, such as "plant," "photosynthesis," or "solar energy." A proposition is two or more concepts linked by words in a phrase or thought. The linking shows how the concepts are related. For example, these terms might be mapped in several ways—see the reverse side of this assignment for an example.

There is no single correct way to develop a concept map. Conversely, concept maps are meant to be rearranged and redrawn. Your first attempt will certainly have gaps and flaws and can be improved. As new information is obtained, new insights of relationships may occur to you. A concept map should draw on the ideas of the entire group.

Here are some tips about common strategies for constructing a concept map:

1. Identify words or series of words representing key concepts. It is convenient to write these words on "Post-it Notes" until the map takes final shape.

2. Rearrange the words (notes) in hierarchies of importance, with more general concepts at the top. The concepts should get increasingly more specific toward the bottom of the map. (Some maps are constructed so that the most general concepts are on the edges and the most specific at the center, or vice versa).

3. Then draw lines between related concepts, and write a word or phrase that establishes the link between the connected concepts above each line (referred to as propositional linkages).

4. Crosslinks can then be constructed—these are connections between concepts in different map areas.

17

PBL, POLITICS, AND DEMOCRACY

Kurt Burch

Chapter Summary

Several features of problem-based learning (PBL) are especially apt for social science courses. With its use of open-ended problems and student groups, a PBL course can, in itself, model political behavior and participatory democracy. This chapter illustrates efforts to underscore these features in a pair of upper-level courses in political science over a seven-year period.

Introduction

In a democracy, compromise . . . lies at the heart of things because you have to accept that people are going to have different views, especially on the most volatile matters and the most important issues.
—Czech dissident upon election to Parliament in 1990

The structure and dynamics of a PBL course advance pedagogical goals and enhance student performance. The structure and dynamics also convey political and ethical *content*. This essay illustrates how the format of a PBL course models political behavior and participatory democracy in several ways. First, PBL problems present students with insufficient information for a ready solution—conditions that mirror political problems. Second, the substance of politics involves crafting policies and solutions via public discussion and deliberation. These features describe student interactions in PBL study groups. Thus, study groups provide a microcosm of political life. Third, the dynamics of PBL group study stimulate students—notably women, minorities, and introverts—who typically remain relatively uninvolved in traditional course formats. That is, PBL formats promote democratic practices and ethical considerations. This chapter describes how these features have been underscored in two upper-level courses in political science over a seven-year period.

What Is Problem-based Learning?

PBL is a teaching strategy that shifts the classroom focus from teaching to learning. The central premise of PBL holds that most students will better learn information and skills if they need them; need arises as students try to solve specific, open-ended problems. Beyond an orientation to problems, a PBL course promotes learning via activity and discovery. Students interact with each other and engage course material in a shared enterprise of learning-by-discovery. As students explore problems, they discover much about their topics and themselves. A discovery-oriented course provides students with opportunities and responsibilities to make significant decisions about what to investigate, how to proceed, and how to solve problems. Teachers guide students by asking Socratic questions about the engaging problems and the research strategy.

Educational research demonstrates that active learning is the most effective technique for students to learn, apply, integrate, and retain information (e.g., Bonwell & Eison, 1991). Also, most people prefer active, problem-oriented learning because it arranges information in students' preferred sequence from concrete to abstract.

Several principles comprise the structure and dynamics of PBL courses (e.g., Burch, 2000). Two central principles are open-ended problems and student study groups. Problems are vehicles for learning; groups are fuel. Problems transport students from the classroom to tangible, real-world situations that stimulate their curiosity and creativity. Well-devised problems provide insufficient information for immediate solution. Instead, students must identify key issues, focus their efforts, marshal resources, and collaborate. Since students immediately apply the knowledge they discover and explain it to others, students learn by doing. In the process, students develop new social and cognitive skills, responsibilities, and understandings. An example of a "problem" follows:

> Why might the International Labor Organization, UNICEF, U.S. labor unions, and a class action lawsuit in U.S. courts join widespread calls to boycott soccer balls manufactured in Asia? Why do you (not) think the criticisms are fair?

The second key principle of PBL is that learning occurs in groups. Student groups investigate problems by coordinating their efforts, cooperating toward a collective goal, and collaborating in writing and presenting conclusions. Indeed, PBL students participate in a four-stage "cycle of learning" (Svinicki & Dixon, 1987). At each stage, group members discuss material and receive feedback from peers and the teacher. The first stage is the "problem," for which students identify questions and apt resources for investigating those questions. Second, students analyze the problem. Students draw on their existing knowledge to identify which aspects of the problem they do (not) understand. They also identify what information they require and what (policies) must exist to proceed. Third, students conduct research. Last, they present findings to each other, other groups, the class, and perhaps the public. Findings may provoke further research, refined policymaking, or other actions.

Problem-oriented learning is active and applied rather than passive and absorbed. As students engage a real-life problem, they first identify what they do not know: these are "learning issues." Some learning issues are quite basic: Do the circumstances that concern critics of soccer balls occur often or infrequently? Occur in few or many places? What is a "class action" lawsuit? Further questions require more sophisticated cognitive skills: What are likely consequences of a boycott of soccer balls? What, if anything, do these protests over soccer balls tell you about Asian countries, economies, culture, and laws? What does one mean by "Asian"? How might you respond to the claim that calls to boycott Asian-made soccer balls represent a form of discrimination? As students address learning issues, they identify basic principles and concepts, develop a stock of knowledge, integrate and organize their knowledge, and develop critical-thinking skills. Students help "teach" each other because they constantly interact in order to share information and ideas, develop and refine points, and offer assistance.

In short, one organizes a PBL course around problems and student groups. Open-ended problems and student groups mirror several features of political life.

PBL Problems Mirror Political Problems

PBL problems are microcosms of political life. PBL problems mirror the complexity, richness, and ambiguity of problems that confront policymakers. Also, students' interactions within their study groups mimic the contingencies and uncertainties of all manner of politics. Social actors in any setting confront other actors with disparate views and differing information. Actors strive to reconcile their disparities to become a coherent group that can then draft cogent rules of behavior, public policies, and solutions to problems. Thus, both politics and PBL problems embrace complexity, ambiguity, and indeterminacy. One familiar definition describes politics as "the art of the possible." PBL problems provoke students to ask, "What is possible?" and "What can be done?"

The striking feature of PBL problems and political problems is that they have indeterminate "solutions." Under what conditions might Congress reform the Social Security system? What consequences might follow if the U.S. government abrogates the Antiballistic Missile treaty in order to pursue "Star Wars" technologies? What sorts of Social Security reform or nuclear defense would you recommend? Possible "solutions" to such questions are political rather than algebraic. One cannot solve for x, deduce the "correct" solution, or conduct laboratory experiments. Solutions are always political, drawn from asserted premises and consequent conflict or debate. Incomplete information complicates indeterminacy. Advocates of Social Security reform cannot know how the stock market will perform in future or how current grade schoolers will feel about tomorrow's implications of today's decisions. Similarly, U.S. strategic policymakers cannot be sure how military analysts in other governments will react to U.S. decisions. Might they build chemical arsenals in response?

Each PBL problem is a political problem; each student group is a political system. The realization that PBL groups *are* microcosmic political systems offers teachers unique opportunities to use the PBL experience as a tool for illustrating political themes. For example, do students' triumphs and tribulations in their groups mirror broader political conditions? What implications for democracy follow from students' choices and experiences?

PBL Group Dynamics Mirror Political Life and Democratic Practices

Experiences in PBL groups illustrate revelatory implications for democracy. For instance, both PBL problems and the demands of politics involve declaring values, creating rules, assessing circumstances, advancing and contesting solutions, allocating responsibilities and resources, making and justifying choices, and questioning the choices of others. Further, PBL group interactions model the practices of participatory, pluralistic democracy because all members must, and should, participate by drawing on their diverse knowledge and experiences. The more diverse and varied the participation, the better a group succeeds and the more democracy flourishes. As one sage notes, democracy is both the cause and consequence of "cultural variety and social pluralism" (Niebuhr, 1947, p. 122). Such democracy is an ongoing process, a result of collective efforts to solve problems by crafting, applying, distributing, limiting, and directing authority in the name of governance and management (Dryzek, 1996, pp. 4, 14).

My initial attraction to PBL was "political" because PBL group interactions are microcosms of participatory democracy and public deliberation. PBL groups promote four features of public life significant for politics and democracy: participation, diversity, public deliberation, and transformative multicultural education.

PBL enhances participation by forming students into groups of three to seven members. The comfortable scale of group work improves participation because people of all ages and skills are typically far more willing to participate in a small group than in a large one. The cycle of learning in PBL also heightens participation because it requires contributions from all group members.

The greater the participation, the greater the range of diverse perspectives. As more students engage each other and the material, the range of views becomes wider and richer. Students learn from the material and from the diversity of other's experiences and impressions. Also, PBL group interactions improve the participation, achievement, and enthusiasm of women, minorities, introverts, and those frustrated by the competitiveness and alienating isolation fostered by typical classroom teaching (Tobias, 1990). Thus, participation enhances diversity and, reciprocally, diversity enhances participation.

By enhancing and widening the diversity of expressed views, PBL courses become models of pluralism, multiculturalism, and equity. The scale, dynamics, and purposes of PBL groupwork promote greater fairness in the classroom because they provide students a greater range of opportunities and a wider horizon of outcomes. This distinction mirrors the familiar difference between procedural justice and substantive justice.

By enhancing participation and diversity, PBL groups also expand the breadth and depth of deliberation. Said simply, more people are pondering and engaging matters of public concern, and they do so with more thoughtfulness. Public deliberation involves sharing reasons that might convince others participating in a given discussion. Such reasons likely extend beyond one's mere self-interest toward a broader general interest (Bohman, 1996, pp. 4–5). Deliberation occurs in two ways in PBL groups. First, the "cycle of learning" that occurs within PBL groups demands public deliberation. Members must reflect upon, share opinions about, engage other opinions, and finally form a consensus about how to proceed. Second, the PBL problem requires a response, an action aimed at addressing the problem. Again, members must deliberate about the characteristics of the problem and potential policies intended to solve the problem.

Discussion, deliberation, and consensus are necessary hallmarks of democracy. Further, as diversity, participation, and equity enhance discussion and deliberation, a more robust participatory democracy emerges. "To allow for and encourage diverse viewpoints is to encourage the value of diversity and open debate" (Sleeter & Grant, 1994, p. 129). Such diversity and debate are essential because "a democracy requires citizens who are capable of critical thought and collective social action" (Sleeter & Grant, 1994, p. 219). Such democratic practice involves more than mere majority rule. As John Dewey (1988, p. 365) wrote many decades ago:

> The means by which a majority comes to be a majority is the important thing: antecedent debates, the modification of views to meet the opinions of minorities. . . . The essential need, in other words, is the improvement of the methods and conditions of debate, discussion, and persuasion (Bohman, 1996, p. 1).

PBL groups provide opportunities for such improvement. PBL students continuously engage in discussion, persuasion, and deliberation. If deliberative democracy requires creating social circumstances and institutions that promote public reasoning (Bohman, 1996, p. 238), then PBL groups are such a creation. Moreover, the task of PBL students—to coordinate themselves, so to manage and direct themselves, so to solve problems—mirrors the functions of public reasoning:

> The basic task of critical public reason should be thought of in more practical terms: the point of political deliberation is to solve social problems and to overcome political conflicts. The criterion for successful deliberation is, therefore, that it restore the conditions of ongoing cooperation in problematic situations (Bohman, 1996, p. 240).

If discussion and equality prevail among participants, then public deliberation becomes workable, thereby improving both PBL groups and public democracy.

In this sense, to form student groups is to make substantial ethical choices. First, a contemporary philosophical debate rages over the merits of communitarian and individualist principles of social interaction. For students to participate in a cooperative group is a valuable tonic for the often lonely, asocial individualism of our contemporary society and education systems. Second, groups and societies are ruled either by dominant ideas, by superior authorities, or by an exchange of promises (rights and duties) among members. In the latter case, democratic principles are often effective means. Yet democracy is under fire; what forms of democracy will or should prevail? Scholars, policymakers, and citizens call for democratic reform (e.g., Elshtain, 1995; Dryzek, 1996; Laidi, 1998, pp. 31–37). One demand cries for radically multicultural democracy (Matustik, 1998), a form of democracy that challenges interlocking forms of oppression—such as ageism, racism, sexism, and resource inequalities—by seeking to overcome narrow "identities" in favor of multiple and fluid identities. PBL groups foster both communitarian interactions and multicultural, pluralistic participation.

In this sense, elements of PBL foster "multicultural and social reconstructionist" education (see Table 17.1) (Sleeter & Grant, 1994, chap. 6). To the extent the dynamics of PBL learning require students to confront problems, conceive the possible, and construct alternatives, then PBL fosters skills to enable students to reconstruct society. Such experiences help students "develop the power and skills to articulate both their own goals and a vision of social justice for all groups and to work constructively toward these ends" (Sleeter & Grant, 1994, p. 210). These educational principles share much with the pedagogies of both John Dewey (e.g., 1938, 1959, 1966) and Paulo Freire (e.g., 1970, 1985, 1994).

In part for these reasons, the PBL strategy is a remarkably adept and adaptable vehicle for advancing the three goals of my courses, to develop in students the following:

1. *Core knowledge* in a content area

2. *Cognitive skills,* such as analysis, synthesis, application, evaluation, and critique

3. *Action skills,* such as managing conflicts, organizing time and resources, coordinating, negotiating, and tolerating

Since PBL group work fosters coordination, collaboration, and cooperation, thereby placing these endeavors on a par with conflict and competition, students possess a wider array of experiences and models for addressing future

Table 17.1. Comparing PBL to Transformative Multicultural Education

	PBL	Transformative Multicultural Education
Audience	All Students	
Social Goal	Promote eager, successful learners; Promote equality and diversity in the classroom	Promote equitable social structures and cultural pluralism
Educational Goals	Promote equal opportunities in classrooms; Promote diversity, pluralism, participation, and deliberation; Promote collaborative endeavors; Enhance the content and applicability of learning; Enhance social and cognitive skills	Promote equal opportunities in schools; Promote cultural pluralism and alternative social arrangements; Prepare citizens to work actively toward equitable social arrangements
Curriculum	Organize content around problems; Organize learning around experiences and perspectives of individual students;	Organize content around social issues/problems; Organize learning around experiences and perspectives of different social groups;
	Use students' personal knowledge and experiences as starting points for analyses; Teach critical-thinking skills, analytic skills, social action skills, and empowerment skills	
Instruction	Use cooperative learning; Adapt to students' levels of skill; Build on students' learning styles; Actively involve students in democratic decision making	
Support	Teacher serves as a facilitator or guide; Teacher helps students adapt to as much diversity as possible	

Adapted from Sleeter & Grant, 1994, p. 211, Table 6-1.

personal and social problems. Such knowledge and skills greatly enhance citizens as members of overlapping communities and democracies in the Information Age of the global political economy.

How PBL Works in Two Upper-level Courses

Although PBL is applicable across the curriculum, I draw examples in this essay from two of my junior- and senior-level courses. In the course entitled International Organization (IO), with an enrollment of 35, students form permanent groups and prepare a formal moot court presentation. In Contemporary Problems in World Politics, typically 25–30 students, students engage a new problem each week and form different groups almost every day. In both courses, students investigate explicitly political problems.

In IO, I use the character of PBL group interactions to model the international system. That is, PBL group interactions illustrate the problematic quality of political life in the anarchic international system. Anarchy means the lack of a ruler. No mayor, emperor, junta, or world government presides over the international system. All governments are formally equal, although they possess unequal resources. This same condition describes a student group. Each of the students is formally equal. No individual student or subgroup rules the larger group. How will these students organize themselves and coordinate their efforts? I turn this anxious proverbial question into an illustration of problematic qualities of the international system. Every student anxiety mirrors an ominous condition of international life.

As students study global capitalism, competing countries, international law, and international organization, they are studying mere academic subjects. Their experiences in PBL groups, however, provide tangible analogies. An "economy" may develop as group members "exchange" tasks, favors, and resources, such as one's promise to buy pizza if another types the group report. Threats of any kind often polarize a group. Group ground rules become similar to international law. Honor and reputation affect how members treat each other. Tensions between fairness and efficiency become central concerns to members. Some seek to lead, others to follow. Students experience in microcosm what world leaders experience on a broader scale.

Since I began using PBL in 1993, no student has noted any similarities between PBL groups and the global system. When I introduce the analogy many weeks into the semester, after they complete a major assignment, their interactions in the groups become richer and more meaningful because they are no longer studying abstract, distant ideas, but building directly upon their own experiences. In the last few weeks of the semester we review the prior material in light of their group experiences.

The second course, Contemporary Problems in World Politics (CPWP), addresses a range of contemporary problems, particularly violence and oppression. If in IO we highlight the student groups as groups, then in CPWP we emphasize individuals in group contexts as a means to illustrate ethical themes: the global contexts and consequences of individual choices. The PBL group interactions model the virtues of personal expression, participation, and deliberation as potential remedies to oppression and as fragile components of democracy. Films and brief novels illustrate the contemporary problems. In each source, the main character is a young adult confronting a dilemma. Making choices is a central theme of PBL, democracy, and this course.

Problems that demand reflection and choice often spark students. In *Imagining Argentina,* Carlos ponders how to confront the regime he suspects of authorizing his wife's abduction and whether to join resolute mothers marching outside the Argentine equivalent of the White House to protest missing loved ones, the "disappeareds" presumably kidnapped by the government. In *Dawn,* Elisha anguishes over whether to execute a captured British officer. In *A Man for All Seasons,* Sir Thomas More weighs whether to compromise his principles and live comfortably or to challenge King Henry VIII and risk death. Each source asks students enduring questions: How can citizens resist tyranny and violent oppression? What consequences follow or resistance or acquiescence?

In one course, few would follow More to the executioner by maintaining principles, but half would protest in Argentina or execute a British officer to advance "the cause." Spirited discussion follows about what is a "good cause" because it is ground in historical events and in the students' vicarious experiences. Ethnic cleansing in Bosnia and massacres in Rwanda, as well as earlier historical atrocities, become more compelling and problematic circumstances. Depictions and subsequent questions in Elie Wiesel's *Night,* Rigoberto Menchu's *I, Rigoberto,* Chinua Achebe's *Things Fall Apart,* and Erich Maria Remarque's *All Quiet on the Western Front* become more harrowing for students because they vicariously participate in the characters' choices as they decide for themselves. For example, I have asked students to apply Wiesel's political principles from *Night* and from his inaugural speech at the Holocaust Museum in Washington, DC to allied strikes in Baghdad and Belgrade.

By the end of the course, we shift our attention from the books and films to the authors and directors. Why would a Central American peasant devastated by civil war bother to learn Spanish and write *I, Rigoberto?* Why would Achebe write a tale of a Nigerian village in the 1880s, but craft the tale in impeccable English and classic Western literary form? Why do virtually all of the protagonists in *Imagining Argentina* pursue a creative hobby or profession—whether painter, jeweler, dancer, choreographer, musician, journalist, writer—but the antagonists are thoughtless and robotic? These individuals are driven to express themselves, to share their experiences and views, to participate in a wider "discussion" that embraces multiple, diverse perspectives. These authors and their characters demand greater public deliberation and wider participatory democracy. As students participate in PBL groups, they enjoy precisely these opportunities.

Conclusion

By decentralizing the classroom, students discover the latitude to explore ideas, form opinions, and express themselves. They also find they must engage others and confront novel ideas. Not every student will appreciate or take advantage of the opportunities, but they will fare no less well than in a conventional course. Those who become engaged will shine because they can radiate their creativity. According to course evaluations, students enjoy and value these courses and experiences. For example: "This course was very valuable for it allowed students to participate in lectures and discussion. I gained a lot of insight from other students' viewpoints. The course required a lot of independent discipline. . . . I've grown" (Spring, 1994). "[The class] allowed students to work through the issues on their own rather than simply presenting conclusions to them" (Spring, 1995). "I *enjoyed* the assignments because they allowed me to 'experience' different perspectives rather than read about them" (Spring, 1996). "I really did learn a lot in the course, not only about World Politics, but also about interacting with people, making a point, and being receptive to other points of view" (Spring, 1997). "I learned more than I thought possible from one course" (Fall, 1998). "I liked the learning process that we used. Forcing us to admit what we didn't know and understand worked well. The group project was difficult, but I learned an exceptional amount from it" (Winter, 1999). Nonetheless, some students may be frustrated, particularly those who dualistically define "learning" as the collection of concrete right-or-wrong "facts."

Research drawn from twenty years of PBL experience conclude that "PBL has done no harm in terms of conventional tests of knowledge and that students may show better clinical problem-solving skills. They also show that students are stimulated and motivated by PBL as a method" (Albanese & Mitchell, 1993; Vernon & Blake, 1993; quotation in Barrows, 1996, p. 10). Students retain information longer and recall it more quickly and accurately

(Barrows, 1984; 1996, p. 6). Thus, the foremost role of instruction should not be to convey information, but to assist students to develop the necessary skills to direct their own learning and to "construct" knowledge in ways that are effective for them (Bereiter & Scardamalia, 1992). This conclusion reinforces my goal to teach substance *and* skills.

Similarly, students valuably learn skills necessary to direct their social and political lives in constructive and enriching directions. Students benefit from personal experiences that illustrate collaboration over competition, participation over indifference, listening and deliberation over knee-jerk reaction, and democracy over disillusionment or despotism. Developing these political and ethical sensibilities is as important as fostering cognitive skills. Fortunately, PBL methods promote political, social, and cognitive abilities.

Author Biography

Kurt Burch is Associate Professor of Political Science and International Relations at the University of Delaware.

References

Albanese, M. A., & Mitchell, S. (1993). Problem-based learning: A review of the literature on its outcomes and implementation issues. *Academic Medicine, 68* (1), 52–81.

Barrows, H. S. (1984). A specific, problem-based, self-directed learning method designed to teach medical problem-solving skills, self-learning skills, and enhanced knowledge retention and recall. In H. G. Schmidt and M. L. DeVolder (Eds.), *Tutorials in problem-based learning*. Maastricht, the Netherlands: Van Gorcum.

———. (1996). Problem-based learning in medicine and beyond: A brief overview. In L. Wilkerson, and W. Gijselaers (Eds.), *Bringing problem-based learning to higher education: Theory and practice* (pp. 3–12). San Francisco, CA: Jossey-Bass Publishers.

Bereiter, C., & Scardamalia, M. (1992). Cognition and curriculum. In P. W. Jackson (Ed.), *Handbook of research on curriculum*. Old Tappan, NJ: Macmillan.

Bohman, J. (1996). *Public deliberation: Pluralism, complexity, and democracy.* Cambridge, MA: The MIT Press.

Bonwell, C. C. & Eison, J. A. (1991). *Active learning: Creating excitement in the classroom.* ASHE-ERIC Higher Education Report No. 1. Washington, DC: The George Washington University, School of Education and Human Development.

Burch, K. (2000 April). A Primer on problem-based learning for international relations courses. *International Studies Perspectives, 1*(1), pp. 31–44.

Dewey, J. (1938). *Experience and education.* New York, NY: Macmillan Press.

———. (1959). *Dewey on education.* New York, NY: Teacher's College of Columbia University.

———. (1966/1916). *Democracy and education: An introduction to the philosophy of education.* New York, NY: The Free Press.

———. (1988). *The public and its problems.* In J. A. Boydston (Ed.), *The later works [of John Dewey]* (Volume 2). Carbondale, IL: University of Southern Illinois Press.

Dryzek, J. S. (1996). *Democracy in capitalist times: Ideals, limits, and struggles.* New York, NY: Oxford University Press.

Elshtain, J. B. (1995). *Democracy on trial.* New York, NY: Basic Books.

Freire, P. (1970). *Pedagogy of the oppressed.* (M.P. Ramos, Trans.). New York, NY: Herder and Herder.

———. (1985). *The politics of education: Culture, power, and liberation.* (D. Macedo, Trans.). South Hadley, MA: Bergin and Garvey Publishers.

———. (1994). *Pedagogy of hope: Reliving pedagogy of the oppressed.* (R. R. Barr, Trans.). New York, NY: Continuum Publishing.

Laidi, Z. (1998). *A world without meaning: The crisis of meaning in international politics.* (J. Burnham & J. Coulon, Trans.). New York, NY: Routledge.

Matustik, M. J. B. (1998). *Specters of liberation: Great refusals in the new world order.* Albany, NY: SUNY Press.

Niebuhr, R. (1947). *The children of light and the children of darkness.* New York, NY: Charles Scribner's Sons.

Sleeter, C. E. & Grant, C. A. (1994). *Making choices for multicultural education: Five approaches to race, class, and gender* (2nd ed.). Englewood Cliffs, NJ: Prentice Hall.

Svinicki, M. D., & Dixon, N. M. (1987, Fall). The Kolb model modified for classroom activities. *College Teaching, 35* (4), pp. 141–146.

Tobias, S. (1990). *They're not dumb, they're different.* Tucson, AZ: Research Corporation.

Vernon, D. T. A., and Blake, R. L. (1993). Does problem-based learning work?: A meta-analysis of evaluative research. *Academic Medicine, 68* (7), pp. 550–563.

18

USING PROBLEM-BASED LEARNING IN GENERAL CHEMISTRY

Susan E. Groh

Chapter Summary

Problem-based learning (PBL) has become the central component of a yearlong Honors general chemistry course for science majors. Real-world, contextual problems are used to introduce concepts; students working together find and master the information and ideas needed to generate a solution. Whole-class discussions of the problems are supplemented by minilectures, demonstrations, and other active learning techniques.

Introduction

The main intent of "general chemistry" is to provide an introduction to the most important principles and applications of chemistry. Its roots lie in descriptive chemistry, which focuses on the physical and chemical characteristics of the elements and their compounds and stresses a practical knowledge of reactivity and applications. Over the years, as the nature of the discipline itself has changed, general chemistry has become more complex, with a strong emphasis on the mathematical and theoretical aspects of the science. Rather than supplanting descriptive chemistry, however, this more abstract material has simply been added, with little integration of the two aspects. In addition, as the clientele taking general chemistry has expanded from mostly potential chemistry majors to a host of students from a wide range of disciplines, the desire to show the role of chemistry in each of these areas has led to the incorporation of even more information, resulting in a situation shared by many other survey courses— a curriculum a mile wide and an inch deep. (Lloyd, 1992)

In attempting to narrow the range of the subject somewhat, the University of Delaware offers seven different general chemistry courses for specific subsets of majors, ranging from "Chemistry and the Environment" aimed at fostering chemical literacy in nonscience majors, to a rigorous Honors course for chemists and chemical engineers. Honors General Chemistry 103-104 (CHEM 103-104H), the course described here, targets first-year students in the University's Honors Program who plan to major in a science or a branch of engineering other than chemistry, biochemistry, or chemical or environmental engineering. Most of the students in the class are biology (including premedical interest) or mechanical/civil engineering majors; other disciplines represented include physics, art conservation, athletic training and physical therapy, animal science, psychology, and even economics and political science. Present as well are a handful of undeclared students who are searching for a major. This course, then, addresses academically strong students with a fairly wide range of interests who are taking general chemistry as a requirement for their chosen field of study.

What do such students need to take away from a course in general chemistry? Defining essential topics and the balance between breadth and depth of coverage become issues difficult to reconcile when dealing both with students for whom this is a terminal course in chemistry (e.g., engineers) and those (biologists) who will go on to take several more courses in the discipline. In taking stock of the learning objectives I had for the students in this course, I realized that memorizing a large body of specific chemical facts and information was not among them; few of these students would go on to situations in which retention of such details would be important. Nor did I particularly value their ability to plug numbers into equations—of more importance was for them to understand the relationship expressed by the equation and its implications. What I wanted them to gain from this course were (1) a deeper (rather than superficial) understanding of the fundamental guiding principles of chemistry; (2) the ability to recognize how one can explain the observable properties and behavior of the material world by understanding the behavior of matter at the atomic and molecular level; (3) the ability to identify chemistry in action in the real world and the role it plays in other disciplines; (4) the ability to think critically and analytically and to solve problems; (5) the ability to learn independently by discerning when information is needed and where/how to find it; and (6) the abilities to communicate clearly and to work effectively with others.

Given these goals, the appeal of PBL became clear. What better way to illustrate the importance of chemistry in the real world than by drawing on real-world situations as a stage for introducing chemical concepts? Similarly, using such situations as a starting point allows students to ground the abstract theories they encounter in a more concrete and meaningful context, making the connection between the observable macroscopic and invisible microscopic worlds more obvious. It becomes easier for students to gain and retain a deeper understanding of these principles when they are able to relate them to more familiar situations. Since PBL requires students to assess their own knowledge, to recognize deficiencies, and to remedy those shortcomings through their own investigations, it provides them with an explicit model for lifelong learning. In addition, the group format can teach students the power of working cooperatively, foster the development of valuable communication and interpersonal skills, and help establish a community of learners enriched by the gifts of each person.

Model
Course Format and Rationale

CHEM 103-104H is a two-semester, four-credit course that includes a laboratory component. The typical fall enrollment is 75–85 students; this drops to 40–50 in the spring, since several majors require only one semester of chemistry. Because this is an Honors course, enrollment in the lecture section is limited to 20–24 students, which results in three to four sections in the fall and two to three in the spring. The relatively small laboratory accommodates only 12–14 people, so there is no correlation between a student's lecture and lab section. Students may encounter a completely different set of classmates in lab and in lecture, making it impossible to keep the same groups of students together in both lab and lecture. Each lecture section meets for 50 minutes, three days a week, with the different sections meeting back-to-back.

Several factors figured prominently in the design of this course. As mentioned earlier, the students in this course are mostly freshmen beginning their college studies. They are very bright, motivated by grade pressure to do well but as nonmajors, are often not particularly interested in chemistry, and may even feel intimidated by it. The material they will encounter is often very abstract and quantitative; furthermore, as an introductory course, general chemistry deals with a wide range of seemingly disconnected concepts that provide the basis for understanding the discipline. Many real-world situations involving chemistry are fairly complex and bring in ideas that are well beyond the scope of an introductory course. Given such factors, I felt that these novice students would need a greater sense of structure and direction than they might be able to find on their own. Without any guidance in generating learning issues, it would become easy for them to be sidetracked by trivialities or over-whelmed by complexity—especially since I would be the only instructor avail-able. With five to six groups of students and a 50-minute time slot, it would be hard for me to guarantee having enough time to spend with each group if they encountered difficulties in moving forward.

For these reasons, it seemed to me that a model in which PBL was blended with lecture would be more suitable to this audience than a totally PBL format. Problems would be used to introduce concepts whenever possi-ble, but some ideas (such as bonding theory and quantum mechanics) that have not lent themselves as well to problems could still be dealt with through interactive/Socratic lectures, to keep students actively involved with the mate-rial. Similarly, problems would be constructed with a few guiding questions to steer students in an appropriate direction, rather than leaving them com-pletely on their own. While less student-centered than traditional PBL, this approach helps to compensate for the lack of the dedicated tutors found in the more traditional setting, while still giving students groups the opportunity to chart their own course within a more restricted domain.

A Sample Problem: "Winter Woes"

Perhaps the best way to illustrate this model is to examine a particular prob-lem, how it is used and how it fits into the context of the course. "Winter Woes" (see Chapter 18 appendix) is a problem whose content issues center on solutions and their properties. In its original form, it comprised four parts, each focusing on a specific set of issues. On the first page of the problem, the reader meets two University of Delaware students who, on an icy winter day, are attempting to coax an old car into running. The chugging engine prompts the suggestion from one that they add some dry gas to the fuel tank to keep the fuel from freezing. Somewhat skeptical about whether the gas might actu-ally freeze, they accept that dry gas apparently does something useful in win-ter and move on. The second page finds the students at a local hardware store, trying to choose from among the various deicers on display. On the third page, they are found in a checkout line at a grocery, passing time by reading a story about the problems with the city water purification system, due to recent tor-rents depositing more debris than usual in the feeder streams; included in the report is a comment from a city official advising people to get rid of the heavy chlorine smell in their drinking water by refrigerating it. Finally, as they head home on the last page, a radio newscast tells of the dilemma faced by a small town where flooding has led to the runoff of thousands of pounds of road salt into the reservoir.

In each case, a few questions are used to lead the students in an appropriate direction. For example, in the first part they are asked to predict whether gasoline might freeze around 5°C based on its structure (which they must find), and to determine how the main ingredient in dry gas (methanol) might interact with gasoline and water. The deicer page asks them to pick the best deicer among three choices and to justify their choice. The news story about water purification asks for comments on the city official's advice, as well as bringing in some other material related to how water is purified. The reservoir dilemma is used to prompt a comparative examination of distillation and reverse osmosis as means of removing the salt.

The "Winter Woes" problem kicks off the second semester of the course; as a result, one of its purposes is to stimulate recollection of relevant material covered in the first semester, such as intermolecular forces and their relationship to molecular structure. This first page of the problem prompts this review, as the students go back to reconstruct their knowledge of this area; it also opens up a discussion of the process of solution formation and sets the stage for a discussion of colligative properties. Colligative properties remain the theme in the deicer story and appear again in the discussion of osmosis and distillation. Ideas concerning the effects of temperature and pressure on solubility, as well as a discussion of ways to express concentration follow from the water purification story.

This example is one of the few cases in the course where an entire unit is covered solely through problems. In recent practice, not all parts of the problem are used in class every year because of time constraints: going through all four took around 10 class periods, which was more time than I felt could be allotted to this subject. Generally, just the first and last pages are now used with groups in class, and the other two worked into other assignments or discussions. (The deicer comparison, for example, was transformed into a lab experiment.)

A Typical Learning Cycle

For most of the broad topics covered in this course (e.g., kinetics, stoichiometry, equilibrium, etc.), one to three PBL problems are used to introduce the concepts of interest. Most problems are one to two pages in length, include a few leading questions, and are designed to take about one to two class periods to work through and discuss. Generally, only standard chemistry texts or reference works are necessary resources for these problems, although students are not limited to those; a cartful of such books is made available in the classroom, and the chemistry library (including Web access) is close enough to the classroom that students can make use of it during class if they so choose.

New chapters or topics typically begin with a problem. After the instructor provides a brief introduction to set the stage, groups of students work through the problem either to completion or to the end of that class period. As the students work, the instructor wanders from group to group, listening to get a sense of how the students are approaching the problem, of misconceptions that might arise, and of the general progress being made. If most groups seem to be on the right track, the students may be asked to finish and write a brief report or solution to the problem before the next class. If it seems that more time will be needed, the problem is carried over to the next class. In some cases, especially when time is tight, students may be asked to suspend work on some questions in order to begin reporting on the initial questions. Group work may then be resumed on the remaining questions, or we may switch instead to a whole-class discussion of those points. Having this flexibility is useful since, even with problems that have been used in previous semesters, predicting how much time an individual class section will take to finish is tricky.

Reporting may proceed in different ways. One technique that has been quite successful has been to have each group present a summary of their solution on an overhead transparency. The realization that all of their peers will see their work provides more incentive for them to do a good job than one might have expected! Transparencies have the advantage, particularly when calculations or graphs are involved, of preserving the oral report in a form that can be easily photocopied and duplicated for the class. Students are then free to listen to one another without scrambling to take notes during the presentations. During the reporting phase, the instructor can join in with questions to probe their understanding and to connect ideas that emerge in the discussion with concepts that either have already been seen or will be forthcoming.

Once a problem is finished, a new problem may be introduced to address the next set of concepts. Alternatively, some material may be presented through a lecture, especially in order to model particular types of calculations or analyses, to deal with more abstract topics (e.g., atomic orbitals) that are difficult to address with problems, or simply to touch on ideas that are not revealed through the problems. Chemical demonstrations and hands-on activities are also important components of the course and can be used as the basis for a problem. For example, in a discussion of aqueous reactions, solubility rules are introduced as an empirical guide to predicting salt solubilities. The class is then challenged to apply these rules in identifying two different unlabeled solutions, given a number of possible choices. A number of different known solutions are available to use in cross reactions with the unknowns; in the interest of safety, these reactions are run as a demonstration for the whole class. Each group then examines the precipitation patterns and uses those patterns to identify the unknowns. One unknown gives ambiguous results, so another charge for the group is to suggest other tests that can be tried on the spot to resolve the ambiguity. This combination of PBL problems, lecture, and other activities provides a good balance between group and individual work, and contains components that appeal to a range of learning styles.

Groups

During the first two weeks of a semester, students are still dropping and adding courses; for this reason, collaborative work during this period is done through informal groups pulled together as needed. Once the registration has stabilized, permanent groups of four are formed and maintained for the rest of the semester. In constructing the groups, there is an attempt to balance gender and majors, as well as to spread out the students who report having had two years of high school chemistry (vs. only one). This changes a bit in the spring; since at that point more is known about many of the students, the instructor can better distribute the stronger (and weaker) students, being mindful as well of potential personality conflicts.

The use of groups in CHEM 103-104H is fairly standard. Information about group work is provided in the course syllabus and discussed at the beginning of the course. Each group is asked to meet outside of class to prepare a list of ground rules and consequences (see Chapter 6 of this volume), a copy of which, signed by each group member, must be given to the instructor. The roles of discussion leader, reporter, recorder, and advocate/resource person rotate among the group members at the start of each new problem. Twice during the semester (midterm and at the end), group members evaluate each person's contribution (including their own) to the group (see Chapter 6). After the midterm report, students receive feedback from the instructor concerning their perceived strengths and weaknesses. This feedback is a distillation of constructively phrased comments made by their peers and is presented as coming from the instructor, with student contributions remaining anonymous. The second report counts toward the course participation grade (5% of the total). In general, group assessment and accountability is more informal in this class than in many other PBL courses—most group reports and presentations receive "check/plus/minus" acknowledgments rather than a letter grade. As a consequence, perhaps, there have been virtually no problems with dysfunctional groups. (Interestingly, these qualitative ratings do provide motivation for the group to improve their products—no group has ever received a second "check minus" rating!)

Assessment

Most of the assessment procedures in this class are aimed at the individual student. The final grade is based on the items and weightings in Table 18.1.

Hour exams are blue book based and include essays, interpretation and application questions; calculations are worked into the context of these questions, rather having them stand alone. A periodic table and appropriate constants are always provided, as are certain equations. Students have the limited option of "buying" information, such as equations or formulas that they want for their solution. The information is written into the blue book by the instructor so that it will be noticed at grading time. At that point, the amount of credit that would have been allotted to that piece of information is deducted. This practice allows a student to proceed with the remaining sections of a multipart problem and show his or her abilities to deal with the other concepts addressed by the question. It is up to the instructor to determine the propriety of when and what information to provide; help is limited to specific factual information, as opposed to strategies for solving problems. Three hours are allotted for these exams, and partial credit is used in grading.

The final exam uses multiple-choice questions, due to time constraints in preparing course grades at the end of the semester. The hour and final exams are coupled through a system known as point recapture, modeled after a procedure originally reported by Herschbach and Pickering (1991). The idea of point recapture is that points lost on hour exams are not lost permanently; they may be regained if the student is able to demonstrate mastery of that material on the final exam. The rationale here is to encourage students to revisit concepts they did not understand and learn them before the end of the semester. Each part of a question on an hour exam addresses a particular concept or concepts in a certain way. Once the exams have been graded, a spreadsheet is constructed to keep track of each student's score for each question or part. Questions on the final are correlated to many of the hour exam questions, especially those for which the class average fell below 75%. They are designed to address the same concept(s) from essentially the same direction. If

Table 18.1. Basis for Final Grade Determination in CHEM 103-104H

Item	Percent of Final Grade
Hour exams (three)	45
Final cumulative exam	15
Problem sets and assignments	15
Laboratory reports	20
Class and group participation	5

the student demonstrates mastery by answering the final exam question correctly, the points lost on that question in the hour exam are awarded, raising the score on that exam. The student's final grade is then calculated using these revised hour exam scores.

The laboratory component of CHEM 103-104H is integrated with the rest of the course; assessment here is based largely on lab reports. These are graded using a manuscript revision system (Herschbach & Pickering, 1991): reports are "accepted," "accepted with minor revision," "accepted with major revision," or "rejected." Each category is defined by a rubric made available to the students. Minor revision generally encompasses a limited number of "technical" (rather than conceptual) errors, whereas major revision implies several conceptual errors or a multitude of technical problems. Each category is awarded a set number of points. Students then have the option to revise the reports by correcting the areas in error and resubmitting the original report; revised reports, if done correctly, can earn back most of the points available. This policy, like point recapture, encourages students to deal with their areas of ignorance, rather than discounting them.

Fifteen percent of the grade is allotted to problem sets and other assignments. Three problem sets of five to six questions each are assigned each semester. Students are allowed to work on these together, provided that any consultations with others are documented and that each student provides solutions in his or her own words. Other assignments vary and may include reports, web searches, or other projects. While this has not yet been used, it is feasible to consider converting group projects graded on a check/plus/minus scale into numerical scores to include in this category. The participation component of the grade covers class attendance (roll is taken discreetly at each class); individual participation in class (noted after each class); and group participation (based both on peer evaluations and the instructor's assessment).

Outcomes

Instructor's Observations

It is impossible to declare that student understanding of general chemistry has greatly improved since the introduction of PBL into CHEM 103-104H, in the absence of some way to measure any changes in an objective and reliable fashion. Exam questions and other means of assessment in this course are coupled tightly to how the course plays out in class during a particular semester. Certain topics that are stressed one year may not be emphasized as heavily the following year, depending on what sort of discussions evolve from the problems. Because of the point recapture grading system, it is possible to compare class averages on similar questions from year to year; unfortunately, however, enough data are not available from the pre-PBL period to enable any meaningful comparisons. Qualitatively, it seems that student learning of fundamental concepts is not significantly different with or without PBL. Certainly, student performances (in terms of overall course averages) since the change in course format have been at least as good as those before the change. With many uncontrolled factors contributing to a final grade, however, such comparisons have little validity.

Where the differences are more obvious, however, are in behaviors and skills. While it's hard to tell whether higher-order thinking skills have improved, because those were not really being assessed before the introduction of PBL, I have found that, on average, students do quite well in meeting my expectations in their answers to critical-thinking questions. I have found that the type of exam questions that might have stumped classes from earlier years are now being handled more easily by the majority of the class. Students seem better able to make connections between what they are learning in chemistry and their other classes, particularly among the biologists, and frequently bring up such connections both in class and on exams. Their ability to work together effectively in groups clearly improves throughout the year, as does their facility in using texts and other available resources to find information related to the problem at hand. Perhaps the most obvious difference, though, becomes apparent in comparing class meetings in which students are working on a problem, with those that are predominantly lecture-based. In the former, students need to be told when time is up and the class is over, and often a group or two will remain and continue to work until the next class comes in to displace them. When the class has been all lecture, attention flags, and students are quite aware of quitting time! Even if it were to do nothing else, PBL assures that students spend some time grappling with the material at hand, thinking, and discussing.

Student Response

Student reaction to the PBL format has been quite positive. In final course evaluations, they comment that group work, in particular, is helpful. They benefit from seeing that their peers often have the same questions and misunderstandings that they do; from being able to share scientific ideas with equals; and from the chance to try out their ideas and interpretations without fear of ridicule or dismissal. Groups provide a sense of community that is particularly valued by these first-year students: many report continuing to work together in later classes with their group and classmates from CHEM 103-104H.

The emphasis in the course on critical and conceptual thinking over memorization is also valued. Discussions with students a year or two after they have finished CHEM 103-104H almost invariably include the sentiment that they both learned and retained a lot of information from the course. Premedical students often assert that they anticipated (and/or found) no trouble with the chemistry portion of the MCAT because of the preparation afforded them by this course. While in the minority, a number of students do suggest that they would have preferred a greater amount of structure in the course, with more lecturing, more detailed working out of problems by the instructor in class, and more assigned end-of-chapter problems. On the whole, though, the combination of PBL and lecture used in this course seems to be quite effective.

Summary

A course format that uses a more directed form of PBL in conjunction with lectures and other activities has been found to be an effective way to give first-year students a powerful learning experience in general chemistry. Using problems to introduce concepts provides students with a motivation for learning, as well as the opportunity to share ideas and information with their peers. Using problems with directed questions developed by the instructor provides a structure and focus for the learning issues that might otherwise be lacking among this group of novice nonmajor learners in a somewhat intimidating subject. Lecture segments tie together issues generated in a problem with prior and future concepts, as well as demonstrate "expert" strategies and ways of thinking in the field.

Author Biography

Susan E. Groh is Assistant Professor in Chemistry and Biochemistry and an affiliated faculty member of the University Honors Program at the University of Delaware.

References

Herschbach, D., & Pickering, M. (1991). Making grading less painful. *Journal of College Science Teaching, 21,* 377–379.

Lloyd, B. W. (1992). A review of curricular changes in the general chemistry course during the twentieth century. *Journal of Chemical Education, 69,* 633–636.

APPENDIX TO CHAPTER 18

WINTER WOES

Part 1

For nearly a week, the Eastern seaboard had been blasted by what weather forecasters euphemistically called a "wintery mix" of snow, sleet, and freezing rain. The resulting ice-glazed streets and sidewalks sent residents scurrying for shovels, ice choppers, salt, sand, dirt, cat litter—anything to make transportation possible.

Chris and Lee, the only two of a group of housemates left in Newark during winter session, tried to avoid the problem for a while, until their dwindling supply of Doritos and Diet Coke made a shopping trip imperative. They gingerly made their way out to the car and, after two hours of hacking away ice from the door and windows, managed to get in. Twisting the key in the ignition, Chris was delighted to hear the battery turn over immediately, and mentally posted a note of congratulations for taking advantage of a battery sale just a few weeks earlier. The engine, however, didn't "catch" for a while and, when it finally did, ran very roughly, surging and chugging.

"It acts like it's not getting enough gas," Lee noted. "Have you added any 'dry gas' recently?"

"Huh?" Chris responded.

"It's some stuff that you can add to the fuel tank of the car—it's supposed to keep the fuel lines from freezing up," Lee said. "You just toss a bottle's worth in when you tank up, and it eliminates the chugging. My folks swear by it—kept our old car running forever in the winter. We can get some at the gas station."

"But that doesn't make sense," said Chris the theoretician. "Gasoline doesn't freeze at these temperatures—5°F is cold, but that isn't enough to freeze gasoline—is it?"

"I think it has something to do with the gas getting wet. At least, I thought that's why they called it 'dry gas.' I don't know—I just know that dry gas always worked for us. Whatever the reason, it can't hurt to try."

Questions to Consider

1. In chemical terms, what is gasoline? Given the chemical nature of gasoline, what general expectations do you have about its freezing point? Why?

2. Suppose some water did get into the fuel lines. How would you expect water and gasoline to interact? Will the presence of water change the freezing point of gasoline?

3. The chief ingredient in dry gas is methanol. How might the presence of methanol perturb the gasoline-water system?

Part 2

After tanking up at the gas station, Chris and Lee slide down to Agway on Main Street to pick up some salt for deicing their sidewalk. They've lucked out—a new shipment just came in. The board over the counter reads:

Rock Salt	$5.00/100 lbs.
Calcium Chloride	$18.95/80 lbs.
Urea	$8.00/100 lbs.

"Now what?" Lee said. "I thought salt was salt; I didn't know there were different kinds!" "Beats me," Chris agreed. "I heard the traffic guy saying something about it being too cold for salt to work. Maybe one of these other things would work better."

Questions to Consider

1. Draw up a general description of a good deicing agent for streets. Be prepared to back up your description using chemical principles.

2. Which material do you think they should buy? How much will they need to clear 100 feet of sidewalk? (The sidewalk is 2.5 feet wide, covered by 1 inch of ice. Make any other assumptions you feel are necessary.)

Part 3

Next, they headed for College Square. While waiting in the checkout line at Pathmark, Lee picked up a copy of the Newark Post and saw the following article:

> RECENT RAINS TIED TO STRANGE TASTE
> IN LOCAL DRINKING WATER
>   Newarkers experienced the taste of a summer day at the pool in their drinking water this week. David DeNagy, commercial manager at Wilmington Suburban Water Treatment Plant, said last Friday's heavy rain caused flood conditions at the plant. Water, ice, trees and sticks ran off the streets into the water supply, and turbulent conditions caused a lot of mud to be churned into the water. Chlorine and ferric chloride were increased to combat a high bacteria level.
>   "If customers don't smell chlorine they should be more concerned because it's an inhibitor for bacteria," DeNagy said. DeNagy suggested that customers bottle their water and refrigerate it for a couple of hours to dissipate the chlorine.
>   "The highly treated water. . . . "

"You were right about the chlorine smell, Chris," Lee pointed out. "Better go back for some Evian; I'm not drinking *this* stuff."

Questions to Consider

1. Do you agree with the plant manager's suggestion for getting rid of the chlorine in tap water? Explain.

2. The water purification code specifies that the chlorine content of tap water, at the point of delivery, must be at least 1 g of Cl_2 per

1000 kg of water. Express this concentration in units of molarity, parts per million, and molality.

3. How do chlorine and ferric chloride "combat a high bacteria level"?

Part 4

Driving back from their errands, Chris and Lee listen to the latest reports of storm-related mishaps on the radio. One in particular catches their attention: a small coastal town farther south had thought itself lucky to catch the warm side of the most recent storm. The resulting torrential rains, however, caused a creek retaining wall to fail. The rampaging creek, cresting a dozen feet above flood level, washed tons of temporarily stockpiled rock salt into the town's reservoir. Tests showed the salinity of the reservoir to be nearly 3%—almost as salty as ocean water. The news report indicated that the town was considering its options for repurifying the water, including using the facilities of a nearby chemical plant for distilling the water. In the meantime, the local naval base had sent the townspeople an emergency shipment of reverse osmosis desalinators, normally stocked in life rafts, for purifying water at home.

Questions to Consider

1. Describe what would happen during distillation of the reservoir water. What would the initial boiling point be for a sample of this reservoir water? Why?

2. Suppose the reservoir had been contaminated by a spill of methanol instead of salt. Would this change your answer to the first question in any way?

3. What is meant by reverse osmosis? What is the molecular-level basis for this process?

4. Why isn't salt water drinkable?

<p style="text-align:right">

19

A SKEPTIC'S LOOK AT PBL

Elizabeth M. Lieux

Chapter Summary

The author compares lecture and problem-based learning (PBL) teaching methods in a course for junior-level dietetics majors. Students are shown to achieve comparable test scores on a nationally administered exam. Student evaluations of the course are different for PBL and lecture-based classes.

Introduction

Dietetics, like many other professions, requires a certification examination upon completion of the four-year undergraduate program and a six- to nine-month post-baccalaureate internship. Although undergraduate programs are not driven to teach to the examination, for an academic program to remain accredited students from the college or university must have an 80% pass rate on the exam among other criteria. One of the areas of expected competence for dietitians is an understanding of how foods are prepared and served to large groups of people. Even though most dietitians do not practice as managers of foodservice organizations, they still must have an appreciation of how meals are planned, prepared, and delivered in a variety of settings, including hospitals, nursing homes, university and school dining facilities, and many other sites. For as long as I had been teaching the foodservice management courses, the average score of University of Delaware students was above the national mean in the foodservice component of the Registration Examination for Dietitians. I was unwilling to relinquish this level of success as I considered changes in teaching methods.

The course offered in most schools providing a dietetics program that addresses some of these concepts is Quantity Food Production and Service. This course is viewed negatively by many students because they cannot see why they need to take it, and they cannot imagine themselves working in a large foodservice operation. They struggle through the course with little enthusiasm but with an expectation of earning a good grade because they need it to achieve a place in an internship. A second major constraint in teaching this course is student's limited knowledge of food. Many of them have not tasted a wide variety of foods and are not adventurous about trying new flavors. Few of them have food preparation skills. In recent years, cooking has been reduced in many American homes, and few families share the production and consumption of meals together. Some students have developed a dislike of many foods either through fear of gaining weight or through adoption of a vegetarian lifestyle. Many students are oblivious to the fairly obvious concept that consumption of food is the delivery method of choice to achieve good nutritional status. They naively do not recognize the need to have a comprehensive knowledge of food to be able to provide competent advice to consumers about nutrition.

For 12 years I taught Quantity Food Production and Service to 25 to 80 students per year in a lecture format. Class met twice a week for 75 minutes. Evaluation of learning was through quizzes, exams, and abstracts of foodservice literature. I provided a great deal of information, and students busied themselves with taking excellent notes. I was proud of my lectures, which were encyclopedic and humorous. I told many stories about the *real world* to illuminate the concepts. End-of-semester course evaluations rated the course and me as very good to excellent. The pass rate for the credentialing exam was high, so I was doing my job and the students were learning the material. There was no reason to make any changes in the course except I was bored, and the students were bored. Teaching was just not fun anymore. The final straw came on a day when I was lecturing in a very large tiered classroom that would have held 250 students, and 50 students were present. In the midst of the lecture, a young man took orders from his row of students, left the classroom, and returned with coffee and doughnuts for his neighbors. This experience suggested to me that I was not capturing the interest and attention of students and something different was needed.

A few colleagues in Biology and Physics had adopted PBL and were offering workshops to interested faculty. I attended several before I began to see PBL as an approach that would challenge me and my students to become more connected to a discipline that always has problems and emergencies that must be addressed. What better way to learn Quantity Food Production and Service than working with real problems that occur in a variety of food-service operations?

Model
Problem Development

In 1994, the course included both nutrition and dietetics students and students majoring in Hotel, Restaurant, and Institutional Management (hospitality). It seemed important to write problems that could appeal to both groups because they have different orientations to foodservice. Dietitians tend to view food-service from a nutritional perspective, and hospitality students view foodser-vice from a marketing and profit-making perspective. Problems written about hospitals or nursing homes would not appeal to hospitality students. Problems about fine dining or limited-service restaurants would be dismissed by dietet-ics students. I decided to develop problems that would have some interest to both groups (Lieux & Luoto, 2000).

Both groups needed to understand food safety, so I used a highly publi-cized outbreak of food-borne illness in a quick service restaurant as the basis for three problems. The first was to learn about the microorganism that caused the illness, the second to identify methods that would have prevented the outbreak, and the third investigated the effect of the outbreak on the com-pany. These three problems were very successful with both groups. The dietet-ics students, who have a strong science background, were able to teach the hospitality students about microbiology. The hospitality students helped the dietetics students understand how the stock market, marketing and public relations, and franchise relationships work, and how to read and use the infor-mation from a profit and loss statement.

With the help of a registered dietitian who manages the Child Nutrition Program for a nearby school district, I created another set of problems around the school lunch program. The six problems focused on menu planning, pur-chasing, production controls, and food production methods.

Finally, there was a problem about a business and industry foodservice account that investigated inventory control and another in a hospital setting that explored food delivery systems.

Generally, both groups of students found the problems interesting and learned the intended material. About three years after I began using PBL, the hospitality program developed their own course in Quantity Food Production and Service so their students no longer were a part of this PBL class. My class is now offered exclusively to nutrition and dietetics students.

Comparing PBL and the Lecture Method

I was concerned that students who took the revised course would learn as much as previous students had learned. Certainly, it was evident that PBL students would not be exposed to as many topics because in the lecture format much more information can be presented. I was granted the opportunity to teach the same course in both formats during the fall semester, 1994 (Lieux, 1996). A PBL section and a lecture (LB) section were offered two times a week at 8:00 A.M. When they registered, students did not know there was a difference between the courses. For each course there were 26 sessions, each 75 minutes in length. I used the same course objectives and textbook. Requirements in the LB section were submission of six abstracts of foodservice articles, two group miniprojects, three quizzes, two hour exams, and a final exam. In the PBL section, the students, working in groups of six, studied the problems for two class sections and then turned in a well-referenced group report reflecting what they had learned. Peer evaluations were conducted twice and contributed to the grade in the course. There were two hour tests and a final exam, which used problems. For both classes, a major portion of the final exam was the same. It was an essay exam consisting of eight questions. Students chose five questions to answer. I collected a variety of data, which were used, along with the final exam results, to compare the effectiveness of the two teaching methods. For both sections, there was a pretest of expected knowledge about food and nutrition; a Learning Environment Survey (LES), which provided information about the student's intellectual and ethical maturity administered as a pre- and posttest (Woods, 1994); attendance; and a course evaluation using the Instructional Development and Effectiveness Assessment instrument (IDEA, 1991).

In the fall of 1995, the study was repeated with minor modifications. In the PBL section, the class met three times a week for 50 minutes, worksheets on topics in the textbook were an added requirement, and brief essays were added to the two hour tests. The LES instrument was not repeated.

Outcomes
Demographics

PBL classes were limited to 36 students based on the size of the available PBL classroom. Male students were equally divided between both sections (see Table 19.1). The first time the class was offered twice as many hospitality

Table 19.1. Demographic Characteristics of the Quantity Food Production and Service Classes

	Major and Gender		LB	PBL
1994	Dietetics		24	26
	Hospitality		21	10
1994	Male		7	7
	Female		38	29
1995	Dietetics		41	22
	Hospitality		12	13
1995	Male		8	7
	Female		45	28

Table 19.2. Scores on a 22-Item Pretest of Food Principles and Basic Nutrition

Year		Lecture-based	Problem-based
1994	Number	38	36
		11.9 (± 2.4)	12.5 (± 2.6)
1995	Number	50	32
		12.8 (± 2.9)	12.6 (± 2.8)

students were in LB as were in PBL, and the second time twice as many dietetics students were in LB.

Prerequisite Knowledge
Courses in nutrition and food are taken before students enroll in Quantity Food Production and Service. There was no statistical difference in the knowledge of food and nutrition between the students in LB or PBL sections based on a pretest administered early in the semester (see Table 19.2).

Intellectual Maturity
The Learning Environment Survey measures the maturation of the learner based on Perry's model of intellectual and ethical development (Perry, 1970). The PBL students had a higher level using the Perry model than did the LB students (see Table 19.3). I believe this was because, due to scheduling incompatibilities, all of the Coordinated Program in Dietetics (CP) students were in the PBL class. This group was selected for CP through a rigorous admission process and tended to be more mature and focused than traditional students.

Table 19.3. Learning Environment Survey Comparing Lecture-based Students and Problem-based Students before and after a Quantity Food Production and Service Course

Average Perry Position	Lecture-based	Problem-based
Before	2.45[a]	2.97**
After	2.48	2.83**

[a]1 = dualist, 3 = multiplist, 5 = relativist
**$p < 0.01$

Table 19.4. Average Percentage of Classes Attended in Lecture-based and Problem-based Sections of Quantity Food Production and Service

Year	Lecture-based	Problem-based
1994	67%	90%
1995	82%	92.5%

Neither PBL nor LB increased LES scores. Both groups started at a relatively low level of intellectual and ethical development and remained there. They were in transition between the dualist position (Level 1) and the multiplist position (Level 3). For these students, the preference is for a teacher-centered environment with limited discussion. They prefer to view the teacher as the source of right and wrong answers and wish to learn what they need to know in order to get good grades. This level of student is uncomfortable with an unstructured environment and when forced to take responsibility for his or her own learning. Many students know how to be successful in a lecture-based classroom, but they find the PBL class to be anxiety producing.

Attendance

There were significantly more students coming to class in the PBL sections in 1994 than those who attended the LB section (see Table 19.4).

In 1994, students in the lecture-based class attended an average of 17.5 (± 5.1) classes of 26 sessions offered (range = 6–26). Students in the PBL class attended an average of 23.5 (± 1.9) classes (range = 18–26). In 1995, LB students attended an average of 23 classes of 28 offered (range = 12–28). Students in PBL attended an average of 37 classes of 40 offered (range = 33–40). PBL students are much more likely to attend class even when sessions meet three rather than two times each week.

Table 19.5. Final Exam—Frequency of Answering an Exam Question and Scores for Each Question in Lecture-based and Problem-based Sections of Quantity Food Production and Service, Fall 1994. Students Chose Five of Eight Questions.

Question	Frequency LB%	Frequency PBL%	Points Possible	Average Score ± std LB	Average Score ± std PBL
1	67	64	9	8.4(0.9)	7.3(1.4)*
2	84	92	9	5.0(1.8)	5.6(2.1)*
3	49	47	9	6.9(2.4)	7.1(1.5)
4	13	19	9	5.0(2.5)	7.2(2.1)
5	87	78	9	5.6(1.7)	6.1(1.7)
6	87	81	4	2.9(1.2)	2.9(1.1)
7	49	39	4	1.5(1.2)	2.5(1.1)*
8	62	81	4	2.8(1.3)	3.0(0.9)

*$p < 0.05$

Student Learning as Measured on a Common Final Exam

A major portion of the final examination in both courses was an essay test. Students were offered a choice of questions to answer. The frequency of choosing to answer each question and the scores for each question were collected and analyzed (see Table 19.5 and Table 19.6). All of the students answered the questions in blue books that were merged and graded anonymously.

The first time LB was compared with PBL there were significant differences in the scores for three exam questions but no differences for the total scores on the exams. For questions 2 and 7, PBL students did better. LB students performed better on question 1. Students chose to answer questions at approximately the same frequency. Questions 2, 5, and 6 were answered by over 75% of the students in both classes. Question 4 was chosen by less than 20% of the students in both classes. Only question 8 was chosen by many more PBL than LB students. A linear regression of independent variables (major, GPA, gender, and section) developed a two-variable model as the best fit, $F_{(2,27)}=7.57$, $p < 0.005$, $R^2 = 29.0\%$. That is, 29% of the variance in the final exam total score was accounted for by the grade point average (GPA) and major. Students with higher GPAs and students majoring in hospitality performed better on the final exam. Whether the students took the class LB or PBL did not have an effect on the final exam total score.

Table 19.6. Final Exam—Frequency of Answering an Exam Question and Scores for Each Question in Lecture-based and Problem-based Sections of Quantity Food Production and Service, Fall 1995. Students Chose to Answer Five of Eight Questions.

Question	Frequency LB%	Frequency PBL%	Points Possible	Average Score ± std LB	Average Score ± std PBL
1	44	80	6	5.2(1.3)	5.1(1.2)
2	86	97	6	5.1(0.8)	4.8(1.0)
3	86	86	6	4.7(1.3)	4.0(1.2)*
4	55	26	6	4.5(1.6)	4.7(0.9)
5	46	34	6	4.4(0.9)	4.3(0.9)
6	40	51	6	3.6(2.1)	2.9(2.0)
7	73	35	6	5.4(1.1)	5.0(1.0)
8	75	55	6	4.4(1.3)	4.3(1.3)

*$p < 0.05$

In 1995, for only one question was there a significant difference between the scores of LB and PBL students. There was, once again, no difference between the two sections total scores in the final exam. Linear regression of the independent variables (GPA, GPA in major, number of credits in the major, and section) found that only GPA served as a predictor of the final exam total score. Twenty-nine percent of the variance was accounted for by the GPA.

Student Perceptions of the Course

The IDEA rating form was completed both years. IDEA is a nationally referenced instrument that allows comparison with courses from similar disciplines offered at many institutions. In 1995, the results were compared statistically (See Table 19.7). Only those items for which the sections were different in 1995 are reported.

The percentage of students completing the survey instrument is lower in the LB class, mirroring the attendance rate. Questions 1 through 3 look at the student's perception of their improvement in subject matter mastery and skills as a result of taking the course. LB students thought that they gained more factual knowledge and more professional skills and viewpoints than did PBL students, but PBL students perceived that they enhanced their communication skills much more than did LB students.

Questions 4 and 5 look at the course description. PBL students felt they had more reading and other work than did LB students. The difference

Table 19.7. IDEA Rating-Comparison of Quantity Food Production and Service Taught by Either Lecture-based or Problem-based Learning in 1994 and 1995.

	1994 LB	1994 PBL	1995 LB	1995 PBL
Percentage of students completing the survey	58%	97%	71%	94%
1. Factual knowledge	4.0@	3.3	3.9(0.66)	3.5(1.09)*
2. Professional skills and viewpoints	3.7@	3.5	3.9(0.81)	3.6(1.12)*
3. Effective communication	3.0@	3.7	2.6(1.12)	3.8(1.25)****
4. Amount of reading	2.5#	2.7	2.5(0.82)	3.0(0.81)**
5. Amount of other work	3.2#	3.6	3.1(0.77)	4.2(0.71)****
6. Worked hard	2.8†	3.2	2.7(0.86)	3.9(0.79)****
7. Promoted student-teacher discussion	3.7‡	4.1	3.5(0.94)	4.3(0.85)***
8. Helped student answer own questions	3.6‡	4.1	3.3(0.81)	4.3(0.94)****
9. Encouraged student to express themselves	4.0‡	4.2	3.9(0.89)	4.4(0.86)*
10. Demonstrated the significance of the subject	4.4‡	3.8	4.6(0.59)	3.9(1.01)***
11. Made it clear how each topic fit	4.3‡	3.4	4.6(0.55)	3.9(0.95)***
12. Clearly stated objectives of the course	4.5‡	3.5	4.3(1.10)	3.7(0.98)*
13. Explained course material clearly	4.3‡	3.1	4.3(0.77)	3.7(1.01)**
14. Related material to real life situations	4.6‡	4.0	4.7(0.46)	3.8(1.21)***
15. Stimulated students to high intellectual effort	3.2‡	3.9	2.9(1.18)	3.6(0.90)**
16. Introduced stimulating ideas about the subject	3.7‡	3.5	3.9(0.68)	3.4(1.00)*
17. Gave exams stressing unnecessary memorization	2.5‡	2.6	2.2(1.23)	3.0(1.33)**
18. Exam questions were unreasonably detailed	2.6‡	2.2	1.9(1.09)	2.7(1.07)*

****$p < 0.0001$, ***$p < 0.001$, **$p < 0.01$, *$p < 0.05$
@ 1 = Low, 5 = High
# 1 = Much less than most courses, 5 = Much more than most courses
† 1 = Definitely false, 5 = Definitely true
‡ 1 = Hardly ever, 5 = Almost always

increased from 1994 to 1995 when requirements were added to the PBL class. Question 6 looked at student's self-rating, and here again PBL students thought they worked harder than LB students did. I do not view more reading, more other work, and working hard negatively and am encouraged by these results.

Questions 7 through 9 looked at methods of involving students, and PBL students reported more instances of involvement in discussion, answering their own questions, and expressing themselves. Questions 10 through 14 addressed communication of content and purpose. Here PBL students awarded lower scores than LB students, both in 1994 and 1995. When I looked at these results in 1994, I tried to do a better job in this area, and there was some improvement in 1995. I suspect these scores will never be as high in a PBL course as in a LB course because the students have a greater responsibility for developing their own learning issues and conducting the research. When faculty no longer tell them everything they need to know, the students are likely to believe they have to create the structure of the course themselves.

Questions 15 and 16 look at creating enthusiasm. PBL students believed they were stimulated to high intellectual effort but did not believe that there was an introduction of stimulating ideas about the subject. The last two questions were about preparing exams. PBL students were less satisfied with their exams than LB students and thought they had to remember more details.

What may be seen from these results is a preference on the part of less mature students for an instructor-centered course. They still would like to learn in ways that are comfortable with less responsibility for their own learning. They do recognize that their communication skills are greatly improved. Along with this are greater opportunities for teacher-student discussion and self-expression. They yearn, however, for the teacher to tell them what they need to learn and how everything fits together. We can hope that increases in the use of active learning methods at all levels of education will relegate using primarily lecture-based teaching methods to the scrap heap. Then perhaps students will expect to share responsibility for their own learning with the faculty instead of expecting the instructor to shoulder most of the burden.

Performance on the Registration Examination for Dietitians

Scores in foodservice management for our students have, with very few exceptions, been above the national average (see Table 19.8). The first time Quantity Food Production and Service was offered as a PBL course was fall semester 1994. Not all of the dietetics students were in the PBL section. This was

Table 19.8. Comparison of Test Scores in Foodservice Management for University of Delaware Graduates and All Test Takers Nationally in the Registration Exam for Dietitians

Year	Month	Total	Passed	UD Score (± std)	National Score (± std)
1991	May	4	4	18.75 (1.41)	16.01 (4.45)
1991	October	8	7	18.50 (2.55)	17.51 (4.11)
1992	May	4	4	18.00 (0.71)	16.58 (4.35)
1992	October	9	9	19.88 (3.48)	17.84 (4.30)
1993	May	2	2	21.0 (2.0)	18.0 (4.2)
1993	October	13	12	18.5 (3.3)	18.4 (4.1)
1994	May	5	4	21.80 (1.33)	17.95 (4.44)
1994	October	10	10	20.60 (3.23)	18.81 (3.91)
1995	October	16	15	18.38 (3.50)	18.86 (4.00)
1996	May	1	0	12.00 (0.00)	18.44 (4.13)
1996	October	13	12	18.15 (4.47)	18.34 (4.06)

Standard and Exam Were Changed

Year	Total	Passed	UD Score (± std)	National Score (± std)
1997	17	17	18.88 (2.14)	17.66 (3.82)
1998	28	25	18.50 (3.74)	18.15 (3.72)
1999	18	17	17.50 (4.35)	17.11 (4.13)

true in 1995 as well. Students who had the PBL experience, however, started challenging the registration exam in 1996 and, from then on, more and more of the test takers would have had their Quantity Food Production and Service as a PBL class. Only in 1995 and 1996 were scores for University of Delaware students not above the national average. Since then, these scores have been above the national average in foodservice management. This clearly indicates that students are as well prepared using PBL methods of teaching as they were using LB methods.

Ways the Course Has Changed Since Its Inception

Every semester I find some modification to make to the course, most of which have improved it. Group size has been decreased from six to four students. This has placed added responsibility on each member of the group, and there is less opportunity for a student to resist contributing to the group. Groups are not willing to carry unproductive members, and this is more evident in a group of four.

Quizzes are given after each problem is completed. The content of the quiz is based on the problem and the worksheet that supports the problem. Seventy percent of the quiz is for individual effort, but there is always one question that is completed by the group working together.

I developed technology enrichments for the course a couple of years ago that seem to have had a positive impact. A web page contains the syllabus and resources for each problem. I identified a variety of Internet sites that provide useful information. Many of the periodical articles that I had previously placed on reserve in the library are now available through electronic reserves in the library. I present the wrap-ups for each problem using multimedia presentation software (PowerPoint™). This has increased the student's interest in the information.

Deliverables for each problem are usually a written group report. For some problems, oral reports are presented. This has helped students improve their presentation skills. Of late, most groups elect to use PowerPoint™ as their method of providing the information visually. The PBL classroom used for this course has fine multimedia capabilities. I make a laptop computer available, and students bring their presentations on disks they have created elsewhere. They are developing great skill in utilizing this medium and delivering more effective presentations.

Peer tutors have been used in many semesters to work with the groups as they develop an understanding of each problem. This has been particularly effective when one tutor is responsible for two to three groups. The tutors are able to communicate to students my expectations in ways that help them to learn.

Lessons Learned

Over the years, I have gained a great deal of confidence in PBL. I find that the students are certainly capable of learning much information on their own and applying it to real-world situations. PBL has great advantages in helping the students develop team skills, improve their oral and written communication skills, and help them to think critically. Many students would still prefer that I revert to previous teaching methods and tell them everything they need to know. I continue, however, to believe that using active teaching methods is key to helping the students become lifetime learners. No profession allows members to use only the information they acquired as students. It is crucial for members of the profession to continue to learn. I believe the PBL helps students acquire the skills they need to continue their education on their own.

Author Biography

Elizabeth M. Lieux is an Associate Professor in the Department of Nutrition and Dietetics at the University of Delaware.

References

Instructional Development and Effectiveness Assessment. (1991). IDEA system, Center for Faculty Evaluation and Development, Kansas State University.

Lieux, E. M. (1996) *The effect of teaching method on student's knowledge of quantity food production and service, course evaluations, and propensity for participative management.* Unpublished Doctoral Dissertation. Virginia Polytechnic Institute and State University, Blacksburg, VA.

Lieux, E. M., Luoto, P. K. (2000). *Exploring quantity food production and service through problems.* Upper Saddle River, NJ: Prentice Hall, Inc.

Perry, W. G. (1970). *Forms of intellectual and ethical development in the college years. A scheme.* New York: Holt, Rinehart and Winston, Inc.

Woods, D. R. (1994) *Problem-based learning: How to gain the most from PBL.* Hamilton, ON: Griffith Printing Limited, Adapted from Moore and Fitch Inventory for Learning Preference reprinted with permission.

20

PBL IN PRESERVICE TEACHER EDUCATION

Eugene Matusov, John St. Julien, and James A. Whitson

Chapter Summary

Two courses in the preservice elementary teacher education were revised, initially, to develop models that might be used throughout the program. While useful models were developed in a variety of problems within these courses, the instructors conclude that differences between "schoolish" and authentic problems are more essential to the success of problem-based learning (PBL) than are the "models" provided by successful PBL problems and courses.

Introduction

In this chapter, we report and discuss our experience revising two courses in the undergraduate program in elementary teacher education. We initially intended that these two revised courses might provide models for using PBL in preservice teacher education—models that could be replicated throughout other courses in our ETE program. Our experience leads us to conclude, however, that although effective PBL problems or courses do provide models that might be adopted and adapted in designing other effective problems and courses, it is a mistake to focus on these models, forms, and design structures as the key to effectiveness in PBL.

From the "Model Problem" to the "Model" Problem

There is a crucial difference between our project and others reported in this volume. While others provide models for using PBL in teaching physics, biology, nursing, and other disciplines, we are attempting to assist our students in their own preparation as teachers, so they will be able and disposed to use PBL in teaching social studies, reading, science, and math to their own students in the elementary grades. Hence, while our courses might be seen as providing models for the use of PBL in other college education courses; within our courses, we were also setting out to model PBL as an approach that our own students could use in their elementary school teaching.

Modeling PBL in the Elementary Social Studies "Methods" Class

In survey after survey, elementary and secondary students invariably identify social studies as the school subject they like least (or dislike most). This is routinely attributed to the familiar practice of teaching history, geography, or civics by having students read one chapter after another in their textbook, without any motivation other than curricular mandates, and then answer questions found at the end of each textbook chapter.

The challenge of designing and implementing units on a wide variety of social studies topic areas, in ways that are interesting, engaging, and effective for student learning, is a huge problem for elementary school teachers. Our students face this challenge in the form of their requirement to design and teach a social studies unit in the elementary or middle school classroom where they have been placed for the semester. The topic for their unit is determined by the curriculum for the classroom in which each pair of our students has been placed. In other words, a team of two preservice teachers may be responsible for planning and teaching a unit on a topic area in history, geography, civics, or economics that they may never have studied in their own college or precollege careers and that may be different from the topics to be taught by any of their classmates in the methods course.

As noted earlier, the routine or default way of dealing with this problem is reliance on the textbook. Our students have always known that this would not work for them, simply because it would not satisfy their professor in the college methods class. Before our revision of the course using PBL, students generally tried to deal with this challenge by brainstorming and scrounging around for activities related to their topics that would be more fun and more engaging than a slavish reliance on the textbook. Often, they did come up with clever and inventive ideas for activities that could really be a lot of fun for their students. Almost as often, though, it would be hard to see the value of those activities—beyond their entertainment value—in terms of learning outcomes that would result for their students. Moreover, when their units did include activities that could be expected to produce some real learning benefits for their elementary or middle school students, those activities often did not build on one another in a progressive or coherent way to advance the students' understanding of the topic or their ability to understand comparable topics in the social studies subjects.

Preservice teacher education students are often at a loss to understand why plans like this will not receive the grade they feel that they deserve, and the students feel that they are entitled to be told explicitly what they need to do to earn an "A." The directions they seek, and typically are given, often take the form of formalistic criteria, such as the number of "objectives" to be stated for each lesson in the unit; how many of these objectives should be stated in the form of Bloom's (Bloom, 1956) "higher level" objectives; how many different student grouping arrangements, or types of student activities, should be included over the course of the unit; how many (and what types) of resources should be included in their list of references for the unit, etc.

Of course, there is a good chance that explicit and detailed directions of this kind will result in better units being designed by methods students. This, however, fails to solve the problem of the methods course itself, since those "better units" might be produced by students who have only learned how to follow formalistic directions and not how to design their own units on the basis of their own assessment of how to treat a given social studies topic in a way that will be most beneficial for the students in their classrooms later in their careers. This prospect can be seen, in fact, in the units that have met all the formalistic criteria (number and variety of activities, etc.) but still fail to add up to a coherent unit that will provide real learning benefits for the elementary school students. In these cases (and even in many cases where those formalistic directions actually *did* result in better unit plans), the problem that the preservice teacher education students were focusing on, and the problem that motivated and organized their efforts, was the "schoolish" problem of how to satisfy their professor, rather than the authentic problem of how to design the most effective unit to promote learning by their elementary school students.

We were able to transform this situation by revising our course using PBL. Instead of giving them formalistic criteria for better unit plans and then letting them focus on the "schoolish" problem of how to satisfy our criteria, we let them take on, for themselves, the problem of designing their best unit on their topic for their students—and the constituent problem of figuring out the standards, criteria, and requirements demanded by that task. Instead of them asking us how many objectives should be stated in each lesson plan, or how many and what kinds of resources would be required for their unit, we would now ask them to figure out the answers to such question in the course of working through their own problem of designing their best unit on the topic for their students.

Of course, we could not do this just by telling them, "It's your problem now, you need to figure it all out for yourselves." That is precisely what they needed to learn how to do in our class, and what they had never before learned how to do. This is, however, where the PBL model would provide just the help that they would need.

Our plan was that we would introduce a PBL model for group problem solving at the beginning of the course and then provide problems that would serve as opportunities for them to practice using this PBL model over the semester—with at least one extended problem that would serve almost as a direct rehearsal for the culminating problem of their final unit plans.

We first introduced PBL to our students, at the beginning of their social studies methods class, by giving them a version of the plea negotiation problem that had been developed by Dr. Valerie Hans for a course in criminal justice at the University of Delaware (UD) (see Chapter 13 of this volume for discussion of the Plea Negotiation problem). For about two weeks, along with reading and discussing other introductory materials for the course, our students worked in four-member negotiating groups as prosecutors, defendants, defense counsel, and surviving victims, doing research on criminal and case law, sentencing guidelines, and conflicting arguments on public policy, while negotiating toward a plea agreement within each of their groups. We intended that this process would provide a model that our students could use in groups working through other problems throughout this course, and in their careers, including their final social studies unit plans for the semester.

We also intended that by working through the Plea Negotiation problem, they would get the experience of PBL learning with a problem designed for students at their own (i.e., college undergraduate) level, which could serve as helpful background for them in designing PBL experiences for students in the elementary and middle school grades. This also provided an opportunity for reflecting on the importance of specific learning goals as the basis for how any given problem should be used. In this case, our students could see that the same Plea Negotiation problem could be appropriate in both the criminal justice and the social studies classes but that it should be used differently to serve the differing purposes of each class. Criminal justice majors are learning how to perform the roles within that system, so some aspects of the process may have more importance in that context. As an opportunity for learning about civics within the elementary or middle school social studies curriculum, however, it would be more important for students to discover how the three branches of government interact within particular cases, such as this one, to serve and protect the conflicting principles, values, and interests that our governmental and legal systems are designed to orchestrate.

After their introduction to this PBL model with the Plea Negotiation problem, our students were given a larger problem to work on over several weeks, in which they worked together in planning units or lessons on a topic area shared by the entire class. In the spring semester of 1999, the topic area was presidential impeachment. This really was a problem area for elementary school teachers at the time. Children were hearing about impeachment at home, on the streets, and in the news. On the one hand, this generated a level of interest and curiosity that would normally be a teacher's greatest asset. On the other hand, some of the seamier and more controversial aspects of the conflict over President Bill Clinton's impeachment made the topic seem extremely perilous to many grade school teachers. Children would not let this topic simply be ignored (and an attempt to do so would have taught the children questionable lessons in any case), and the topic involved so much rich content in history, government, and politics that in some ways this was a social studies teacher's dream come true. How could this topic be handled, with *particular* classes of grade school children? This was the problem that our students grappled with that semester. Since all groups in the class were working in the same problem area, they could discover from each other the wide variety of possible approaches to a single topic. It also was possible to provide more coaching, scaffolding, and peer support for everyone, while they could work through a unit planning process that was almost a rehearsal for their research and development of final social studies unit plans, which each pair of methods students would need to work on more independently.

Beyond Modeling: Instructional Strategies and Reflective Practices

Instructional Strategies and Reflective Practices (ISRP) is a course that focuses on instructional strategies, classroom management, lesson plans, and educational philosophies. One concern in this class is for students to learn how to provide sensitive guidance for all children with diverse educational needs. Students often raise this issue of dealing with "slow learners" in their teaching practicum associated with this class, while providing challenging instruction for all of the children. Many believe that the only way to provide sensitive guidance is through one-on-one teaching or through tracking children by their abilities. However, they know that one-on-one teaching or tracking is logistically not always possible in the classroom. Besides, many of these students are aware of negative consequences of tracking, which has often resulted in an increasing gap between "high" and "low" tracks, and in low-track children being stigmatized and losing self-esteem and motivation for their academic learning.

Having participated in the UD Winter Institute, the instructor was eager to design a PBL unit in which students would develop sensitive instruction for a group of children with diverse levels of educational abilities and skills. As a model for designing this unit, the instructor referred to the Plea Negotiation problem (discussed previously) that had been used as an introduction to PBL for faculty participants during the first two days of the Institute. Along with the other Institute participants, we were all impressed by the design of the plea negotiation problem and its effectiveness as a learning experience within the Institute. On this basis, it appeared that the Plea Negotiation problem provided an exemplary design that could be directly replicated in designing a problem on sensitive guidance and instruction for diverse learners. Unlike the social studies methods course discussed previously, in which the Plea Negotiation problem itself was given to the students for them to work through, in this case the students were *not* given that problem to work on. In this case, the instructor looked to the design of the Plea Negotiation problem as a model for the design of a different problem for this class.

Following the Plea Negotiation problem as a model, the instructor developed a problematic scenario that he calls the "Sitting Disability" problem. According to this scenario, the second grade teacher referred her student, Mike, for medication, because of his assumed Attention Deficit Disorder (ADD) problem evident in his distracting other children in the class during independent reading/writing classroom activities. From time to time the student was taken from class to learn the alphabet because he could not read or write. It was suspected that the student's distracting behavior was not caused by ADD but was his way of trying to get help (or some alternative activities) from his classmates in the reading/writing classroom activities, in which he could not participate on his own.

Following the model of the Plea Negotiation problem, the scenario for this problem described four specialists: an instruction specialist, a curriculum specialist, a child psychologist, and a language arts specialist, who are supposed to design a language arts lesson (or an unit) for a group of second grade students, including Mike, that should involve sensitive guidance for all the students in the group.

The rest of the two-week Sitting Disability unit followed the structure of the Plea Negotiation problem and involved class meetings of the four specialist teams, their work outside of the class using Internet sources to address questions that emerged in the teams' meetings, team meetings in class for bringing information together, and finally, reassembling the groups to design an inclusive language arts lesson.

The unit did not work. Students complained about the work required outside of class (despite the fact that they did weekly miniprojects at home on a regular basis); they asked how many questions minimum each student should take care of and how much writing they should do in reply to the questions; student questions were very shallow; they cut and pasted texts from suggested Internet websites without much thinking about whether and how the texts address their questions; they never went beyond the suggested websites; they worried how much the group project would contribute to the final grade for the class for each group member; their designs for inclusive lessons were not informed by the searches they did and were reduced to tracking at best and to low-quality drills in reading and writing at worst; and so forth. It was anything but active learning. It was a somewhat torturous experience of getting through, for them and the instructor.

Why? Why did the model work so beautifully for Dr. Hans in criminal justice and so badly for us in this course? Of course, we could focus on differences in educational attitudes and motivation between criminal justice and education students, and blame our students for being lazy, dull, and disinterested—PBL was simply not for them. We know, however, that this would not be true, fair, or productive. What makes the difference between successful PBL and its failure? We know that the answer is not in the structure of the PBL lesson, since that was directly copied from the model of the Plea Negotiation lesson. We could blame the instructor for ineffective implementation of a basically good model. Our reflection on this experience, however, convinces us that a focus on the structure of successful PBL problems, taken as models, is not the key for understanding what will make the difference between successful and unsuccessful uses of PBL.

PBL is often discussed in terms that suggest there is a choice to be made between problem-based learning and learning that is not problem-based. We would argue to the contrary that *all learning is problem-based*. The question is not *whether* learning will be problem-based or not, but rather *what kind* of problem will motivate and determine students' learning. Will student efforts be addressing "schoolish" problems (e.g., problems of figuring out how to satisfy the instructor's arbitrary requirements with a minimum of effort), or authentic problems (e.g., for our preservice teacher education students, the real problems they will be dealing with as teachers, as well as—in the case of social studies, for example—real problems in the social world or in the history and social science disciplines)?

In the case of the Plea Negotiation problem, both the instructor's and the students' concerns centered on the plea negotiation issues. In contrast, in the case of the Sitting Disability problem, despite the fact that the problem was structured on the same model, the instructor's and students' concerns were mutually exclusive to each other and did not consider each other as legitimate. Of course, the instructor's and students' concerns are not the same and should not be the same because the instructor is supposed to focus on guiding the students, while the students are supposed to focus on learning and on accomplishing learning activities. However, the relationship between the instructor's and students' concerns has to be shared, supportive, compatible, and open for public negotiation in the class to make PBL authentic. *PBL emerges from the relationship between the instructor's and students' concerns in the classroom activities—this relationship defines whether PBL is "schoolish" or authentic.*

In the Sitting Disability lesson, the instructor worked against, rejected, and overruled the students' vision of how to provide sensitive guidance for children with diverse educational needs, rather than working with students' visions of the problem. The starting point of the Sitting Disability lesson was for the students to reject their own approach to sensitive guidance resulting in tracking and one-on-one tutoring and, instead, to focus on the instructor's agenda of how to design inclusive guidance in this problematic situation. The students were precluded from working on the real problem, as they understood it, so instead they devoted their efforts to the "schoolish" problem of satisfying the demands of their instructor.

Based on this analysis of the experience with PBL in ISRP one semester, the instructor revised the use of PBL for the following semester, with a focus on working *with* students' concerns and visions rather than struggling *against* them. For example, at the very beginning of the teaching practicum, the instructor asked the students to discuss with children in their elementary school classes what their favorite book is in their class and then to reflect on this learning activity. The students' opinions about the activity were split from high excitement and endorsing the activity as extremely educational, to disparagement of the activity as having very low educational value.

In the next class meeting, each group was asked to report on pedagogical aspects of the activity, such as pedagogical values, classroom management, organizational transitions, concerns and problems that they had, and the children had had, during the favorite book activity, and their emerging relations with the children. To their surprise, their replies fell into the two patterns that fit the two groups. For example, the group that considered the activity as successful emphasized how their children were supportive, cooperative, and collaborative, while the other group reported disciplinary problems.

When the activity profiles for the two groups were completed, the students shifted their attention to why these two different patterns occurred. Initially, some students suggested that the difference was in the children, since the activity was the same. However, many students quickly noticed that the activities actually were *not* the same! In the group where the activity was successful, the activity goals for the children centered on sharing their favorite books with their classmates and on persuasive speech. In the group where the activity was not successful, the activity goals for the children centered on competition and on imposing their choices on the other children.

After the class, many students commented that they were surprised to learn so much from the their own unsuccessful teaching activity. Students in this activity repeated to some degree their instructor's own teaching experience, described previously. At this point, they join the community of educators learning how to design authentic PBL in their classrooms.

Assessment of Student Learning

Assessment of student learning in the courses has been done partly on the basis of the same kinds of student products that have been used for grading purposes in the past. For example, students have continued to develop and implement lesson plans and unit plans in social studies, which must not only demonstrate mastery of the principles of curriculum design and planning for instruction, but must also demonstrate an understanding of teacher strategies for addressing the problems that elementary school students have in mastering the skills and conceptual content of social studies subjects, such as civics, history, geography, and economics. We believe that such products from the past two semesters demonstrate superior mastery as compared with comparable products from previous semesters.

The most striking improvement in student learning was seen in their final units and in their lesson plans for teaching. ECSS is the course in the final block before student teaching in which units are required. As such it has traditionally been the first place where a large number of the complex elements of teaching and curriculum design are brought together in the production of a practical project. Short of student teaching itself, this can be regarded as the capstone activity of the student's academic career of on-campus coursework prior to their student teaching, and as a foundation for their student teaching internships. To construct a viable unit the lessons must be sequenced, build students emerging competencies and provide a satisfying way for students to become aware of their own developing abilities. It is hardly surprising that students regard this as one of the most difficult tasks they engage in, and it is disappointing that professors generally find many of the same problems in student units year after year and in different institutions.

One important difference in the PBL approach is that it naturally lends itself to engaging students in assessing the value and quality of their own learning in the course of their problem-based learning experiences. With PBL, students' decisions about how to respond to problematic situations will depend upon their own active deliberations on the differences between more and less worthy solutions to the embedded problems and the criteria upon which such judgments should be based. In the PBL-revised course, teacher education students have been discovering how student learning can be enhanced through ongoing engagement in assessing the quality and value of their own work and their accomplishments, through informal communication, as well as more formal assessment rubrics. This also supplies them with strategies for engaging their own students in the active assessment of learning in their elementary school classrooms.

Student units in the last two semesters have shown a dramatic improvement in quality in our judgment. Most noticeably, they are more likely to be designed around issues that are actually meaningful, even when the cooperating teacher in the student's field placement dictates the topic. Individual lessons are better written, and the unit is more likely to clearly build, and build on, the emerging abilities of those taught. The complex of reasons for this improvement is difficult to trace in detail, but preliminary analysis appears to show that they are related to the PBL portions of the class.

In the course ISRP, students were assigned an open-ended essay in which they were to reflect on what they've learned in the class. Student statements in the essays were analyzed and tabulated (see Table 20.1), showing that students from PBL classes mentioned that they learned more and experienced richer curricula than students from non-PBL class.

Outcomes

At the beginning of this project, we expected that we would see our students designing PBL problems for the elementary school children in their practicum and (later) student teaching placements, and that this would be the ultimate test of our own project. Although we have seen some impressive PBL units designed and implemented by our students in their practica, our students are still more often designing units that would not be recognized as PBL in the

Table 20.1. Tabulated Results from Student Reflection Essays

Important Aspects of the Class Mentioned by the Students	PBL, N=21	Non-PBL, N=24	P-value, T-test
1. Sharing practicum experiences, ideas, and problems	81%	88%	0.2805
2. Student wants to use the strategies learned in the class in her or his future teaching	57%	21%	0.0127
3. Appreciation of cooperative learning and learning through collaboration	48%	17%	0.0144
4. Discussion of educational philosophies	62%	4%	0.0051
5. Discussion of children's active learning (including PBL)	71%	8%	0.0000
6. Diversity of views and different ways of dealing with problems	33%	25%	0.2758
7. Considering pros and cons of educational strategies, critical thinking	24%	4%	0.0347
8. Focusing on shared ownership for decision making	19%	0%	0.0211
9. Value of reflection	52%	21%	0.0151
10. Discussion of problems and problematic situations	33%	8%	0.0229
11. Educational eclecticism (let's mix all educational philosophies together)*	0%	17%	0.0214
12. Diversity of ways that students learn	24%	4%	0.0321
13. Focus on learning and not on grade	5%	4%	0.4628
14. Stressless class	24%	17%	0.2822
15. Diversity of teaching styles and techniques	76%	17%	0.0000
16. Flexible and open-minded teaching	24%	4%	0.0347

*This item indicates the students' lack of understanding of educational philosophy according to the instructor.
P-value < 0.05 indicates items with statistically significant differences between the classes.

(continued)

Table 20.1. Tabulated Results from Student Reflection Essays—*continued*

Important Aspects of the Class Mentioned by the Students	PBL, N=21	Non-PBL, N=24	P-value, T-test
17. Report a dramatic change in student's perspectives, beliefs, and attitudes	52%	0%	0.0001
18. Critique of transmission of knowledge educational approach	24%	0%	0.0106
19. Reasoning and backing up ideas and opinions in the essay	43%	0%	0.0004
20. Appreciation of learning through PBL and teaching activities in the class	76%	0%	0.0000
21. Appreciation of support from the classmates, feeling of a community	48%	0%	0.0002
22. Increased confidence in teaching	24%	0%	0.0106
23. Emphasis on a connection between instruction and learning	29%	0%	0.0052
24. Positive attitude toward the class	100%	75%	0.0055
Average number of the items mentioned by each student	11.0	3.5	0.0000

*This item indicates the students' lack of understanding of educational philosophy according to the instructor.
P-value < 0.05 indicates items with statistically significant differences between the classes.

classic sense. We do see this as a continuing challenge for our work in these courses and the larger ETE program: i.e., the "problem" of using PBL within our program more effectively in ways that will result in greater use of PBL by our students and our graduates in their own classrooms.

At the same time, we already do see impressive positive results in other forms. As we have revised our courses using PBL, we have found that—even when they are not using a "model" of PBL problems as such—our students are engaged in working more authentically on the real problems of curriculum and instruction, rather than the "schoolish" problems of satisfying course requirements. In designing social studies units, students are far more engaged now than before with the nexus of (a) social and historical problems embedded in the social studies content, (b) the problems that will actually be experienced by their students in the conduct of their lessons, and (c) the teacher's problems of designing experiences for students so that the elementary school students will be progressively developing their capacities for dealing with real historical and social problems while meeting the requirements of state-mandated curricula and standards-driven testing programs.

Suggestions for Adoption

Successful PBL involves more than just repackaging the content of traditional lectures into problematic scenarios and group work; it requires a transformation of students' experiences, concerns, and visions. Authentic PBL lessons can come as direct replies to students' concerns from their practicum, or from experiences initiated by the instructor. In any case, the students' experiences, concerns, and visions are in the center of the classroom activities being accepted, legitimatized, and problematized by the instructor. This seems to make the difference between "schoolish" and authentic PBL.

Authors' Biographies

Eugene Matusov and John St. Julien are Assistant Professors, and James A. Whitson is Associate Professor of Education at the University of Delaware.

References

Bloom, B. S. (Ed.). (1956). *Taxonomy of educational objectives: The classification of educational goals.* New York: Longman.

21

INTRODUCTORY PHYSICS

A Problem-Based Model

Barbara A. Williams

Chapter Summary

This chapter describes a model used to incorporate problem-based learning (PBL) into a two-semester algebra-based introductory physics course. Student reaction to the course is detailed, as well as student achievement results.

Introduction

Introductory Physics is a two-semester Honors course for students majoring in biology, chemistry, biochemistry, premedicine, sciences other than physics, and unrelated disciplines. Set at the level of high school algebra and elementary trigonometry, this course is well-suited for students who can evaluate algebraic expressions, solve verbal mathematical problems, represent functional relations graphically, and manipulate first- and second-order algebraic equations. Designed for freshmen and sophomores, the course in its early offerings attracted students who postponed introductory physics until their junior year; however, in the past two years, dramatic shifts have occurred in the enrollment demographics. In this current year, sophomore students for the first time represent the majority. Enrollments have never exceeded 30 students because small-sized classes are one of the attractive features of the University Honors Program.

In general, Honors students tend to be highly motivated and goal-oriented. Students who enroll in this course are no exception. Some have never studied physics in high school, for most this will be the only formal physics course they will have at the college level, and nearly all have underdeveloped skills and preparation in basic algebra. In recent years, I have tried to quantify and document the mathematical skills of the students who select this course. Each student enrolled in the course since 1998 has taken a 10-item diagnostic covering the fundamentals of basic algebra. The median score on this algebra diagnostic is at the 60% level and supports my earlier undocumented observations that underdeveloped skills and preparation in algebra can be formidable barriers for nearly half the students who take this course.

Brief History of the Course

Barbara Duch was responsible for the initial development of the Honors Introductory Physics course at the University of Delaware. In 1992, she taught a newly combined recitation and laboratory section created to provide a unique experience for Honors students who had a common lecture with more than 200 regular students. This model of a single course director who delivers the lecture and multiple sections of recitation and laboratory taught by different teaching assistants is a popular instructional strategy for teaching large numbers of students in science courses. The present course grew out of that joint Honors recitation/laboratory section, when in 1993, lecture, recitation, and laboratory sections were separated from the larger lecture-driven course, established as an independent, autonomous Honors Introductory Physics course in the University Honors Program, developed and taught by Barbara Duch. During this period, she designed complex real-world problems and open-ended experiments to teach physics principles and their applications to the real world and used cooperative- and problem-based learning strategies to develop critical-thinking and problem-solving skills.

In 1994, I inherited the teaching duties of this course and continued to use the cooperative- and problem-based learning strategies initiated by Barbara Duch. When I discovered that some students could do well on the real-world problems and open-ended laboratories without a complete understanding of the underlying physics principles, I introduced that same year conceptual assignments as part of the course content to help students make explicit connections among the physical concepts, their mathematical representations, and the physical world. Conceptual assignments are carefully selected to expose students' alternative conceptions, in particular, those that have proven to be highly resistant to instruction. Qualitative questions that probe for conceptual understanding were included in group assignments, individual homework assignments, group and individual examinations, real-world problems, and the laboratories. After teaching the course for more than five years, I have made new contributions to the course materials in the form of laboratory activities, experiments, and real-world problems.

Introductory Physics Model
Instructional Strategies

I continue to use both cooperative- and problem-based learning strategies to teach basic physics principles and their applications to the real world. During the first class meeting, permanent groups of three to four students are formed using a random process and a gender template to ensure that at least two female students are assigned per group. Gender-based educational research has shown that female students tend to be more verbal and assertive in academic interactions that involve other females (Hall & Sandler, 1984; Gabriel & Smithson, 1990). Members work together on each activity until they all understand and complete the assignment in each learning cycle described in the following sections. In order for the group learning to be truly cooperative, the following elements must be present: positive interdependence, individual accountability, face-to-face promotive interaction, and interpersonal skills (Johnson, Johnson, & Smith, 1991).

Single submissions of group assignments, solutions to real-world problems, laboratory reports, and group examinations are course requirements that foster positive interdependence. I have found that group solutions resulting from a consensus encourage dialogue that challenges alternative conceptions of the physical world and promotes the use of critical-thinking skills in defense of arguments and positions taken by members of a group. Each year, I see students teaching other members inside and outside their groups. These cooperative tasks stimulate impromptu teaching moments among students. In addition, to collaborative tasks, students must adopt a collaborative role (e.g., discussion leader, recorder, and skeptic) within the group as another means of building positive interdependence. Assigned roles that rotate among members help students shape their behavior and identify their specific contributions to the collaborative effort.

To encourage individual accountability, groups are instructed to generate by consensus a set of ground rules and consequences for any violations, shortly after each group becomes stable and before conflict arises. The level of individual performance within the group is assessed through formal peer evaluations that occur three times per semester during individual examinations. Attaching the peer evaluation form at the end of each written examination ensures confidentiality and promotes more candid constructive responses. To receive credit for group activities, each person must sign his or her name to an academic honesty statement (Table 21.1) that accompanies each group assignment, laboratory report, and problem solution. If this cover sheet is not completed and attached to the group submissions, they will not be graded. Should a student sign his or her name to the document without having met the three conditions described in Table 21.1, the incident would be reported to the Dean of Students and processed under the university's academic dishonesty policy.

One of my responsibilities as instructor is to monitor the social skills needed to cooperate effectively in groups, as well as the student's understanding of physics. I circulate among the groups and intervene when necessary to suggest more effective ways to interact and avoid conflict. When I join the group to assist with the task and to query students about their understanding of the material, this is an opportunity to model and teach social skills. An example of some of the questions I use, as suggested by Barrows and Tamblyn (1980) are "Why did you come to that conclusion?", "If what you suggest is true, then how would you explain . . . ?", "What are the hidden assumptions being made in your analysis?", "Are you sure of what you are saying?". To ensure that groups are able to process their effectiveness, I provide six opportunities during the semester for students to evaluate their performance as a group and to set goals for improving their subsequent group interactions.

I have not fully embraced the medical school model (Boud & Feletti, 1997) of problem-based learning because the students that I teach lack the necessary ability and/or confidence in their problem-solving and mathematical skills. These students become anxious and offer considerable resistance when they encounter a real-world problem without some preparation, i.e., reading, homework assignment, and/or hearing a lecture about the physics concepts. Students find it difficult to define the broad nature of the problem and organize their ideas when they feel constrained by and fearful of their limited knowledge of physics. For these reasons, I use condensed minipresentations that introduce physics principles and integrate the learning units, i.e., a body of integrated physics principles that define the content of the course (e.g., kinematics, dynamics, conservation laws, fluids, and optics). In most cases, the students engage the real-world problem after some preparation, for example, the minilecture, homework, and conceptual assignments. After acquiring increased confidence in their conceptual understanding of the physics principles, the students use the PBL process as described by Barrows (1985) to work through and solve the real-world problem encountered in each learning cycle. These modifications to the medical school model have been successful because the minilectures, homework, and conceptual assignments support the students

Table 21.1. Cover Page of an Academic Honesty Statement

ACADEMIC HONESTY STATEMENT
PHYS 201-080

My signature below indicates that I have (1) made an equitable contribution to _____ as a member of this group, (2) read and fully agree with the contents (i.e., results, conclusions, analyses) of this document, and (3) acknowledged by name anyone outside this group who assisted this learning team or any individual member in completing this document.

Today's date_____

Active Members

(1)_____ (reporter)   (2)_____

(3)_____   (4)_____

Acknowledgment of individual(s) who assisted this group in completing this document:

(1)_____   (2)_____

(3)_____   (4)_____

through the development of the skills needed for the more complex real-world problems they encounter later.

Course Objectives and Learning Cycle

In addition to the content mastery objectives, the following process objectives are set for the course: (1) to encourage students' responsibility for their learning; (2) to identify and address what a student does not know or understand; (3) to increase the students' discussion of physics principles; (4) to encourage the students' use of logic; and (5) to develop students' reasoning skills. In order to meet these objectives, the students' learning of physics is structured around cycles of in-class activities, each of which includes a minilecture, a conceptual assignment, real-world applications (problem and laboratory), and an overview. Each learning cycle (Figure 21.1) encompasses many activities that help students learn—regardless of their preferred learning style. Typically, the cycle, as shown in Figure 21.1, takes more than a week for the students to complete. To develop the learning format and the instructional approach described here, I recommend class periods longer than 50 minutes. This Honors physics class meets three times a week as two 75-minute sessions, plus one three-hour time block formed by scheduling the traditional laboratory and recitation sessions together. The individual conceptual homework, not shown in Figure 21.1, is completed outside of class, precedes each minilecture, is used to monitor the reading assignment, and to ensure that each student is prepared to participate in the group activities. The order in which the components of the learning cycle are completed in class varies according to the objectives of the teacher, the concept being introduced, and the needs of the students. Overview discussions and minilectures involve the whole class, whereas the conceptual assignments, experiments, and the real-world problems are performed in small collaborative groups. When a new learning unit is introduced, the learning cycle repeats, sometimes with new starting points.

Minilecture and Conceptual Assignment

Minilectures help students to understand the framework of the physical concepts and to connect the knowledge just learned to the new concepts being introduced. Condensed presentations and whole-class discussions have been extremely useful in providing all students with a common base of knowledge to guide self-study in preparation for the other activities that occur in the learning cycle. During the whole-class discussions, I explain difficult concepts, e.g., tension, "massless" strings, "passive" forces, and circular motion.

In the medical school model, there is one tutor/facilitator per learning group. This student-to-teacher ratio allows constant monitoring of student learning within the groups. With 20–25 students in five or six groups with one instructor, the medical school model was not an option for this course. To monitor students' learning more closely in my course, the instructor serves as a "roving" tutor/facilitator during group activities. Because the roving instructor cannot monitor all the students' learning constantly, whole-class

THE LEARNING CYCLE

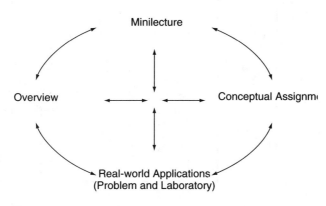

FIGURE 21.1.   The learning cycle

discussions and minilectures ensure students' understanding. When students are given this kind of support through whole-class discussions and minilectures, either before or while they are using groups to solve complex problems, they are less anxious, fearful, or suspicious of the process. Since my attention is distributed over multiple groups, I require an activity log (Table 21.2) indicating how each group used class time to work through group assignments, experiments, group problems, and group functioning. The activity log is handed in after each class meeting and is used to set realistic due dates for the group activities.

Since 1998, I have used undergraduate peer tutors to augment the roving instructor. Peer tutors help guide the groups through the conceptual assignments and real-world problems during the 75-minute class periods. The peer tutors are drawn from a pool of successful, more experienced students who have already taken the course or who are physics, engineering, or physics education majors. As the instructor, I still roam freely among the groups to assist peer tutors, monitor understanding of physics principles, identify learning issues (anything a student does not understand or know), address alternative conceptions, and model the skills needed for critical thinking and problem solving. The class has provided an opportunity for the physics education majors to gain teaching experience in the classroom, learn about one form of active learning, experience PBL techniques, and reflect on their dual roles as tutor and learner.

With some prompting or incentives, students in introductory physics courses find it easier to discuss physics principles. The conceptual assignment consists of provocative questions that students must answer and is a formal

Table 21.2. In-Class Activity Log

Group #	Assignment			Problem		Laboratory		Group Functioning
	Date	Item	Time	Item	Time	Item	Time	
BEGIN								
END								
BEGIN								
END								
BEGIN								
END								
BEGIN								
END								
BEGIN								
END								
BEGIN								
END								

mechanism for generating discussion of physics principles among students in their respective groups. Afterward, the group is required to submit one set of written responses to the questions that appear on the conceptual group assignments. The responses are graded for clarity, consistency, the use of logic, and explicit connections made between the physics principles and the physical world. The following are examples of the types of questions I have used from various textbooks to generate lively group discussions.

> *Suppose that a body acted on by exactly two forces is accelerated. Does it then follow that (a) the body cannot move with a constant speed?; (b) the velocity can never be zero?; (c) the sum of the two forces cannot be zero?; (d) the forces must act in the same line? Explain your response.*
>
> *In the early days of rocketry, it was assumed by many people that a rocket would not work in outer space because there was no air for the exhaust gases to push against. Explain why the rocket works in outer space.*
>
> *To ease the pain, should you catch a fast-moving softball while your hand is moving toward the ball, while it is at rest, or while it is moving in the direction of the incoming ball? Explain using physics principles.*

Real-World Applications— Problems and the Laboratory

Opportunities for combining conceptual understanding of physics with critical-thinking skills occur when the students encounter the real-world applications. Whenever possible, problems and experiments relate the basic physics principles to the real world—especially biology, medicine, and the physiology. Students who acquire scientific knowledge in the context in which it will be used are more likely to retain what they learn and apply that knowledge appropriately (Albanese & Mitchell, 1993; Boud & Feletti, 1997). The problems developed for this class are very different from typical end-of-chapter problems or exercises. In general, the end-of-chapter problems are too directive, supply the relevant unknown parameters, and can be solved with little understanding. Mazur (1996) notes that "most textbook problems test mathematical, instead of analytical, thinking skills" while the more meaningful problems are those that give students the opportunity to make assumptions and estimates and to develop and work out models. The problems that have been developed for this class demand that students do several things: (1) connect new knowledge to old; (2) recognize what they know and understand and what they do not; (3)

learn concepts thoroughly enough so they can explain them in their own words; and (4) be able to teach them to their peers.

Some examples of problems used in this course follow: students use conservation of energy, moment of inertia, and kinematics to design fast model derby racers; they apply the principles of rotational dynamics to evaluate the stability of different bicycles during braking; and Ohms' law, electrical power, and resistance must be applied to design a safe outdoor lighting system. An example of a problem that I have used to teach kinematics is Bare Accidents shown in Appendix 21.1. This is the first problem that students encounter in the first learning cycle organized around kinematics. The first two questions in the problem are open-ended, require little knowledge of what has been taught in the course to this point, and give each student regardless of his or her knowledge an opportunity to contribute to the group discussion. As the students progress deeper into the problem, questions 3, 4, and 5, they use the physics principles and skills developed through repeated applications and encounters in homework, group assignments, whole-class discussions, and minilecture. In question 6, the students interpret their quantitative responses, compare them to each other and to their intuitive predictions, question 1. Most of the instructional objectives that I set for kinematics can be met in this one problem. In order to respond to questions 3, 4, and 5, the students must be able to generate qualitative graphs of motion from written descriptions; describe motion mathematically, using the appropriate kinematical equations; represent the motion of multiple objects on a single qualitative graph; and know what explicit and implicit information can be extracted from motion graphs.

The experimental investigations are open-ended and less structured than most undergraduate teaching laboratories. Students are asked to design an experiment that would answer a question posed to them; identify sources of uncertainty in the data to be gathered, plan ways to minimize that uncertainty, and explain reason for discrepancy in the results. Some of the experimental investigations ask students to simply explain a familiar everyday phenomenon. In order to explain that phenomenon, students must take data, analyze that data, and respond to a series of questions that stage conflict between the students' perception of the physical world and basic physics principles. Riding an Elevator (Appendix 21.2) is an example of this kind of investigation. To experience the sensory effects of acceleration, students ride the elevators in a 15-story high-rise dormitory. Using the data collected, they respond to a series of questions that probe their understanding of acceleration, net forces, passive forces, contact forces, weight, and Newton's three laws of motion.

Overview

During this phase of the learning cycle, the entire class becomes a single group that reflects upon the difficulties encountered in the learning cycle. Everyone benefits from further discussion of concepts and remaining unresolved learning issues that confront the class. I use this time to acknowledge and appreciate the diversity of ideas generated by the groups to solve the physics problem and to design their experiments. This reinforces the idea that there is a variety of ways to solve physics problems. In addition to being a format for the entire class to process their learning experience, the overview is used to preview and link the next learning unit with the current one. This will help students build an integrated and coherent view of the physical world.

Assessment of Student Performance

The overall performance of a student is evaluated by using a weighted average of the grades generated from written group and individual examinations, group problem solutions, group laboratory reports, conceptual assignments, individual homework, and group participation. Before instruction begins, the students are given on the course syllabus the performance levels I use to assign the final grade, e.g., A, A–, B+. Grading is by design independent of the class performance and is never done on a curve.

All examinations, including the final, contain individual and group components. Thirty-five percent of the grade on each written examination is acquired through group effort; the rest is individual effort. All examinations except the final are administered on Wednesdays during the three-hour class period. The first hour is reserved for the group examination, and the students use the remaining two hours to complete the individual portion. The collaborative activities, the group portion of written examinations, conceptual assignments, problem solutions, laboratory reports, and group participation account for 60% of a student's final course grade. The individual working alone is responsible for the other 40%.

Student Attitudes

Student response to various aspects of this course on final course ratings forms has continued to remain positive. Over the past 6 1/2 years, students still feel comfortable working in groups and still identify group work as the most important aspect that contributed to their learning. The following are typical comments made by students:

> "The ability to work in groups is definitely beneficial."
> "Learning by working with peer group and peer tutor is much better than trying to struggle through the material alone."

"Working problems out as a group; the distribution of labor."

"The fact that we could discuss things in groups and the application to real world problems."

The application of physics to real-world problems continues to nearly tie with group work as the most beneficial to student learning. In many responses, students cite both group work and real-world problem solving but consistently rank group work first and then real-world problem solving. Typical comments from students regarding the real-world problem solving follow:

"I liked being drilled with many different problems as opposed to being lectured to."

"Very repetitive problems. Stress on concepts and real world problems."

"The homework and problems—they make you think about Physics in a logical, practical sense rather than just in a quantitative sense."

"The real world applications made great use of that which we learned."

"Applying physics to real world situations—through the real world problems—made me start to think about physics outside of class."

The question, "Have the skills learned in this class made a difference in your other academic or social situations?" elicited a variety of responses. A few of the representative response follow:

"For everything I look at physics principles pops in my head."

"Physics principles apply to everything. It will help my understanding of the human body as I pursue a career in medicine. . . ."

"Better ability to reason and more confidence that my approach is correct sometimes."

"I can better analyze problems and work in group situations."

"I don't have examples (specific ones) but I know I learned how to take turns and really listen to other members of the group and how to not be in control all the time."

"This course focused on understanding, applying, the same principle in many different situations. This can be carried into other courses and thesis research."

"No."

Every year, there are some students who dislike the class format and call for more support through lecturing and more structure to the class. Typical responses follow:

"More lecture before assignments. If necessary, actually use the book."
     "More lecturing so I could grasp the concepts better. More 'out of the book' type problems for a basic understanding of concepts and math."
     "More direct instruction."
     "More lecture less problems."

Evaluation of Instruction

To measure the effectiveness of the instructional method previously described, I administered the Force Concept Inventory (Hestenes, Wells, & Swackhamer, 1992) to approximately 100 students enrolled in the Introductory Physics course from fall 1993 to fall 1999. The Force Concept Inventory (FCI) is an instrument designed to probe students' understanding of Newtonian mechanics and has been given to more than 2000 high school and university students. Hestenes et al. (1992) have collected abundant evidence to support their claim that the FCI is an accurate and reliable instrument for evaluating instruction. Each of my physics classes were given the FCI as a pretest before instruction and as a posttest at the end of the semester. The posttest is always administered on the last day of class, and the students' performance on this diagnostic never counts toward their final grade. The posttest consists of the same questions as the pretest but looks different because the questions have been reordered. The Honors physics students' pretest and posttest mean scores and their standard deviations are given in Table 21.3.

Hestenes et al. (1992) conclude from their study that only posttest scores are essential for evaluating effective instruction. "Pretest/Posttest gains will be large if the pretest scores were low but small if pretest scores were high" (Hestenes et al., 1992). Using their data, Hestenes et al. (1992) conclude that below a conceptual threshold near a score of 60% on the FCI, student's understanding of Newtonian concepts is too inadequate for skillful problem solving. If instruction is indeed effective, the results on the FCI will be nearly the same, that is, above this threshold (Hestenes et al., 1992). How effective was the instruction using the criterion set by Hestenes et al. (1992)? The data in Table 21.3 shows that the posttest mean scores measured for the Honor physics students are all above the conceptual threshold. The posttest mean

Table 21.3. Pre- and Posttest Scores for Force Concept Inventor.

Sample N	Pretest Percentage Scores (S. Dev.)	Posttest Percentage Scores (S. Dev.)
1994 Honors 23	39.7 (16.5)	70.2 (12.0)
1996 Honors 21	39.2 (15.6)	72.4 (14.5)
1997 Honors 20	41.2 (19.7)	70.5 (16.9)
1998 Honors 16	41.0 (18.6)	79.1 (10.9)
1999 Honors 21	40.6 (14.3)	67.2 (13.4)

N is total number of students taking the posttests.
1995 was a sabbatical year.

scores met and exceeded the Hestenes et al. (1992) criterion for demonstrating effective instruction.

Hake (1998) uses the average normalized gain g, defined as the ratio of the actual average gain (%post – %pre) to the maximum possible average gain (100% pre) of a class, as a rough measure of the average effectiveness of a course in promoting conceptual understanding. The average normalized gains for the honor physics students are between 0.45 and 0.64. These values are consistent with the average $g = 0.48 \pm 0.14$ (Hake, 1998) measured for 48 other physics courses that use interactive-engagement methods and twice as high as the average $g = 0.23 \pm 0.04$ measured for 14 traditional physics courses that use little or no interactive engagement methods. Assuming that g is a valid measure of course effectiveness as Hake (1998) does, then it appears that the Introductory Honors Physics course is twice as effective in building basic concepts as traditional physics courses. These results seem to indicate that active group learning and connections to real-world applications did help students learn physics and apply that knowledge appropriately as measured by the FCI.

Author Biography

Barbara A. Williams is an Associate Professor of Physics and Astronomy and an affiliated faculty member of the University Honors Program at the University of Delaware.

References

Albanese, M. A., and Mitchell, S. (1993). Problem-based learning: A review of literature on its outcomes and implementation issues. *Academic Medicine, 68,* 52–81.

Barrows, H. S. (1985). *How to design a problem-based curriculum for pre-clinical years.* New York, NY: Springer Publishing Company.

Barrows, H. S., & Tamblyn, R. M. (1980). *Problem-based learning: An approach to medical education.* New York, NY: Springer Publishing Company.

Boud, D., and Feletti, G. (1997). *The challenge of problem-based learning.* London: Kogan Page.

Gabriel, S., & Smithson, I. (Eds.) (1990). *Gender in the classroom: Power and pedagogy.* Urbana, IN: University of Illinois Press.

Hake, R. R. (1998). Interactive-engagement versus traditional methods: A six-thousand-student survey of mechanics test data for introductory physics course. *Am. J. Phys., 66,* 64–74.

Hall, R., & Sandler, B. (1984). The classroom climate: A chilly one for women? Project on the Status and Education of Women. American Association of Colleges, Washington, USA.

Hestenes, D., Wells, M., and Swackhamer, G. (1992). Force Concept Inventory. *The Physics Teacher, 30,* 141–153.

Johnson, D. W., Johnson, R. T., & Smith, K. A. (1991). Cooperative learning: Increasing college faculty instructional productivity. ASHE-ERIC Higher Education Report No. 4, Washington, USA.

Mazur, E. (1996). The problem with problems. *Optics and Photonic News, 7,* 59.

APPENDIX I TO CHAPTER 21

BARE ACCIDENTS

Barbara A. Williams

At the Albemarle Zoo, animals are free to roam in a five-square-mile park. The visitors to the zoo are kept in cages or on trains well isolated from the animals that roam in their simulated natural habitats. Trains have been built on bridges over the open territories of roaming animals. Several sections of the rail system have been built on trestle bridges that cross man-made lakes through sections of the zoo occupied by the bear population. Unfortunately, trestle bridges should not have been built over these sections because bears are good climbers and intensely curious. A bear playing in the lake below a trestle decided to climb atop the bridge. Shortly after the bear reached the top, a tourist train began to approach the bridge. Startled by the vibrations of the track, the bear begins running on the rails. When the driver of the train sees the bear, the front of the train is as far away from the edge of the bridge as the bridge is long. The driver makes no attempt to change his speed because he assumes the bear will have enough time to escape onto the elevated land off the bridge. The bear moves at constant velocity but cannot travel at a speed equal to or greater than the train's speed.

As you work through the problem, generate a list of learning issues.

1. What factors do you think should be considered in deciding whether the bear can survive or not? Include any assumptions the group thinks can be reasonably made.

2. Generate a list of different outcomes that are possible, assuming the bear remains on the track over water but does not remain on the track over land.

3. Select one of your outcomes. Make use of the old proverb, "A picture is worth a thousand words" and decide within your group the best way to represent graphically the action leading to your selected outcome.

4. Identify regions on your graph where the bear can survive and where there is a chance the bear might die. Explain your selections and describe how they differ.

5. If the bear is to survive, how can the bear avoid a head-on collision? If the bear is to survive, how can it avoid being run over from behind? (Provide qualitative and algebraic responses.) Are the conditions the same for both cases? Explain.

6. Did your solutions to the bear's dilemma depend on the factors you selected as relevant in question 1? Explain.

7. Assuming that there are bears of all ages in the zoo and nearly all of the young ones are excellent climbers but slow runners, would you be comfortable employing this driver if the zoo officials wanted to maintain a stable bear population? Explain.

8. Make a list of the learning issues that this problem generated for your group. Which are still unresolved?

APPENDIX 2 TO CHAPTER 21

Riding an Elevator

Barbara A. Williams

Part I. Measurements

1. Select a member of the group whose weight will be monitored, and record his or her weight when the elevator is at rest.

2. As the elevator starts to move upward and downward, describe in detail the physical sensation you feel and where you feel it.

3. Record the maximum change in the member's weight when the elevator moves upward and downward.

4. During the ride, did the scale measure the same value it did when the elevator was at rest?

Part II. Analysis

1. Identify the forces acting on the member standing on the scale, and specify their directions. Identify the corresponding reaction forces.

2. Describe how a bathroom scale works, i.e., what specific action has to occur in order for the needle to move. What exactly does the scale measure as a result of this action?

3. Which of the forces acting on the member does the scale measure during the motion? Support your reasoning with physics principle(s).

4. What is the relation between the acceleration of the person inside the elevator and the acceleration of the elevator?

5. Determine the maximum upward and downward acceleration of the elevator. What principle(s) do you need to use in order to answer this question? State assumptions.

6. If placed blindfolded in the elevator, could you distinguish between upward and downward acceleration? Explain in words.

7. How it is possible when the elevator is in motion for the scale to measure the same value as that recorded when the elevator was at rest?

8. If the elevator cables were to break, what would the scale read? Explain.

9. If the elevator cables were to break, could a person save him- or herself from serious injury by jumping up from the floor just before the elevator hits the bottom of the shaft. Comment on the feasibility of this suggestion.

10. For all five cases (at rest, accelerating up and down, free fall, and moving with a constant velocity) determine the force that the person exerts on the scale and the force that the scale exerts on the person. How do the five values compare, i.e., rank the five cases from maximum force to minimum force? Are your determinations counterintuitive?